COMPLICITY

"This tough-minded book reveals Northern slavery to have been neither a marginal nor a short-lived institution but a central element of the region's economy and society."
—IRA BERLIN, *The Washington Post*

"This is history worth remembering. . . . The width and breadth of the exploitation they describe is impressive. . . . The hardest question is what to do when human rights give way to profits. The authors have clearly shown that historical amnesia is not an option."
—*San Francisco Chronicle*

"Here is a book you may not want to pick up but won't be able to put down. It is history written with the urgency of breaking news, a journalist's ear for the perfect quotation, and an unflinching sensitivity to the human dimensions of a most intentionally inhuman institution."
—*Chicago Tribune*

"*Complicity* may be an eye-opener for finger-pointing Northerners."
—*The Virginian-Pilot*

"This is history at its best . . . [and] a rich history of slavery in the North that adds new dimensions to what you might have learned in school."
—*The Boston Globe*

"Essential reading."
—*Library Journal*

COMPLICITY

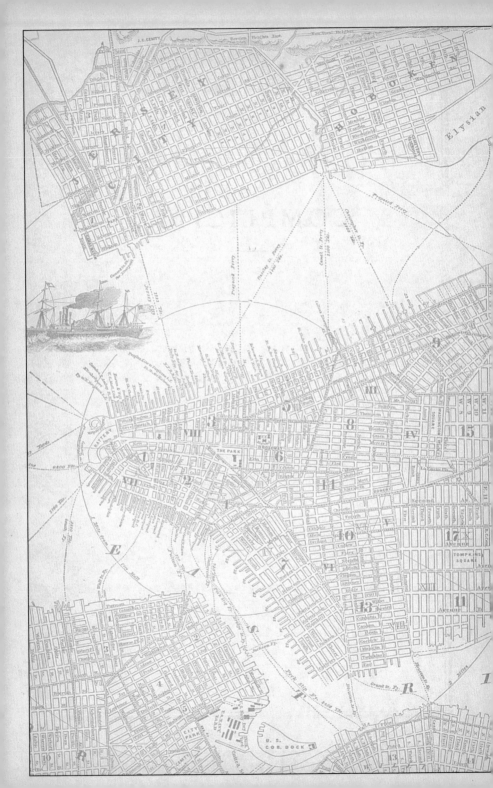

COMPLICITY

HOW THE NORTH
PROMOTED, PROLONGED, and PROFITED
FROM SLAVERY

Anne Farrow, Joel Lang, and *Jenifer Frank*

of

THE HARTFORD COURANT

with

Cheryl Magazine, IMAGES EDITOR

Foreword by *Evelyn Brooks Higginbotham*

BALLANTINE BOOKS • NEW YORK

To the memory of my father, Charles William Farrow,
and the experience of Africa.
I no go forget.

A.F.

———•·•———

To Maxine and Donna, for their generosity

J.L.

———•·•———

To Kenton, Gigi, and Max
(who said of this dedication: "You better not just say 'To my family'").
You mean more to me than a million bales of cotton.

J.F.

———•·•———

To Philip, Jonathan, and Daniel Moeller

C.M.

The Northern slaveholder traded in men and women whom he never saw, and of whose separations, tears, and miseries he determined never to hear.

HARRIET BEECHER STOWE
"The Education of Freedmen"
The North American Review, June 1879

FOREWORD

by Evelyn Brooks Higginbotham

My first real knowledge of the Civil War and its aftermath came from seeing a photograph of my great-grandfather Albert Royal Brooks. A former slave, Brooks served on the Richmond grand jury convened to consider evidence against Jefferson Davis for treason. Davis never came to trial; he was pardoned in 1868 by President Andrew Johnson. In fact, the only visual record I have of my great-grandfather comes from this extraordinary photograph of him, sitting proudly among the black and white jurors.[1] As a child, and for years thereafter, I wondered why the trial had not occurred and also what my great-grandfather might have felt about it. Later in life, I would come to understand Davis's amnesty from the perspective of a professional historian—a perspective far more complex than that of a young girl.

The granting of amnesty was not simply the act of a Southern president whose sympathies ran opposite to those of the many Northerners and Radical Republican Congressmen who sought to see Davis tried for treason and murder. Other Northerners joined Southerners in sending petitions and memorials for Davis's release. The *New York Herald* and *New York Tribune* both printed editorials sympathetic to secession and to the fate of Davis. Wealthy, influential Northern men, including Cornelius Vanderbilt, Horace Greeley, and once-radical abolitionist Gerrit Smith, put up the money for Davis's bail. Even more ironic, the fiery black clergyman Henry McNeil Turner, who had served as a chaplain in the Union army, presented an earnest supplication for mercy for Davis.

---

1. For the photograph of the grand jury, see Marie Tyler-McGraw, *At the Falls: Richmond, Virginia, and Its People* (Chapel Hill: University of North Carolina Press, 1994), p. 171.

Jefferson Davis himself was never repentant about the war, nor did he ever petition for amnesty, as did thousands of both ordinary and prominent ex-Confederates.[2] Historian David Blight has noted that in the decades after the war the "drive for reunion both used and trumped race."[3]

Unlikely alliances and strange bedfellows often create ironic stories. In 1641, for example, the Massachusetts Bay Colony became the first of the American colonies to give legal recognition to the institution of slavery. Its Body of Liberties permitted the enslavement of "lawful captives taken in juste warres, and such strangers as willingly sell themselves or are sold to us."[4] Although the Virginia colony had already begun the practice of using black slaves, the Massachusetts statute preceded Virginia's legal sanctioning of servitude. It seems ironic that clergy-led Boston, this seventeenth-century "city on a hill," would soon become a bustling port for the trade in human flesh. Religion proved no match for profits. In Rhode Island, in the Narragansett Bay area, large landholdings used sizable numbers of slaves to provision the mono-crop plantations in the Caribbean with foodstuffs. Such cities as Boston, Salem, Providence, and New London, bustled with activity; outgoing ships were loaded with rum, fish, and dairy products, as slaves, along with molasses and sugar, were unloaded from incoming ships. Up until the American War for Independence, the slave trade was a profitable element of the New England economy.[5]

It is little wonder, then, that England looked askance at Americans' demands for independence in the early 1770s. The British had published Phillis Wheatley's book of poetry in 1773, while simultaneously chiding the people of Boston for failing to free her from slavery. "We are much concerned to find that this ingenious young woman is yet a slave," the British admonished the liberty-loving American patriots, and they also asserted that "one such act as the purchase of her freedom, would, in our opinion, have done them more honour than hanging a thousand trees with

2. Jonathan T. Dorris, *Pardon and Amnesty under Lincoln and Johnson: The Restoration of the Confederates to Their Rights and Privileges, 1861–1898* (Chapel Hill: University of North Carolina Press, 1953); Roy Franklin Nichols, "United States vs. Jefferson Davis, 1865–1869," *American Historical Review* 31 (January 1926):266–284; Clarence A. Bacote, "Truth from the Point of View of the Investigator," *Journal of Negro History* 25 (October 1940):460.

3. David Blight, *Race and Reunion: The Civil War in American Memory* (Cambridge: Harvard University Press, 2001), p. 2.

4. Quoted in A. Leon Higginbotham Jr., *In the Matter of Color: Race and the American Legal Process: The Colonial Period* (New York: Oxford University Press, 1978), p. 62.

5. On slavery and the slave trade in New England, see Lorenzo Johnston Greene, *The Negro in Colonial New England* (New York: Atheneum, 1968).

ribbons and emblems."[6] In the early years of the American Revolution, the Massachusetts legislature was bombarded with petitions submitted by the colony's slaves requesting, in no uncertain terms, the right to freedom; this right of petition was part of the "liberties and Christian usages" that the Puritans believed slave owners should allow their slaves. Yet, in 1777, in reaction to one such petition, the legislature felt duty bound to emphasize regional conciliation as opposed to black freedom. In a missive on the subject of slavery and freedom to the Continental Congress, which was sitting in Philadelphia, these descendants of the Puritans opined that "we have such a sacred regard to the union and harmony of the United States as to conceive ourselves under obligation to refrain from every measure that should have a tendency to injure that union which is the basis and foundation of our defense and happiness."[7] Remaining sensitive to the happiness of Southern slaveholders, the Commonwealth of Massachusetts never formally abolished slavery, but rather left it to acts of private manumission and the withering effect of court decisions that questioned the legality of human ownership. To the credit of Massachusetts, however, as of the first federal census in 1790, it was the only state in the new republic to register no slaves in its population.

In slave-free Massachusetts, the fight for the immediate rather than gradual abolition of slavery was launched, with William Lloyd Garrison's *Liberator* in 1831 and the alignment of the New England Anti-Slavery Society in 1832 with the state's free blacks in their commitment to immediatism. If New England represented the heart of the antebellum abolitionist movement, it also represented a complex mixture of antislavery sentiment and virulent racism.[8] Indeed, Harriet Beecher Stowe portrayed this complexity in her now-classic abolitionist novel, *Uncle Tom's Cabin*. The book's designated racist is none other than the pious antislavery New Englander Ophelia, who, while visiting her slave-owning cousin Augustine St. Clair in Louisiana constantly criticizes him for his participation in the evil of slavery, yet cannot bring herself to touch the black "uncivilized" Topsy. Amused by Ophelia's New England hypocrisy, Augustine offers her a challenge: "If we emancipate, will you educate?" Ophelia eventually accepts but, after adopting and educating Topsy in

6. *The Poems of Phillis Wheatley.* Revised and Enlarged Edition. Edited with an Introduction by Julian D. Mason Jr. (Chapel Hill: University of North Carolina Press, 1989), p. 25.
7. Massachusetts Legislature's letter to the Continental Congress, printed in *Proceedings of the Massachusetts Historical Society*, vol. 10, pp. 332–33.
8. On New England antislavery sentiment, see Donald Martin Jacobs, ed., *Courage and Conscience: Black and White Abolitionists in Boston* (Bloomington: University of Indiana Press, 1993).

New England, sends her along with the majority of the novel's major black characters, including Liza, George, Harry, Emmaline, and Cassie, to Africa. That the plot ended with colonization permitted Stowe's readers to advocate the abolition of slavery while forestalling the question of what to do with the ex-slaves.[9] For most Northern whites in the 1850s, the desire to end slave labor did not equate with a belief in racial equality. Thus blacks might be freed, eventually, but they would not be welcome to remain. For most free blacks in the 1850s, colonization failed to offer a realistic, or desirable, "solution." Northern blacks had clearly flirted with the idea in the late eighteenth and early nineteenth centuries, and a small minority continued to prefer colonization to racism in America well into the twentieth century. However, the majority was determined to stay on American soil, where they built viable and cohesive black communities.[10]

The process of black community-building began in the years immediately after the Northern states signaled their complicity in slavery by agreeing to those sections in the Constitution that, in crucial ways, gave tacit support to the "peculiar institution." Not coincidently, this era has also been called the "first emancipation."[11] With the exception of Massachusetts and tiny Vermont, which had joined the union in 1791 with a constitution outlawing slavery, all of the other states in New England and the Middle Atlantic adopted gradual-emancipation statutes. Such laws made provisions for those freed after a certain date to work as indentured servants for their "masters" until adulthood. Thus, the North's moral repugnance to slavery was compromised by a deeper respect for property rights, even those inclusive of the right to hold men and women of African descent as chattel.[12]

And yet, complicity and complexity went hand in hand. It was in Pennsylvania and New York, both of which gradually emancipated their slaves, that the very first American antislavery societies were formed. The Pennsylvania Abolition Society (PAS) and the New York Manumission Society were both founded in the late eighteenth century by white

9. Harriet Beecher Stowe, *Uncle Tom's Cabin: Authoritative Text, Backgrounds and Contexts, Criticism*, Elizabeth Ammons, ed., (New York: W. W. Norton, 1994). For black responses to the novel and specifically to the colonization plot device, see Dickson D. Bruce Jr., *The Origins of African American Literature, 1680–1865* (Charlottesville: University of Virginia Press, 2001), pp. 285–87.

10. On black community life in the antebellum North, see James O. Horton and Lois E. Horton, *In Hope of Liberty: Culture, Community, and Protest Among Northern Free Blacks, 1700–1860* (New York: Oxford University Press, 1997).

11. Arthur Zilversmit, *The First Emancipation: The Abolition of Slavery in the North* (Chicago: University of Chicago Press, 1967).

12. Ibid.; also see Ira Berlin, *Many Thousands Gone: The First Two Centuries of Slavery in North America* (Cambridge: Harvard University Press, 1998), pp. 233–37.

Northerners of property and political power. These men were the allies, and sometimes the financial backers, of blacks who were in the process of forming institutions—mutual-aid societies, fraternal lodges, schools, and churches—around which to orient their nascent communities. Among them were such illustrious men as Alexander Hamilton and John Jay, in New York, and Benjamin Franklin and Benjamin Rush, in Philadelphia. In these early years of black community-building, free blacks realized that the racist society of the North also included persons and institutions of good will.[13]

African Americans were careful to distinguish degrees of complicity from blatant disrespect and disregard for the rights of blacks, free and slave. Black leaders in the North attacked a complex cast of characters in their protest literature. The extraordinary black Boston pamphleteer and antislavery militant David Walker denounced Thomas Jefferson for his insulting remarks. Thomas Jefferson, who wrote the Declaration of Independence proclaiming the equality of all men, also wrote of the natural inferiority of blacks in his *Notes on the State of Virginia*. Walker raged in 1829, "Do you believe that the assertions of such a man, will pass away into oblivion unobserved by this people and the world? . . . I say, unless we try to refute Mr. Jefferson's arguments respecting us, we will only establish them."[14]

Nineteenth-century black protest literature, too, exposes the contradictions inherent in what historians term the Jacksonian Democracy of the 1830s, since the era's extension of "universal" manhood suffrage was accompanied by the disfranchisement of black freeholders. Even earlier, in Connecticut in 1818 and New York in 1821, state laws significantly enlarged the white male electorate, while simultaneously reducing the number of black male voters through property requirements and harsh residency laws specific to blacks.[15] Such scholars as David Roediger reveal that the Northern free blacks stood alienated both literally and figuratively from white workers, who violently chased African Americans from public parks on the Fourth of July. The legacy of black soldiers who had fought in the Revolutionary War was too often unob-

13. Richard S. Newman, *The Transformation of American Abolitionism: Fighting Slavery in the Early Republic* (Chapel Hill: University of North Carolina Press, 2002).
14. David Walker, *Walker's Appeal in Four Articles; Together with a Preamble, to the Colored Citizens of the World* (Boston, 1929), quoted in Henry Louis Gates and Nellie McKay, eds., *The Norton Anthology of African American Literature* (New York: W. W. Norton, 1997), p. 188.
15. Leslie M. Harris, *In the Shadow of Slavery: African Americans in New York City, 1626–1863* (Chicago: University of Chicago Press, 2003); Michael Warner, "A Soliloquy 'Lately Spoken at the African Theatre': Race and the Public Sphere in New York City, 1821," *American Literature* 73 (March 2001):1–46.

served and unwelcome in public commemorations of American Independence.[16]

Doubtless aware of the complicity of Northern whites with regard to slaves and free blacks alike, African Americans also criticized fellow blacks. When David Walker asked, " Are we not Men?" he railed against the complicity of his own people, those who had become silent in the face of injustice, "*submissive* to a gang of men, whom we cannot tell whether they are as good as ourselves or not." No less controversial, black antislavery activist Henry Highland Garnet believed Southern slaves themselves complicit, if they did not rebel against their continued enslavement. Praising the heroism of Denmark Vesey and Toussaint L'Ouverture, Garnet challenged the slaves: "Let your motto be resistance! *resistance!* RESISTANCE! No oppressed people have ever secured their liberty without resistance."[17]

"Complicity" is a loaded word, pregnant with complication and irony. Thus it is a word appropriately chosen as the title for this book by Anne Farrow, Joel Lang, and Jenifer Frank. In this study of how the North promoted, prolonged, and profited from slavery, the authors give a fascinating account of racial inequality in America, revealing that positions do not fall neatly into categories such as North versus South, antebellum versus postbellum, and virtuous versus complicit. Although *Complicity* calls attention primarily to slavery, the North and South continued their complicitous relationship with regard to white supremacy into the late nineteenth century and the twentieth. It is worth remembering that the litigants who appealed to the Supreme Court in the *Civil Rights Cases of 1883* brought charges of national, not simply Southern, discrimination, suing establishments in New York, San Francisco, Kansas, and Tennessee. Decades later, in the 1940s through 1960s, the fight to end Jim Crow and disfranchisement would be waged not only in Southern cities and deltas, but also in Northern cities, where African Americans and their white allies fought for racial justice in regard to education, housing, and hiring. The authors of *Complicity* have rendered a story full of new and interesting facts about an earlier time in this nation's history, and by so doing they speak powerfully to present-day America and the continuing quest for freedom and justice for all.

16. David R. Roediger, *The Wages of Whiteness: Race and the Making of the American Working Class* (New York: Verso, 1991), p. 57; David Waldstreicher, *In the Midst of Perpetual Fetes: The Making of American Nationalism, 1776–1820* (Chapel Hill: University of North Carolina Press, 1997); see also Shane White, "'It Was a Proud Day': African Americans, Festivals, and Parades in the North, 1741–1834," *Journal of American History* 81 (1994):13–50.

17. Walker, *Appeal*, in Gates and McKay, *Norton Anthology*, p. 189; Henry Highland Garnet, *An Address to the Slaves of the United Sates of America* (New York, 1848), in Gates and McKay, *Norton Anthology*, p. 283.

PREFACE

SEVERAL YEARS AGO, ON ITS FRONT PAGE, *THE HARTFORD COURANT* published a story with an extraordinary headline—"Aetna 'Regrets' Insuring Slaves"—concerning an overdue admission and apology from one of Connecticut's oldest and most prestigious companies.

The next day, *Courant* reporters began to investigate the newspaper's own role in slavery. After giving such prominence to the Aetna story, it seemed only fair that we try to determine whether we, as an institution, were also culpable. As America's oldest continuously published newspaper—the *Courant* dates from 1764—we thought it likely that we were.

Four months later, we ran what we'd learned across the top of the front page: "Courant Complicity in an Old Wrong—Newspaper's Founder Published Ads in Support of the Sale and Capture of Slaves." The response was immediate and fierce: The story was picked up by media across the country, and we received calls even from overseas. Adding spice to the story, a *Courant* spokesman apologized for the newspaper's role in slavery.

The following year, in partial response to a lawsuit seeking reparations that had been filed against Aetna and several other companies (though not against the *Courant*), the newspaper's editor, Brian Toolan, e-mailed a challenge to the staff. Would it be possible, he asked, to learn the identity of a slave, any slave, who had been insured, and to write of his or her life?

The staff of *Northeast*, the *Courant*'s Sunday magazine, decided to look into it. Longtime writer Joel Lang headed to Yale for an exploratory talk with Robert P. Forbes, associate director of the Gilder Lehrman Center for the Study of Slavery, Resistance, and Abolition. A handful of scholars, Lang discovered, were starting to look at slavery through a global economic lens. As they did so, it was becoming clear that Connecticut's role in slavery was not only huge, it was a key to the success of the entire institution. Finding an insured slave suddenly became secondary. We were now looking at nothing less than an altered reality.

Our first response was confusion: Hold on, weren't we the good guys in the Civil War? Wasn't the South to blame for slavery? After all, Southerners had plantations, we had the Underground Railroad. They had Simon Legree, we had his abolitionist creator—Harriet Beecher Stowe's house is literally up the street from the *Courant*.

But the more we looked, the more we found what appeared to be unshakable proof of Connecticut's complicity in slavery. What's more, it quickly became obvious that our economic links to slavery were deeply entwined with our religious, political, and educational institutions. Slavery was part of the social contract in Connecticut. It was in the air we breathed.

There was more. The year before the American Revolution, more than 5,000 Africans were enslaved in Connecticut. Though there were certainly fewer slaves proportionately than in Virginia or South Carolina, the number shocked us. How could we not know this? How could we not know, for example, that in 1790 most prosperous merchants in Connecticut owned at least one slave, as did 50 percent of the ministers? The federal census clearly showed this.

In addition, some Connecticut slaves actually lived on farms as large as many in the South. Another word for such farms could be "plantations."

The story grew bigger, and more damning.

The Triangle Trade between the Americas, Europe, and Africa is a staple of the high school curriculum. But as Lang wrote in the original "Complicity" issue of the newspaper,

> somehow in popular perception, slavery has been cut out of the trade triangle and transferred forward to the Civil War, where it became a moral problem confined to the South. Just as Connecticut was thought not to have "had slavery" because it did not have many slaves or Southern-style plantations, it was thought not to profit from slavery as much as the South did.
>
> The truth, however, which ought to have been plain, is that Connecticut derived a great part, maybe the greatest part, of its early surplus wealth from slavery.

ONCE OUR SPECIAL ISSUE WAS PUBLISHED, REQUESTS FOR EXTRA COPIES flowed in from scholars, educators, and the public.

Literary agent Tanya McKinnon read "Complicity" and came to us with an exciting proposal. We agreed to broaden our thesis to encompass the North, and she sold the idea to Ballantine Books. This book is the result of a year and a half of post-magazine work by Lang, *Northeast* staff writer Anne Farrow, and *Northeast* editor and writer Jenifer Frank.

WHAT WAS TRUE OF CONNECTICUT TURNED OUT TO BE OVERWHELMINGLY true of the entire North. Most of what you'll read here was gleaned from older, often out-of-print texts, and from period newspapers, largely in Connecticut, New York, and Massachusetts.

We are journalists, not scholars, and want to share what surprised, and even shocked, the three of us. We have all grown up, attended schools, and worked in Northern states, from Maine to Maryland. We thought we knew our home. We thought we knew our country.

We were wrong.

CONTENTS

FOREWORD by *Evelyn Brooks Higginbotham*   xi

PREFACE   xvii

INTRODUCTION   xxv

One   COTTON COMES NORTH   3
*New York City and New England boomed as the South's
business partners in a national economy that the Civil War
threatened to ruin.*

THE CARRIAGE TRADE
*In the horse-and-buggy age, New Haven vehicle makers catered
to customers in the South.*

Two   FIRST FORTUNES   45
*Massachusetts Puritans led colonial farmers and merchants to
their best market, the West Indies' plantation islands, which were
worked by tens of thousands of slaves.*

TRANSPLANTED YANKEES
*Nathaniel Russell moved from Rhode Island to South Carolina,
sold rum and slaves, and founded the New England Society
of Charleston.*

Three   A CONNECTICUT SLAVE   61
*Venture Smith's autobiography is the narrative of his journey from
bondage to freedom, and a portrait of slavery in the North.*

Four **REBELLION IN MANHATTAN** 77
Two of the earliest slave uprisings occurred in New York, where violent resistance was avenged by dozens of executions.

Five **NEWPORT RUM, AFRICAN SLAVES** 95
For almost a century, the nation's busiest fleet of slave ships sailed from Narragansett Bay in tiny Rhode Island.

HELL'S GATE
Over 130 years, as many as 12,000 Africans may have been transported to America from Sierra Leone's Bunce Island, a favorite port-of-call for New England slave ships.

Six **NEW YORK'S SLAVE PIRATES** 121
When Congress outlawed the slave trade, entrepreneurs moved to where they could better operate undercover.

LAST SURVIVORS
In 1908, an anthropologist photographed Africans who were children when they were packed aboard a slave yacht from New York.

Seven **THE OTHER UNDERGROUND RAILROAD** 139
Free blacks all over the North feared, and fought, abduction to the South by kidnapping gangs.

Eight **HATED HEROES** 155
The radical abolitionism of Prudence Crandall, Elijah Lovejoy, and John Brown incited Northern mobs to riot and murder.

Nine **PHILADELPHIA'S RACE SCIENTIST** 179
Dr. Samuel Morton was a collector of human skulls and a pioneer in the research that served to confirm whites' worst beliefs about blacks.

Ten **PLUNDER FOR PIANOS** 193
From before the Civil War until close to the twentieth century, two Connecticut companies imported tons of elephant ivory in a trade that destroyed the lives of 2 million African slaves.

AFTERWORD   215

CHRONOLOGY   217

NOTES   221

BIBLIOGRAPHY   235

ACKNOWLEDGMENTS   251

INDEX   257

INTRODUCTION

COMPLICITY IS THE STORY OF HOW THE NORTH HELPED CREATE, strengthen, and prolong slavery in America.

We're telling this side of the story because we already know the story of the South. The South's story is set on a plantation in Mississippi or Louisiana or any other Southern state where overseers brandished whips over slaves picking cotton.

In contrast, the North's story is thought to be heroic, filled with ardent abolitionists running that train to freedom, the Underground Railroad. The few slaves who may have lived in the North, it has been believed, were treated like members of the family. And, of course, Northerners were the good guys in the Civil War. They freed the slaves.

Not all of the above is exactly mythology, but it is a convenient and whitewashed shorthand.

The history of the United States is typically told backwards, as a means of explaining to members of the current generation how their country grew to be the way it is. In such an account, slavery is a single chapter, a background event limited to one region of the country and overwhelmed by the more recent events of pioneers moving west, railroads spanning the continent, and great cities growing up around stockyards and steel mills.

A history told frontwards, however, pushes slavery into the foreground, inserting it into nearly every chapter.

The truth is that slavery was a national phenomenon. The North shared in the wealth it created, and in the oppression it required.

While it may seem incredible that the depth of the North's role in slavery is largely unknown to the general public, only since the civil rights movement have many historians themselves begun to recognize how central slavery was to our history. Our intention in *Complicity* is to demonstrate that centrality. By the American Revolution, slavery was already a vital part of the national economy. In the decades after the Revolution, particularly after the patenting of the cotton gin, slavery's importance escalated, and the institution expanded to where, on the eve of the Civil War, there were nearly 4 million people living in bondage in America.

Well before that point, however, slavery had become the foundation of a network of interdependent economic systems throughout the country that rested on the premise that it was acceptable to view black human beings as property. The natural consequences of this deeply racist premise were resistance and violence.

The North was in the perfect position, however, to deal with resistance and violence. By and large, the region's relationship with slavery, though extraordinarily profitable, was a distant one. That distance allowed the North to minimize and even deny its links with the institution that fueled its prosperity.

Consider:

- New England and the Mid-Atlantic began their economic ascent in the eighteenth century because the regions grew and shipped food to help feed millions of slaves—in the West Indies.

- Northern merchants, shippers, and financial institutions, many based in New York City, were crucial players in every phase of the national and international cotton trade. Meanwhile, the rivers and streams of the North, particularly in New England, were crowded with hundreds of textile mills. Well before the Civil War, the economy of the entire North relied heavily on cotton grown by millions of slaves—in the South.

- Even some smaller industries had these distant, but vital, links to slavery. Starting before the Civil War and lasting up to the edge of the twentieth century, two Connecticut towns were an international center for ivory production, milling hundreds of thousands of tons of elephant tusks procured through the enslavement or death of as many as 2 million people—in Africa.

Connecticut's Harriet Beecher Stowe, author of the iconic abolitionist novel *Uncle Tom's Cabin*, said this was slavery the way Northerners liked it: all of the benefits and none of the screams.

As soon as Europeans set foot on this huge, wild continent, they needed help taming it. In the 1640s, John Winthrop, governor of the Massachusetts Bay Colony, received a letter from his brother-in-law Emanuel Downing, who complained about how much work needed to be done. Downing suggested to the governor that a "just war" against Indians could provide the colony with captives to exchange in the West Indies for badly needed "Moores."

Thus, from the very beginning, the nation's experience with slavery was defined by commerce and violence, in the North as well as the South. This is the backbone of *Complicity*, which opens in the time and place where the fruits of hundreds of years of slave labor may have been the most dramatically realized: in New York City, as the country trembled on the edge of civil war.

The antislavery Abraham Lincoln had just been elected president, pushing the Southern states over the edge to secession. The disintegration of America inspired a most curious response on the part of New York's mayor: he publicly declared that his city should secede from the Union along with the Southern states, in large part because of New York's economic dependence on the cotton trade.

Meanwhile, even before the 1860 election, Boston-area manufacturers—though some held antislavery views—were desperately currying favor with the Southern politicians and planters whose millions of slaves delivered the product necessary to their wealth and financial survival. These businessmen were, after all, in textiles, and what would they do without cotton?

Before the Civil War, the North grew rich beyond measure by agreeing to live, however uneasily at times, with slavery. Perhaps as a consequence of striking that bargain, Northerners have pushed much of their early history into the deepest shadows of repression. Many of the facts can, frankly, be shocking:

- In the eighteenth century, even after America won its freedom from Great Britain, even after the writing of the Declaration of Independence, tens of thousands of black people were living as slaves in the North. Earlier in that century, enslaved blacks made up nearly one-fifth of the population of New York City.

- In the first half of the eighteenth century, two major slave revolts occurred in New York City. During the second uprising, with haunting parallels to the hysteria surrounding the Salem witch trials 50 years earlier, 31 black people, all slaves, and 4 white people were either hanged or burned alive at the stake.

- At the same time that the North was selling food and other supplies to the sugar plantations that blanketed the islands of the Caribbean, thousands of acres of Connecticut, New York, and tiny Rhode Island held plantations that used slave labor.

- In the century before Congress finally banned the importation of slaves, Rhode Island was America's leader in the transatlantic trade, launching nearly 1,000 voyages to Africa and carrying at least 100,000 captives back across the Atlantic. The captains and crews of these ships were often the veteran seamen of America: New Englanders.

- In the decades before the Civil War, New York City's bustling seaport became the hub of an enormously lucrative illegal slave trade. Manhattan shipyards built ships to carry captive Africans, the vessels often outfitted with crates of shackles and with the huge water tanks needed for their human cargo. A conservative estimate is that during the illegal trade's peak years, 1859 and 1860, at least two slave ships—each built to hold between 600 and 1,000 slaves—left lower Manhattan every month.

- A Harvard University zoologist was a major figure in the now-discredited field of "race science." His mentor, one of the most eminent physicians in Philadelphia, had a world-famous collection of human skulls that the "ethnologists" said proved that blacks of African descent had the smallest "cranial capacity" among all humans and thus were doomed to inferiority. These influential scientists not only helped justify slavery, they helped solidify the myth of black inferiority. "Race science" may well be the most lasting and devastating legacy of the North's involvement in slavery.

IN 1954, THE BRILLIANT SOCIAL HISTORIAN W.E.B. DU BOIS OF MASSAchusetts penned an apologia upon the republication of his seminal 1896 work *The Suppression of the African Slave Trade to the United States of America, 1638–1870.* He wrote:

> *If the influence of economic motives on the action of mankind ever had a clearer illustration it was in the modern history of the African race, and particularly in America.*

I still saw slavery and the [slave] trade as chiefly a result of moral lassitude. . . . But apparently I did not clearly see that the real difficulty rested in the willingness of a privileged class of Americans to get power and comfort at the expense of degrading a class of black slaves, by not paying them what their labor deserved.

Early Americans needed cheap labor. Coming to a wild and hostile continent in search of religious freedom, they had to find their way and then, eventually, try to compete with much older and established European nations. How could they not have been in a hurry to settle this wilderness, put together a workable way to govern themselves, and, both as a nation and as individuals, earn a living?

Slavery has long been identified in the national consciousness as a Southern institution. The time to bury that myth is overdue. Slavery is a story about America, all of America. The nation's wealth, from the very beginning, depended upon the exploitation of black people on three continents. Together, over the lives of millions of enslaved men and women, Northerners and Southerners shook hands and made a country.

Here's what the Northerners were shaking on.

COMPLICITY

The nation's financial and

manufacturing centers,

New York and Massachusetts,

spun gold from the

slave fields of the South.

One

COTTON COMES NORTH

"The ships would rot at her docks; grass would grow in Wall Street and
Broadway, and the glory of New York, like that of Babylon and Rome,
would be numbered with the things of the past."

The answer given by a prominent Southern editor
when asked by The Times *(London),*
"What would New York be without slavery?"

FERNANDO WOOD THOUGHT HIS TIMING WAS PERFECT.
The election of an antislavery president had finally forced the
South to make good on years of threats, and the exodus of 11 states from
the Union had begun. Militant South Carolina was the first to secede,
after a convention in Charleston five days before Christmas of 1860.
Within weeks, 6 more states had broken off from the Union, and by the
end of May, the Confederacy was complete.

As the most profound crisis in our young nation's history unrolled,
Wood, the mayor of New York, America's most powerful city, made a
stunning proposal: New York City should secede from the United
States, too.

"With our aggrieved brethren of the Slave States, we have friendly
relations and a common sympathy," Wood told the New York Common
Council in his State of the City message on January 7, 1861. "As a free
city," he said, New York "would have the whole and united support of
the Southern States, as well as all other States to whose interests and
rights under the constitution she has always been true."

Although many in the city's intelligentsia rolled their eyes, and the mayor was slammed in much of the New York press, Wood's proposal made a certain kind of sense. The mayor was reacting to tensions with Albany, but there was far more behind his secession proposal, particularly if one understood that the lifeblood of New York City's economy was cotton, the product most closely identified with the South and its defining system of labor: the slavery of millions of people of African descent.

As the Southern states started to secede, the controversial Fernando Wood, sometimes referred to as New York's "Southern mayor," proposed that his city join the cotton-producing states in leaving the Union. *Brady National Photographic Art Gallery, courtesy of James Wadsworth Family Papers, Library of Congress*

Slave-grown cotton is, in large part, the root of New York's wealth. Forty years before Fernando Wood suggested that New York join hands with the South and leave the Union, cotton had already become the nation's number one exported product. And in the four intervening decades New York had become a commercial and financial behemoth dwarfing any other U.S. city and most others in the world. Cotton was more than just a profitable crop. It was the national currency, the product most responsible for America's explosive growth in the decades before the Civil War.

As much as it is linked to the barbaric system of slave labor that raised it, cotton created New York.

By the eve of the war, hundreds of businesses in New York, and countless more throughout the North, were connected to, and dependent upon, cotton. As New York became the fulcrum of the U.S. cotton trade, merchants, shippers, auctioneers, bankers, brokers, insurers, and thousands of others were drawn to the burgeoning urban center. They packed lower Manhattan, turning it into the nation's emporium, in which products from all over the world were traded.

In those prewar decades, hundreds of shrewd merchants and smart businessmen made their fortunes in ventures directly or indirectly tied to cotton. The names of some of them reverberate today.

Three brothers named Lehman were cotton brokers in Montgomery, Alabama, before they moved to New York and helped to establish the New York Cotton Exchange. Today, of course, Lehman Brothers is the international investment firm.

Junius Morgan, father of J. Pierpont Morgan, arranged for his son to study the cotton trade in the South as the future industrialist and banker was beginning his business career. Morgan Sr., a Massachusetts native who became a major banker and cotton broker in London, understood that knowledge of the cotton trade was essential to prospering in the commercial world in the 1850s.

Real estate and shipping magnate John Jacob Astor—one of America's first millionaires and namesake of the Waldorf-Astoria and whole neighborhoods in New York City—made his fortune in furs and the China trade. But Astor's ships, like those of many successful merchant-shippers, also carried tons of cotton.

Cotton's rich threads can even be traced to an ambitious young man who dreamed of opening a "fancy goods" store in New York. The young man's father, who operated a cotton mill in eastern Connecticut, gave his son the money to open his first store, on Broadway, in 1837. But more important than the $500 stake made from cotton was the young man's destination and timing: Charles L. Tiffany had begun serving a city in extraordinary, and enduring, economic ascent.

As with any commodity, trading in cotton was complicated and risky. Businessmen, even savvy ones, lost fortunes, but some made their mark on the city nonetheless.

As cotton was becoming a staple in the transatlantic trade, Scotsman Archibald Gracie immigrated to New York after training in Liverpool, Great Britain's great cotton port. Gracie became an international shipping magnate, a merchant prince, building a summer home on the East River before losing much of his wealth. His son and grandson left the city to become cotton brokers in Mobile, Alabama, but their family's summer home, today called Gracie Mansion, is the official residence of the mayor of New York.

But beyond identifying the individuals who prospered from the South's most important product, it's vital to understand the economic climate—the vast opportunities for wealth that the cotton trade created, and that linked New York City so tightly to the South. Before the Civil War, the city's fortunes, its very future, were considered by many to be inseparable from those of the cotton-producing states.

Secession was not even an original thought with Wood, a tall, charming, three-term scoundrel of a mayor and multiterm congressman. For years, members of New York's business community had mused privately, and occasionally in the pages of journals, that the city would be better off as a "free port," independent of tariff-levying politicians in Albany and Washington. As America unraveled over the issue of slavery, many Northern politicians and businessmen became frantic to reach out to their most important constituency: Southern planters.

New York was not the only area in the North whose future was threatened by the growing secession crisis. In Massachusetts, birthplace of America, and the center of an increasingly troublesome movement called abolitionism, the Southern states' frequent threats to secede had become an ongoing nightmare for the leaders of the powerful textile industry.

By 1860, New England was home to 472 cotton mills, built on rivers and streams throughout the region. The town of Thompson, Connecticut, alone, for example, had seven mills within its nine-square-mile area. Hundreds of other textile mills were scattered in New York State, New Jersey, and elsewhere in the North. Just between 1830 and 1840, Northern mills consumed more than 100 million pounds of Southern cotton. With shipping and manufacturing included, the economy of much of New England was connected to textiles.

For years, the national dispute over slavery had been growing more and more alarming to the powerful group of Massachusetts businessmen that historians refer to as the Boston Associates. When this handful of brilliant industrialists established America's textile industry earlier in the nineteenth century, they also created America's own industrial revolution. By the 1850s, their enormous profits had been poured into a complex network of banks, insurance companies, and railroads. But their wealth remained anchored to dozens of mammoth textile mills in Massachusetts, southern Maine, and New Hampshire. Some of these places were textile cities, really—like Lowell and Lawrence, Massachusetts, both named for Boston Associates founders.

As the nation lurched toward war and the certainty of economic disruption, these industrialists and allied politicians wanted to convince the South that at least some in the North were eager to compromise on slavery. A compromise was critical, for the good of the Union and business.

On the evening of October 11, 1858, a standing-room-only audience of politicians and businessmen honored a visitor at a rally at Faneuil Hall, long the center of Boston's public life. The wealthy and powerful of New England's preeminent city lauded the "intellectual cultivation" and "eloquence" of the senator from Mississippi, and when Jefferson

Davis walked onto the stage, the Brahmins of Boston gave him a standing ovation.

OTHER AMERICAN STAPLES, SUCH AS CORN, WHEAT, AND TOBACCO, HAVE a charged or even exalted status in our nation's narrative. And other resources—whale oil, coal, and gold—were the main characters in defining chapters of American history.

But cotton was king.

On the cusp of the Civil War, the 10 major cotton states were producing 66 percent of the world's cotton, and raw cotton accounted for more than half of all U.S. exports. The numbers are almost impossible to grasp: in the season that ended on August 31, 1860, the United States produced close to 5 million bales of cotton, or roughly 2.3 *billion* pounds. Of that amount, it exported about half—or more than 1 billion pounds—to Great Britain's 2,650 cotton factories.

America's most common cotton plant is *Gossypium hirsutum,* or upland cotton. *Chicago Historical Society*

By then, the Industrial Revolution had spread throughout Europe. Although small compared with Great Britain's, France's textile industry, centered in Lille, was also fed almost entirely by U.S. cotton, 200 million pounds' worth in 1858. And Southern cotton was important to textile industries in the Netherlands, Switzerland, Germany, Austria, Russia, Italy, Spain, and Belgium.

But most of the world's cotton went through Liverpool, the port nearest Manchester in Lancashire, the heart of textile manufacturing. Up until the end of the 1700s, Great Britain had imported most of its cotton from the Mediterranean, its colonies in the West Indies, and India and Brazil. But in 1794 Eli Whitney, the son of a Massachusetts farmer, patented his cotton gin (invented the previous year), and it changed the world.

The problem with cotton is its seeds. Nestled deep in the fibers of every fist-sized boll of upland cotton—the predominant type grown in

COTTON CROP OF THE UNITED STATES.

Statement and Total Amount for the year ending 31st August, 1850.

NEW-ORLEANS.	Bales.	Total.	1849.
Export—			
To Foreign Ports................624,748			
Coastwise.....................913,843			
Stock, 1st September, 1850............16,612	855,203		
Deduct—			
Stock, 1st September, 1849............15,480			
Received from Mobile and Montgomery, Ala...41,148			
Received from Florida..............10,601			
Received from Texas...............6,088	73,317	781,886	1,033,707

ALABAMA.			
Export—			
To Foreign Ports................214,164			
Coastwise.....................128,872			
Stock, 1st September, 1850............12,960	355,996		
Deduct—			
Stock, 1st September, 1849............5,946	5,946	350,052	518,706

FLORIDA.			
Export—			
To Foreign Ports................48,934			
Coastwise.....................131,877			
Stock, 1st September, 1850............1,148	181,959		
*Deduct—*Stock, 1st September, 1849..........615	615	181,344	200,186

TEXAS.			
Export—			
To Foreign Ports.................513			
Coastwise.....................30,937			
Stock, 1st September, 1850............265	31,715		
*Deduct—*Stock, 1st September, 1849..........432	432	31,283	38,827

GEORGIA.			
Export from SAVANNAH—			
To Foreign Ports—Uplands..........144,540			
Sea Islands............8,603			
Coastwise—Uplands.............186,721			
Sea Islands............1,839	341,703		
Export from DARIEN—			
To New-York...................22			
Stock in Savannah, 1st September, 1850........9,599			
Stock in Augusta and Hamburg, 1st Sept. 1850...19,470	29,091	370,794	
Deduct—			
Stock in Savannah and Augusta, 1st Sept. 1849...25,319			
Received from Florida.............1,840	27,159	343,635	391,372

SOUTH CAROLINA.			
Export from CHARLESTON—			
To Foreign Ports—Uplands..........213,265			
Sea Islands............14,366			
Coastwise—Uplands.............152,122			
Sea Islands............2,071	381,764		
Burnt at Charleston................6,146			
Export from GEORGETOWN—			
To New-York and Boston.............1,449			
Stock in Charleston, 1st Sept. 1850.......30,698	33,147	420,057	
Deduct—			
Stock in Charleston, 1st September, 1849.....23,896			
Received from Savannah.............11,647			
Received from Florida.............338	35,792	384,265	458,117

NORTH CAROLINA.			
*Export—*Coastwise................	11,861	11,861	10,041

VIRGINIA.			
Export—			
To Foreign Ports.................183			
Coastwise, and	} 12,067		
Manufactured (Taken from the Ports).			
Stock, 1st September, 1850............1,000	13,250		
*Deduct—*Stock, 1st September, 1849..........1,750	1,750	17,550	

| TOTAL CROP OF THE UNITED STATES........... | | 2,096,706 | 2,728,596 |

Total Crop of 1850, as above............	bales.	2,096,706
Crop of 1849....................		2,728,596
Crop of 1848....................		2,347,634
Crop of 1847....................		1,778,651
Decrease from last year.........	bales.	631,890
Decrease from year before.........		250,928

EXPORT TO FOREIGN PORTS,

From September 1, 1849, to August 31, 1850.

FROM	To Great Britain.	To France.	To North of Europe.	Other Fn Ports.	TOTAL.
New-Orleans.............bales.	397,189	117,413	25,196	84,950	624,748
Mobile.................	162,219	39,968		11,977	214,164
Florida.................	39,594	..	7,165	2,175	48,934
Texas.................	513	..			513
Georgia.................	137,185	14,110	1,848		153,143
South Carolina...........	165,623	33,082	8,944	19,922	227,571
North Carolina...........	..	..			183
Virginia.................	..	..	133	50	432
Baltimore...............	902	..	230		4,053
Philadelphia.............	3,454	..		589	314,680
New-York...............	200,113	85,934	27,796	1,907	1,614
Boston.................	679	..	914	21	
GRAND TOTAL.........	1,106,571	289,627	72,156	121,601	1,590,155
Total last year............	1,537,901	368,259	165,458	156,226	2,227,844
Decrease.............	431,130	78,632	93,302	34,625	637,689

GROWTH.

Crop of 1823–4..bales. 509,158	1832—3.....bales. 1,070,438	1841—2......bales. 1,683,574
1824—5........569,249	1833—4........1,205,394	1842—3......2,378,875
1825—6........720,027	1834—5........1,254,328	1843—4......2,030,409
1826—7........957,281	1835—6........1,360,725	1844—5......2,394,503
1827—8........720,593	1836—7........1,422,930	1845—6......2,100,537
1828—9........857,744	1837—8........1,801,497	1846—7......1,778,651
1829—30.......976,845	1838—9........1,360,532	1847—8......2,347,634
1830—31......1,038,848	1839—40.......2,177,635	1848—9......2,728,596
1831—2........987,477	1840—1........1,634,945	1849—50......2,096,706

CONSUMPTION.

Total Crop of the United States, as above stated.........		bales.	2,096,706
Add—			
Stocks on hand at the commencement of the year, 1st Sept. 1849:			
In the Southern Ports...........	72,468		
In the Northern Ports...........	82,285	154,753	
			2,251,459
Makes a Supply of............		2,251,459	
Deduct therefrom—			
The Export to Foreign Ports.......	1,590,155		
Less, Foreign included.......	1,341	1,588,814	
Stocks on hand, 1st September, 1850:			
In the Southern Ports...........	91,774		
In the Northern Ports...........	76,176	167,930	
Burnt at New-York and Charleston.......		6,946	1,763,690
Taken for Home use.........		bales.	487,769

Quantity consumed by and in the hands of Manufacturers.

1849–50.....bales. 487,769	1841—2......bales. 267,850	1833—4......bales. 196,413
1848—9........518,039	1840—1........297,288	1832—3........194,412
1847—8........531,772	1839—40.......295,193	1831—2........173,800
1846—7........427,967	1838—9........276,018	1830—1........182,142
1845—6........422,597	1837—8........246,063	1829—30.......126,512
1844—5........369,000	1836—7........222,540	1828—9........118,853
1843—4........346,744	1835—6........236,733	1827—8........190,593
1842—3........325,129	1834—5........216,888	1826—7........149,516

In our last Annual Statement, the Estimate of Cotton taken for Consumption for the year ending Sept. 1, 1849, in the States South and West of Virginia, was probably over-estimated—the following for the past year is believed to be very nearly correct. The number of Mills has increased since that time, and is still increasing, but the quantity consumed, as far as we can learn, is, owing to high prices, &c. less than the year previous. The following Estimate is from a judicious and careful observer at the South, of the quantity so consumed, and not included in the Receipts. Thus, in—

	Mills.	Spindles.	Quantity consumed.
North Carolina.........	30	..	20,000 bales.
South Carolina.........	16	36,500	15,000 "
Georgia..............	36	51,150	27,000 "
Alabama.............	11	16,969	6,000 "
Tennessee............	30	36,000	12,000 "
On the Ohio, &c.........	30	102,220	27,500 "
Total to Sept. 1, 1850................			107,500 bales.
Total to Sept. 1, 1849................			110,000 "
Total to Sept. 1, 1848................			75,000 "

To which should be added the Stocks in the interior Towns, the quantity burnt in the interior, and that lost on its way to market; these, added to the Crop as given above, received at the Shipping Ports, will show very nearly the amount raised in the United States the past season—say, in round numbers, 2,212,000 bales.

The quantity of new Cotton received at the Shipping Ports up to the 1st inst. amounted to about 255 bales, against about 575 bales last year.

The Shipments given in this Statement from TEXAS, are those by Sea only; a considerable portion of the Crop of that State finds its way to market via Red River, and is included in the Receipts at New-Orleans.

Editors copying the above, will please give us the proper credit.

OFFICE OF THE SHIPPING AND COMMERCIAL LIST,
AND NEW-YORK PRICE CURRENT,

No. 158 Pearl-street, N. Y.

NEW-YORK, SEPTEMBER 11, 1850.

From 1840 to 1850, the U.S. cotton crop remained steady at about 2 million bales a year, as indicated in this chart from the Office of the Shipping and Commercial List on New York's Pearl Street. By 1860, the crop had more than doubled to 4.8 million bales, or about 2.4 trillion pounds. *Chicago Historical Society*

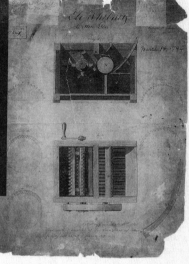

After graduating from Yale, Eli Whitney traveled to the South and invented his revolutionary cotton gin. His simple creation made cotton processing so much easier, and more profitable, that the Deep South became largely a one-crop region. *Portrait of Eli Whitney by Samuel F. B. Morse, New Haven Colony Historical Society*

Whitney submitted this drawing of his gin when he applied for a patent in 1794. His concept was so quickly replicated that he made very little money from his invention. *National Archives and Records Administration*

America—are 30 to 40 impossibly sticky green seeds that must be removed before the white, fluffy fibers can be used.

Before Whitney patented his gin, it took one person an entire day to remove the seeds from a pound of cotton. The gin both mechanized and accelerated the process. The teeth of a series of circular saws "captured" the seeds, allowing the fibers to be pulled away from them. The device increased the production of cleaned cotton an astonishing fiftyfold. In seeking a patent for his invention, Whitney wrote to Thomas Jefferson, then secretary of state, explaining that by using the gin, "one negro [could] . . . clean fifty weight (I mean fifty pounds after it is separated from the seed), of the green seed cotton per day." Jefferson was one of the first plantation owners to order a gin.

Growing cotton suddenly became hugely profitable. Farmers across the South switched over to cotton, and within only about 15 years they were supplying more than half of Great Britain's demand for the product. Well before 1860, the relationship between Great Britain and the South had become ironclad.

A lot of cotton required a lot of slaves. In 1850, some 2.3 million people were enslaved in the 10 cotton states; of these, nearly 2 million were involved in some aspect of cotton production. And their numbers, and importance, just kept growing.

As early as 1836, the secretary of the treasury told Congress that with "less than 100,000 more field hands" and the conversion of just 500,000 more acres of rich Southern land, the United States could produce enough raw cotton for the entire world.

By the eve of the Civil War, Great Britain was largely clothing the Western world, using Southern-grown, slave-picked cotton.

In 1850, the South was home to about 75,000 cotton plantations. Alabama, Mississippi, and Georgia each had over 14,500. The cotton states produced a staggering 2 million bales that year. Even people who saw the trade in action struggled to describe it.

In December 1848, Solon Robinson, a farmer and writer from Connecticut who became agriculture editor for the *New York Tribune*, visited the nation's largest cotton port. "It must be seen to be believed," Robinson wrote of the "acres of cotton bales" standing on the docks of New Orleans. "Boats are constantly arriving, so piled up with cotton, that the lower tier of bales on deck are in the water; and as the boat is approaching, it looks like a huge raft of cotton bales, with the chimneys and steam pipe of an engine sticking up out of the centre."

From New Orleans and the other major cotton ports—Savannah, Georgia; Charleston, South Carolina; and Mobile, Alabama—most of the cotton was shipped to Liverpool. If it did not go directly to Liverpool, it was sent to the North: to Boston for use in the domestic textile industry, or to New York City. From New York, it generally went to Liverpool, or elsewhere in Europe.

But this gives only the slightest hint of the role New York City and the rest of the North played in the cotton trade, or of the lengths the New York business community was forced to go to protect its franchise.

The Union Committee of Fifteen had called a meeting at the offices of Richard Lathers, a prominent cotton merchant. The organizers had planned to invite 200 people, and by written invitation only. But the group that thronged outside of Lathers's offices at 33 Pine Street, a block over from Wall Street, surpassed 2,000. In fact, offices across the street had to be quickly commandeered to accommodate the crowd, and even then the merchants, bankers, and others who gathered that Saturday afternoon spilled into the street.

This was hardly the first time that the worried business community had met to discuss strategies to smooth relations between North and South. But the Pine Street meeting on December 15, 1860, may have represented the group at its most panicky. South Carolina's probable secession vote was days away, and there was talk of Alabama following South Carolina. After that, who knew? The South had to be persuaded to stay in the Union until some kind of compromise in the slavery controversy could be found.

The very spine of nineteenth-century money and power attended the meeting. These "merchant princes" included:

- A. T. Stewart, a cotton merchant who opened the nation's first department store, called "the marble palace," on Broadway. Stewart was thought to be the wealthiest man in New York.

- Moses Taylor, sugar importer, banker, and coal and railroad magnate, whose extensive enterprises made him, for nearly half a century, one of the most influential businessmen in New York City.

- Abiel Abbot Low, whose A. A. Low & Brothers was the most important firm in the new and booming China trade.

- William B. Astor, son of fur and real estate mogul John Jacob Astor, the nation's first millionaire.

- Wall Street banker August Belmont, American agent for the Rothschilds of Germany, who married the daughter of Commodore Perry and whose passion for horse breeding led to the creation of the Belmont Stakes.

Also invited were shipping magnates William H. Aspinwall and his partners Robert Minturn and Henry Grinnell; editors of the *Journal of Commerce* and the *New York Herald;* and several politicians, including two former and future mayors, future presidential candidate Samuel J. Tilden, and former president Millard Fillmore.

Lathers directed his opening comments to Southern planters, urging them to "consider their duties to that part of their Northern brethren whose sympathies have always been with Southern rights and against Northern aggression."

Lawyer Charles O'Conor, longtime defender of slavery, argued that in considering whether to leave the Union, the South was just struggling "to keep its head above the rapidly advancing waters of this black sea of abolitionism, which threatens to drown it."

O'Conor paused, interrupted by applause, then continued, "There is no source of evil whatever in the North except the honest, conscientious mistake of the honest, conscientious people of the North, who have drank into their bosoms this dreadful error—that it is their duty . . . to crush out and trample upon the system of Slavery upon which the prosperity of the South and the permanency of this Union in its present form depend."

As the afternoon lengthened, entreaties to the South grew more emotional. John A. Dix, New Hampshire native, former New York senator, and future New York governor, seemed to sum up the sentiments of the day in declaring: "We will not review the dark history of the aggression and insult visited upon you by Abolitionists and their abettors during the last thirty-five years. Our detestation of these acts of hostility is not inferior to your own."

FROM 1825 ON, IN VOLUME AND VALUE OF IMPORTS AND EXPORTS, THE seaport at South Street outdid the combined trade of its two closest competitors in Boston and Philadelphia. New York's dominance only in-

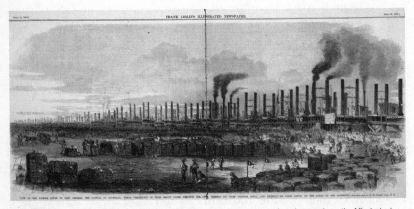

New Orleans's docks were busy in 1860, as the biggest cotton crop ever produced came down the Mississippi for export to Europe and to the North. By that point, the United States had nearly 4 million people in bondage, about 2.25 million of whom labored in the cotton industry. View of the Famous Levee of New Orleans, New Orleans (La.), Frank Leslie's Illustrated Newspaper, *April 14, 1860, Chicago Historical Society*

creased as the nineteenth century progressed. Long before civil war loomed, New York, after London and Paris, had become the third major city of the Western world.

Its glory was built largely of bricks of cotton.

At nearly five feet high and some 500 pounds, a bale of cotton is an impressive presence. In the pre-plastic nineteenth century, bales were bound in tightly woven burlap or held more loosely in place by coarse, large-gapped material from which a sample could easily be sliced and tested for quality. Thin metal bands reinforced the wrapping. But this huge block of soft fibers seemed to burst from its covering, bulging over its tight bands, a muscleman squeezed into a T-shirt.

Their rectangular shape allowed bales to be stacked, stories high, and remain stable while being shipped down the Mississippi River or one of its tributaries, up the East Coast, or across the Atlantic. A bale would be tilted back onto a dolly and wheeled from a dock onto one of thousands of flatboats, sloops, brigs, barks, schooners, clippers, and steamboats. For the half century before the Civil War, cotton was the backbone of the American economy. It was king, and the North ruled the kingdom.

From seed to cloth, Northern merchants, shippers, and financial institutions, many based in New York, controlled nearly every aspect of cotton production and trade.

Only large banks, generally located in Manhattan, or in London, could extend to plantation owners the credit they needed between planting and selling their crop. If a farmer wanted to expand his operations during those boom decades, he required the deep pockets of Northern banks to lend him the money to buy additional equipment, as well as additional labor. Slaves were usually bought on credit.

The power of New York over key aspects of cotton production was wide and deep, and involved many of the most solid and prestigious businessmen of the day.

Nathaniel Prime, for example, one of the half-dozen richest men in New York, was first partner of the largest private bank in the city—Prime, Ward & King—in the early part of the nineteenth century. Prime, a New Englander, was Aaron Burr's broker and reportedly his breakfast companion on July 11, 1804, hours after Burr fatally shot Alexander Hamilton. Samuel Ward was the father of reformer and activist Julia Ward Howe, who wrote the verse for the "Battle Hymn of the Republic." James Gore King was the son of Rufus King—a U.S. senator from New York, a vice-presidential and presidential candidate, and U.S. minister to Great Britain. James King had been a Liverpool banker before moving to New York.

Other Northerners made up the long chain of middlemen linking plantation owner and manufacturer. The first and most important was the cotton "factor," who, through his contacts in New York, helped the isolated, rural planter earn the best price in the volatile world marketplace. Factors, generally New Englanders, were more than brokers or agents. They often bought a planter's supplies, advised him, and took charge of his finances; frequently they knew more about the condition of a plantation than the owner. A factor's success depended on being indispensable, and that required him to provide a high quality of service in return for his commission on a cotton sale. Factors had a lot to juggle.

Take William Bostwick, a Connecticut-born cotton factor based in Augusta, Georgia. On October 27, 1835, Bostwick wrote to Charles Lippitt, a Rhode Island–born factor in Savannah. His letter reflects the breadth and details of the services Bostwick offered his clients:

Dear Sir

Attached is rect [receipt] for 60 Bales Cotton which please ship to Messrs Thad Phelps & Co New York with all the dispatch practible charging them with expenses— As you receive cheese from N York please ship them by such boats as you think will make the most speed *and please use your best exertions to give them every dispatch practicable—*

Yrs
WB

N.B.: The remaining 239 Bales went on board yesterday and I presume will leave here to day or Tomorrow

WB

Northerners' influence and control infused nearly every phase of the trade. Most ships that carried the cotton from plantation to port to market were built in the North, and they were usually owned by Northerners. Their captains and crews were often New Englanders. Northern companies sold the insurance to protect a farmer's crop and all of his property, including his slaves. And hundreds of Northern textile mills clothed those slaves, using what was sometimes referred to as "negro cloth."

As it evolved into a hub of international trade, New York City also became a locus for commerce on an unprecedented scale in the United States.

The docks of South Street are lined with packets. The ship in the foreground, the *Leeds,* built in New York, was part of the Swallowtail Line, cofounded by a New Bedford, Massachusetts, whaling captain with the extraordinary name of Preserved Fish. While leaving London, the ship ran aground in the Thames River on December 24, 1828, the year this etching was created. View of South Street from Maiden Lane, New York City *(54. 90. 130) William James Bennett, The Metropolitan Museum of Art*

New York's physical attributes—including the fact that it was the only East Coast port deep enough in any tide to accommodate the largest vessels of the era—set the stage for the city's preeminence. The city's dominance was further assured in 1825 with the opening of the Erie Canal, which allowed the exchange of goods with the fast-expanding western United States.

But important developments earlier in the nineteenth century also boosted New York's position.

At the end of the War of 1812, with its devastating trade embargoes, Great Britain dumped its huge, pent-up supply of textiles and other goods on the New York market, drastically undercutting the price of anything being produced domestically, and drawing bargain-hungry merchants from all over the country. At about the same time, a new system of sales auctions was implemented—one that further guaranteed great deals for buyers. Nationwide, businessmen quickly came to see New York as a commercial mecca.

But if any development cemented New York's top spot, it was the creation of "sailing packets," shuttles that assured the business world on both sides of the Atlantic of regular delivery of goods. The phenomenon was the brainchild of one of the world's top cotton merchants, the savvy, enormously wealthy Jeremiah Thompson, a Yorkshire Quaker based in Manhattan.

In October 1817, Thompson placed an eye-popping advertisement in the New York trade papers. Topped with a picture of four small ships, the announcement alerted the public that starting in January, the *James Monroe*, the *Amity*, the *Courier*, and the *Pacific* would leave from New York and Liverpool on a guaranteed regular schedule. "The ships have all been built in New York, of the best materials, and are coppered and copper fastened," the ad read. "It is also thought that the regularity of their times of sailing, and the excellent condition in which they deliver

By offering scheduled deliveries on both sides of the Atlantic, the Black Ball Line revolutionized commerce. It also became the model for other oceanic and coastal lines—such as the London Black X, the Red Star, and the Blue and Red Swallowtails—before being superseded by larger and faster steamships. The Black Ball Line survived the Civil War, not stopping its run until 1878. © *Mystic Seaport, Mystic, Connecticut*

This 1857 map shows lower Manhattan lined with wharves labeled by vessel destination. The East Side is dense with docks serving Liverpool, England, and many Southern cities, an indication of New York's dominance in the cotton trade. *[Detail] Map Division, The New York Public Library, Astor, Lenox and Tilden Foundations*

their cargoes, will make them very desirable opportunities for the conveyance of goods."

The launch of Thompson's Black Ball Line also launched a storied era of transatlantic races and daring, colorful captains. Using ships termed "packets," after the leather mail pouches they carried, Black Ball was the first of more than a dozen shipping lines in the United States that transported products and passengers across the ocean—to Liverpool, and to Le Havre, in France—and up and down the East Coast. The ships would carry goods from Europe and the North to the Atlantic cotton ports of Charleston and Savannah, and to ports on the Gulf of Mexico, including the mammoth New Orleans. They would return north with holds full of raw cotton. The Cotton Triangle had been created.

Thus, though geographically improbable, New York became the fulcrum of the international cotton trade. It would have made more sense for Southern ports to trade directly with merchants and manufacturers across the Atlantic. But that would have cut New York out of the loop, and the city's shipping community needed the guarantee of a cargo of cotton to make its shuttles economical.

So for decades Southern cotton was waylaid 200 miles north to the South Street seaport, where it was unloaded and then reloaded onto Liverpool- and Continent-bound vessels. In doing so, myriad costs and jobs were added to the trade, allowing New York to cash in on a crop grown thousands of miles south.

Similarly, packets on their return voyage across the Atlantic were filled with textiles from the mills of Manchester and other European centers. In New York, these goods, too, were unloaded and then reloaded onto other ships that brought European and Northern products to coastal and river ports throughout the United States. The fast-expanding country offered a huge market for these goods.

As early as 1822, only four years after the start of the Black Ball Line, cotton made up 40 percent of New York exports. Clinching New York's reliance on the South was the fact that, except for flour, which was largely a Northern product, slave-grown tobacco and rice were the top exports. The South was providing New York with more than half of its exports.

THE COTTON TRADE DREW HUNDREDS OF OTHER BUSINESSES TO THE city and the region. An 1846–1847 business directory attests to the vibrancy of lower Manhattan. The major arteries, already teeming with immigrants, were South Street, home of the seaport and shipping firms;

Complete List of Merchants and Commercial Houses, Etc.,
Located on South Street in the Year 1851
(Taken from Doggett's New York City Directory for 1851)

	NAME	BUSINESS		NAME	BUSINESS
1	Nehemiah Mason and Foote	Liquor	10	C. V. Spencer	Commission Merchant
	Solomon Foote			Cowing and Company	Commission Merchant
	M. H. Mead	Clothing		J. A. Cowing	
	Samuel Noyes	Grindstone			
	W. W. Townsend	Accountant	11	P. J. Nevius and Sons	Commission Merchant
	Asa Blake	Refectory		J. R. Nevius	
				P. J. Nevius, Jr.	
2-3	Robert F. Sage	Commission Merchant		E. Fish and Company	Commission Merchant
4	J. S. Whitney and Company	Commission Merchant	12	B. Hook	Liquors
	J. F. Whitney			Thomas Birdsall	Bowling
	Smith and Boynton	Commission Merchant			
	Life Smith		13	S. and D. S. Bloomfield	Ship Chandlers
	John Boynton				
				A. VanOrden	Harbormaster
5	A. D. Baker	Cider			
	A. M. Keeler	Measurer	14	I. H. Graft	Liquors
	E. W. Dunham and Son	Merchants			
	Edward Dunham			**Here Broad Street Intersects**	
6	Sturges and Company	Commission Merchant	15	William Parker and Son	Liquors
	T. T. Sturges			Wallis Parker	
	J. S. Sturges			Alanson Cash	
				L. W. Brainard	Agent
7	P. P. Demarest	Provisions		W. M. Cahoon	Grain Measures' Office
	J. J. Schoonmaker	Agent			
	William Schuyler	Agent		William Osborn	
	Durant, Lathrop and Company	Agent		J. G. Ketcham	
	T. C. Durant			R. Cahoon	
	James McDonnell	Agent		W. Beach	
	J. W. Burnham	Agent		O. T. Smith	
				R. Vaughan	
	Here Moore Street Intersects			M. Gray	Agent
				J. S. Conklin	Agent
8	Alva Whedon	Agent		C. P. Tappen	Flour Inspectors' Office
	H. T. Holmes	Agent		Thomas Hadden	
	Henry Arppen	Liquors		John Marshall	
	Thomas Kimball	Agent		J. B. Oakley	
	C. C. Nukerck	Agent		Daniel Brinkerhoff	
				Henry Shields	
9	Lefferts and Benson	Commission Merchant		W. W. Yardley	
	R. B. Lefferts			P. T. Chamberlin	
	Robert Benson, Jr.				
	J. B. Wright and Company	Commission Merchant	16	Wicks and Douglas	Flour
	D. Ryder and Company	Cider		F. J. Wicks	
	J. J. Ryder			R. J. Douglas	
				J. H. Redfield and Company	Agents of Swiftsure Line
				N. VanSantvoord	Agents

Pearl Street, longtime base for brokers of dry goods and other commodities; and already-influential Wall Street, the financial heart.

The marvel was that it could all be contained in a few square miles before development spread north up the island. By the second decade of the nineteenth century, New York City was developing into the nation's shopping paradise.

In the eighteenth century, Wall Street contained several slave markets named after prominent New York families who participated in the international slave trade. *Picture Collection, The Branch Libraries, The New York Public Library, Astor, Lenox and Tilden Foundations*

Lower Manhattan had 66 auction houses, along with firms that imported virtually anything, from linens to toys to steel to coffee to perfumes. One could find the ordinary (rice, tea, buttons, watches, twine) and the more exotic (precious stones, marble, "essential oils," and "Russia goods"). There were 86 importers of hardware and cutlery; 89 importers of wines and liquors; and 45 sugar importers, continuing the North's long-standing trade with the West Indies. There were 9 importers of olive oil and 5 places that offered musical instruments. There was even an importer of oil paintings.

Wholesalers, or "jobbers," provided every type of clothing, from boots to fine laces to furs. There were 46 druggists, 221 grocers, and 93 shops that sold "china, glass & earthenware."

There were dozens of distillers and coffee roasters.

The district provided employment in hundreds of jobs and trades, including, of course, many related to shipbuilding. There were 19 boatbuilders; 35 sailmakers; 16 makers of mathematical and nautical instruments; 43 "weighers"; 8 publishers of maps and charts; and 3 shops that sold barometers and thermometers. There were 45 consulates, and 70 boardinghouses for sailors.

As New York became the nation's commercial center, people were drawn there not only to conduct business but also to have fun. By early in the nineteenth century, the city was already an exciting place, offering theater and other cultural events.

And it sure beat Alabama in August. Each summer, thousands of Southerners would leave their farms and plantations and head for New York City and elsewhere in the North— Newport, Rhode Island, and Saratoga, New York, were also popular—to escape the heat and diseases that were the scourge of the Southern summer. They couldn't have been more welcome. They filled the finest hotels in New York and other Northern cities, and Northern businesses aimed newspaper advertisements at their captive, and captivated, Southern audiences.

The July 1859 issue of *De Bow's Review*, the most widely circulated Southern commercial journal during the antebellum era—and a veritable lifestyle magazine for slaveholders—carried ads for products to help a planter's business and every other aspect of his life. The journals

Charleston-born James D. B. De Bow launched his influential journal in New Orleans in 1846, moving it to Washington, D.C., from 1853 through 1857, when he also served as superintendent of the U.S. Census. *De Bow's* was published until the editor's death in 1867. De Bow was an ardent supporter of slavery, even proposing, in the 1850s, the reopening of the African slave trade. *Courtesy, American Antiquarian Society*

TO COTTON PLANTERS.

We would introduce to your notice the

LOUISIANA CYLINDER GIN, FOR SHORT STAPLE COTTON.

A machine which has been long sought for. This Gin has a Roller of a peculiar construction, filled with teeth composed of "Angular Steel Wire," and placed in the Roller tangentially to its axis, so that they always present needle points with broad backs, and are so close together that nothing but Cotton can be secreted between them, leaving the Seeds and Trash upon the surface, and the Sand and Dirt, instead of dulling the teeth in the Roller, sharpens them. In connection with this Roller is a "Stationary Serrated Straight-edge," which acts in concert with it (in effect) the same as the Revolving Rollers do upon the "Sea Island Cotton," combing it under the Straight-edge, and thereby STRAIGHT ENING THE FIBRE, preventing ALTOGETHER the Napping of the Cotton, and in NO MANNER shortening the Staple. The Cotton is taken from the Roller with the Brush, and thrown into the Lint Room in the usual way. The machine is simple in its construction, having but two motions, the "Roller" and the "Brush," and is not so liable to get out of order, nor to take fire, as the Saw Gin, and occupies much less space, and requires *less* power than a Saw Gin of the same capacity. A Gin of the capacity of 500 pounds of Lint in two hours, occupies a space of five and a half by three feet, and can be driven with three-mule power, *easily*. Another peculiarity of this Gin, is. that it takes the Cotton from the *surface* of the Roll, and presents it to the Brush in a thin sheet, as it passes beyond the Straight-edge, enabling the Brush to mote the Cotton in a superior manner, whilst the Roll in front of the Straight-edge is carried upon the top of it, dividing the two at that point, and following a Curved iron or Shell, is returned again to the Cylinder, forming a Roll of about eight inches diameter; the Seeds, Bolls and Trash, being retained in the Breast by an adjustable front board, and discharged at the will of the operator, the same as the Saw Gin. The Curved Iron or Shell is capable of being adjusted so as to press the Roll as hard upon the Ginning Roller as may be desired. Anything can be placed in the Breast of this Gin, such as Sticks, Trash, Bolls, &c., as the Roller receives and takes forward *nothing* but the Lint, and rejects ALL extraneous matter. This is a novel feature in the Gin, and peculiarly adapts it to the wants of large planters who are short-handed, and gather their Cotton trashy, as it increases the value of the Cotton from 1 to 1½ cents per pound more than that ginned upon any other machine.

There is a Roller Gin that has been in the Market for several years but the Louisiana Gin is on an entire different principle, and there being no agents for this Gin, apply direct to

ALFRED JENKS & SON,
BRIDESBURG, PA.,
MANUFACTURERS OF ALL KINDS OF

COTTON AND WOOLEN MACHINES.

sep-1y.

were thick with notices, largely from New York, Pennsylvania, and Connecticut companies, for everything from cotton gins, made in Philadelphia, to "guano," or fertilizer (said to provide "PERSISTENT fertility to the soil"), available through a Fulton Street firm in New York City. There were groceries from a company on Manhattan's Vesey Street, medicines from Boston, and iron railings ideal for verandahs from a Philadelphia firm.

Three insurance companies advertised in the same issue of *De Bow's*, including Aetna of Hartford, already an "old established and leading Insurance Company." Two New York insurers listed as their agent William A. Bartlett at 81 Gravier Street in New Orleans. Manhattan Life's ad mused, "The practice of Life Insurance, in any country, indicates a state of society where high moral feeling and commercial confidence exist." Knickerbocker's ad was less philosophical: "Insures the Lives of White Persons & Slaves."

Other Northern firms competed for the Southern dollar with fine china, fine furniture, and fine cutlery. Also: candles, soaps, French plate glass, pumps and fire hoses, pianos, pickles, liquors, and account-room "weighing books," specifically for cotton, grain, sugar, and molasses.

Finally, any Southern planter who wanted to provide his daughter with "a solid education of the highest order" may have considered sending her to New York to study at the Rutgers Female Institute, located "in one of the most healthful, quiet, and moral neighborhoods in the city."

If nothing else, the advertisements in *De Bow's* and other journals were indicators of a thriving nation, one where the good life was possible (if one was white and prosperous).

But more to the point—what with fees and commissions, the manufacture of farm machinery, and the provision of everything else Southerners needed for a comfortable life—by some estimates the North took 40 cents of every dollar a planter earned from cotton.

It is little wonder that 2,000 worried New Yorkers gathered that winter afternoon on Pine Street. And although Mayor Wood quickly backed away from his proposal that New York secede from the Union, it is understandable that he and his party continued to murmur sympathetically about the plight of the South and to condemn the "antislavery forces of the North."

As threatening as the regional differences over slavery were, the profits of America's system of enforced servitude were hard for anyone at any level of government to dismiss.

In 1853, Israel D. Andrews, an expert on commerce and trade, told

Insuring slaves was as common as insuring other kinds of property, as indicated in these advertisements. Charter Oak Life Insurance Company was based in the nation's longtime insurance capital.

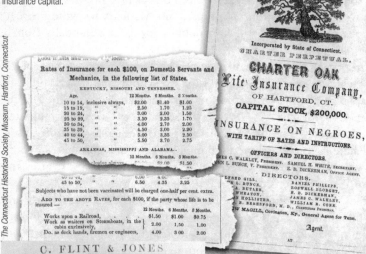

Congress that "the soils, seasons, climate, and labor of no country can successfully compete with those of that vast region of this confederacy which has been appropriately styled the 'Cotton Zone.' "

"It is proper, however," Andrews, who worked for the secretary of state, said, "to state that many of the most intelligent cotton planters of that region insist that their now generally conceded superiority is not so much attributable to any radical difference of the soil or dissimilarity of the climate in that region . . . as it is to the advantages, afforded by the aggregated and combined, and cheap, and reliable labor they derive from that patriarchal system of domestic servitude."

The South grew the cotton, with the help of its "reliable labor." The North handled virtually everything else. Ours was a prosperous, highly symbiotic, highly functioning economy. As long as we stayed united.

"Lords of the Lash" and "Lords of the Loom"

THERE WAS NOTHING LIKE IT ANYWHERE IN THE WORLD. POET JOHN Greenleaf Whittier called it "a city springing up like the enchanted palaces of the Arabian Tales." One European visitor asserted that the only thing comparable in America was Niagara Falls.

By 1840, Lowell, Massachusetts, America's first planned city, was indeed a marvel. Thirty miles northwest of Boston, the city built specifically to manufacture textiles boasted nearly a mile of tall, imposing mill buildings, which stood along the Merrimack River like brick sentries. It had nearly six miles of "power canals," which, as they flowed through the city, turned waterwheels that drove 320,000 spindles and 10,000 looms. Its 10,000 inhabitants, most of whom were young, unmarried women—"mill girls"—produced 1 million yards of textiles every week.

Lowell, Massachusetts, became famous for its "mile of mills" on the Merrimack River. The city was still growing in 1834, the year this etching was made. That same year, the U.S. slave population surpassed 2 million, while Lowell's 22 textile mills were consuming 235,700 pounds of cotton weekly. *American Textile History Museum, Lowell, Massachusetts*

Lowell was extraordinary. Revolutionary. And it required a river of cotton.

Amos Adams Lawrence, son and nephew of two of the key men who built Lowell, Amos and Abbott Lawrence, estimated that by 1850, mills in New England used 150 million pounds of Southern cotton a year.

Although textile manufacturers existed elsewhere in the country, the industry was concentrated, overwhelmingly, in the North, and even more overwhelmingly in New England. In 1860, mills in Massachusetts and tiny Rhode Island manufactured nearly 50 percent of all the textiles produced in America. Altogether that same year, New England mills produced a full 75 percent of the nation's total: 850 million yards of cloth.

The number of slaves involved in cotton production had grown to meet the increasing demand. The first U.S. Census, in 1790, conducted three years before Whitney's invention of the cotton gin, recorded just under 700,000 slaves. By the Civil War, there were nearly 4 million black people in bondage, with 2¼ million involved, directly or indirectly, in growing cotton.

In almost a paradigm of the symbiotic relationship between North and South, Lowell shows how it all came together.

The mill city's 11 textile companies made different products, to minimize competition among them. One specialized in calico prints, for example, another in a heavy fabric called "drillings," yet another in fine fabrics. But the mills at Lowell also made "negro cloth"—coarse, simple material. In other words, slaves in the South picked the cotton, which was sold to Northern textile manufacturers, who wove the cotton into "negro cloth," which was sold to plantation owners to clothe their slaves.

Elegant in its simplicity. And complicity.

THE START OF AMERICA'S TEXTILE INDUSTRY WAS A HEADY TIME FOR Massachusetts industrialists. As Amos Lawrence wrote to his son Amos A. Lawrence in 1831, "Our local affairs are very delightful in this state and city. We have no violent political animosities; and the prosperity of the people is very great." Amos A. Lawrence was optimistic about building on his patrimony. "If I have mercantile tact enough to carry on the immense though safe machine my father and uncle have put in operation," he wrote, "it will turn out gold to me as fast as I could wish."

The time was right for the Lawrences. The three decades before the Civil War were an era of volcanic change in America. Major new industries, such as railroads and steel, were born; the nation stretched

Right: Amos Lawrence *by Chester Harding, given in memory of the Rt. Rev. William Lawrence by his children, Image © 2005 Board of Trustees, National Gallery of Art, Washington, D.C.*

AMOS A. LAWRENCE
of Boston, *Founder of L. University.*

Above: *From the collection of Lawrence University Archives, Appleton, Wisconsin. Used by permission.*

The Massachusetts mill city was named for Amos Lawrence and his brother Abbott, key members of the Boston Associates. Amos Lawrence's son, Amos A., followed in his father's footsteps in business and politics until he felt forced into abolitionism by the South's intransigence on slavery.

westward to fulfill its "manifest destiny"; and political giants like Henry Clay, Daniel Webster, and John C. Calhoun strode the land and clashed in power struggles that had national implications. The young nation was exploring and pushing its limits in far more than a geographical sense. America was shouldering itself onto the world platform alongside the traditional European powers.

Earlier in the nineteenth century, a years-long conflict between England and France had led to the War of 1812 between England and the United States—a war largely over neutral shipping rights. The war had badly hurt the U.S. economy through trade embargoes, blockades, and ship seizures, and no area had been squeezed more than Massachusetts, with its heavy dependence on maritime commerce.

The war's end in 1815 would be the start of an era of growth. But a few years earlier, during the time of economic strangulation, a wealthy young merchant named Francis Cabot Lowell, of Newburyport, Massachusetts, presumably frustrated by trade restrictions, had taken his family for an extended stay in England. For health reasons, he said, but he had an ulterior motive.

The Industrial Revolution, which had begun in Great Britain a half century earlier, started with the invention of a series of machines that spun cotton and wool fibers into thread. More significant was the next step, when Richard Arkwright's invention of a waterpowered spinning frame spurred Edmund Cartwright to invent the power loom. Work that had been done by hand for thousands of years could now be done by machines. The speed and uniform quality with which textiles could be produced soared.

As the textile industry boomed, the British government prohibited the emigration of anyone with knowledge of it, and banned the export of information about the technology—laws that proved impossible to enforce. In 1789, the young superintendent of a cotton mill disguised himself as a farmer, slipped out of England, and headed for America. In Providence, Samuel Slater met Moses Brown, of the wealthy Rhode Island mercantile and slave-trading family. Moses, the abolitionist brother in the family, persuaded Slater to help him start a textile mill, and their partnership led to America's first power-driven mill, on the Blackstone River. Within a few years, mills dotted the banks of fast-moving streams throughout Rhode Island and eastern Connecticut.

But those mills only spun the thread. It took Francis Cabot Lowell to pirate Britain's textile machinery—which he did, almost unbelievably, by memorizing its complicated design while touring the mills in Manchester, England. Lowell then took the Industrial Revolution a step forward. When he and his partners built the first cotton mill in America on the Charles River in Waltham, Massachusetts, its operations were "integrated." That is, for the first time, every step of the manufacturing process took place under one roof. This increased efficiency and, of course, slashed costs. It was America's first factory—the

FRANCIS CABOT LOWELL.

This silhouette is the only known likeness of the Massachusetts-born Francis Cabot Lowell, for whom the first planned city in America is named. *Illustrated History of Lowell and Vicinity, 1897, courtesy of Lowell National Historical Park*

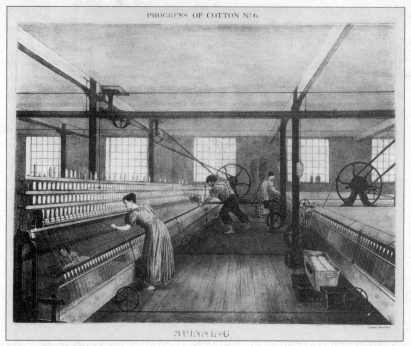

PROGRESS OF COTTON Nº 6

SPINNING

This early nineteenth-century "mule" was a hybrid that blended aspects of various types of spinning machines. Introduced in Rhode Island in 1805, the mule was one of many developments in cloth-making technology. *Slater Mill, A Living History Museum*

beginning of America's version of the Industrial Revolution. And, like the revolution across the Atlantic, it was fed by cotton.

Lowell died in 1817, but his partners poured the profits from Waltham into their new city of mills on the Merrimack River, and they named the city after him.

The Spoiler

AS THE BOSTON ASSOCIATES BEGAN OPENING ONE TEXTILE COMPANY after another—by 1846, there were 40 major mill buildings in Lowell alone—another Newburyport native was launching his own enterprise. With the publication of the first issue of the *Liberator* from the borrowed offices of a Christian newspaper, a twenty-five-year-old former printer ignited an antislavery crusade that would last more than three decades, until the passage of the Thirteenth Amendment to the Constitution in

If Francis Cabot Lowell sparked the American industrial revolution, William Lloyd Garrison, another native of Newburyport, Massachusetts, helped launch the revolution called Emancipation.

1865. On January 1, 1831, William Lloyd Garrison slammed down the gauntlet and became, almost instantly, one of the country's most polarizing figures.

He was aware, Garrison wrote in the *Liberator,* that some would find his language "severe." But he made no apologies for his belief that slaves should be freed immediately, a position that set him in conflict with the then-popular liberal stance of "gradual emancipation." For Garrison, plodding progress in the struggle to eliminate bondage was unacceptable, immoral.

"On this subject, I do not wish to think, or speak, or write, with moderation. No! no!" Garrison's words jumped off the front page. "Tell a man whose house is on fire to give a moderate alarm; tell him to moderately rescue his wife from the hands of the ravisher; tell the mother to gradually extricate her babe from the fire into which it has fallen;—but urge me not to use moderation in a cause like the present. I am in earnest—I will not equivocate—I will not excuse—I will not retreat a single inch—and I WILL BE HEARD."

He was. Nat Turner's failed slave revolt in Virginia occurred eight months after that first issue, and despite the lack of any evidence that the Southampton County slaves had ever seen the journal, Southerners blamed Garrison, among others, for inspiring the uprising. An influential Washington newspaper blasted the *Liberator,* and actions were taken across the South to try to silence "Yankee fanatics." Georgetown, then a town in the District of Columbia, passed a law that any free black who took copies of the *Liberator* from the post office could be fined $20, jailed for 30 days, and sold back into slavery for four months if they failed to meet those penalties.

By 1835, Garrison's "immediatism" had helped make abolitionism part of the national conversation. Several prominent Northerners had joined the antislavery struggle. The textile industrialists were forced to be on watch against threats to their cotton-dependent industry. The prominent, charismatic British abolitionist George Thompson had even spoken in Lowell, the heart of Northern textile manufacturing, during his U.S. tour.

"There is much excitement in the whole South upon the subject of Abolition," Louisiana planter Colonel William Sparks warned Amos Lawrence. "There will be strong measures taken in this state during the winter, some which I can not now mention but which will be alarming to the people of the North."

Antiabolitionist rallies were held, including a huge one, in August

1835, at Faneuil Hall in Boston at which Harrison Gray Otis, the city's former mayor and a major investor in textiles, warned the crowd of 1,500 that the abolitionist movement could lead to war.

As elsewhere in the North, merchants and others invested in the status quo pointed to the Constitution, and compromises that had been made to ensure its approval, to justify their stand on slavery. Rufus Choate, a congressman, then a senator, from Massachusetts, and a founder of the conservative Whig Party, agreed, for example, that slavery was a "great evil," but asserted, "I feel it to be my duty distinctly to say that I would leave to the masters of slaves every guaranty of the Constitution and the Union."

After the Faneuil Hall rally, Garrison wisely kept a low profile for a few months. By October, however, he thought it safe to continue his activities. A meeting of the Boston Female Anti-Slavery Society was scheduled for October 21. Before the meeting, a rumor spread that George Thompson, the British abolitionist, was to address the society. A mob of 1,000 people gathered in front of the meeting place, near City Hall and Quincy Market. Although Thompson was not there, the agitated crowd broke into the hall, tore down an antislavery sign, and raced after Garrison. Chased, captured, roped, paraded through the streets, then escaping with the help of several pitying members of the mob, the abolitionist ended the night in jail, the only place the mayor could ensure his safety.

Abolitionism could be as controversial in Boston, its birthplace, as anywhere in the United States during the fractious prewar decades. In October 1835, Garrison narrowly avoided being lynched, or at the very least tarred, on Boston Common. © Bettmann/CORBIS

IT'S HARD TO ACCEPT THAT IN THE DECADES BEFORE THE CIVIL WAR, Northerners did not know something of the horrors of Southern slavery. Abolitionists were doing everything possible to inform the nation in pamphlets and newspapers filled with exclamation-point-studded prose and dramatic italicized words.

In 1838, for example, the American Anti-Slavery Society published the *Narrative of James Williams, an American Slave*. Williams was the "driver" of other slaves on a cotton plantation in Alabama until he escaped in 1835. Williams's story is filled with harrowing accounts of whippings and other acts of brutality, of extreme overwork, and of bloodhounds chasing down runaway slaves with horrific results.

The same pamphlet contains extended passages quoting slaveholders on how best to control their captives, such as these, made by the Honorable W. B. Seabrook to the Agricultural Society of St. Johns, in Colleton County, South Carolina:

> "*If to our army the disuse of THE LASH has been prejudicial, to the slaveholder it would operate to deprive him of the MAIN SUPPORT of his authority.*
>
> "*For the first class of offences, I consider imprisonment in THE STOCKS at night, with or without hard labor [by] day, as a powerful auxiliary in the cause of good government. Experience has convinced me that there is no punishment of which the slave looks with more horror than that upon which I am now commenting, (the stocks,) and none which has been attended with happier results.*"

The abolitionists' pamphlets reproduced numerous runaway-slave ads, such as this, from the October 10, 1837, Vicksburg, Mississippi, *Sentinel and Expositor:*

> $50 REWARD. —*Ran away from the subscriber, a negro fellow named Dick, about 21 or 22 years of age, dark mulatto, has many scars on his back from being whipped. The boy was purchased by me from Thomas L. Arnold, and absconded about the time the purchase was made.*
> JAMES NOE.

Or this, from the *New Orleans Bee:*

> $10 REWARD. —*Ran away, on the 9th of October, CAROLINE, aged about 38 years; had a collar on with one prong turned down.*
> T. CUGGY,
> Callatin st., Between Hospital and Barracks.

sonable charges paid, by ASHBEL WELLS, jun. of Hartford, or   OVID BURRALL.
Canaan, October 20, 1785.

ON Tuesday evening the 25th instant, ran away from my Tan Works, my Negro MAN JACK, aged about 24 years, about 5 feet and half high, marked with a large gash or cross on each cheek, and part of his scalp taken off the back part of his head, he cannot straiten his right little finger.—— Whoever will take up said servant and return him to me or confine him in some Jail, shall have all necessary charges paid and be handsomely rewarded.
THOMAS DENNY.
Wethersfield, October 31, 1785.
*** Any intelligence about the Negro sent either to Mr. Joseph Webb or me at Wethersfield, will be chearfully acknowledged.

To NEHEMIAH ANDREWS,

The Connecticut Courant
and The Weekly Intelligencer

The Connecticut Courant

This sampling of runaway-slave and slave-sale ads, published in various editions of the *Connecticut Courant* over a quarter century, contains references to a number of prominent families. Joseph Webb of Wethersfield, for example, was a well-known merchant and slave owner whose house is now part of a museum. William Wadsworth is related to the family whose endowment helped establish the Wadsworth Atheneum, the nation's oldest public art museum. The frequency and almost casual placement of the ads reveal how common slavery was in this New England society.

RUN-away from their master last Saturday night a yellow Negro Man and Mongarel Squaw; the man about 26 years old, 5 feet 8 inches high, lame in his right knee, goes a little halt; had on brown coloured cloathing, and carried with him a violin, a brown great coat, some striped shirts and other small articles. The Squaw about 21 years old, pretty likely, well built, strait and rather slim; carried with her a callico goun and short goun, a black drawboy old cloak, a red ... crape habbit, a black bonnet and a ... Whoever will take up and return ... Ten Dollars reward for both, or ... ble charges, by
WILLIAM WADSWORTH.
... for life; the squaw is bound for a

HEZEKIAH MERRILL, Cashier.

RUN-away from the subscriber on the 10th of May inst. a NEGRO MAN by the name of *Newport*, a short thick fellow; wore away a long blue coat, between 50 and 60 years of age, grey-headed, speaks bad English, a sail-maker by trade. Whoever will take him up and return him to me, shall have Ten Cents reward and necessary charges paid. All persons are forbid harbouring, aiding, assisting, or employing him as they would avoid the penalty of the law.
ELISHA CALLENDER.
Wethersfield, May 22.

TO BE SOLD,
Cheap for Cash or Morris's Notes,
At MIDDLETOWN, Upper-Houses, by the Subscriber.

AN elegant black English HORSE, very large and strong, very gentle in a carriage and carries himself well.
A second hand riding Chair and Harness, with an iron Axletree.
A Windsor chair Sulkey, and Harness.
A single Sleigh.
A neat mahogany Desk and Book-Case.
A sett of mahogany Chairs with black hair bottoms.
Two mahogany dining Tables.
Two and a half dozen Pictures, Landscapes and Faces.
One pair sconce Looking-Glasses, 18 by 24 inches, open gilt frames.
A number of Books on various subjects.
ALSO,
A very valuable NEGRO MAN, who understands farming business, has been used to ship carpenters work and coopering, and very handy at using any kind of tools. ALSO, his Wife, who understands all kinds of house work.
ALSO,
A number of pieces of coarse and fine Cambricks and Lawns, from 30s to 6s. per piece. And a bolt of Osnabrigs.
THOMAS HAZARD.
December 6, 1785.

The Connecticut Courant, *The Connecticut Historical Society Museum, Hartford, Connecticut*

250 DOLLARS REWARD.

RUN away from HACHALIAH BAILY, on the 10th of last June, a negro, boy named DONT or JONATHAN, 20 years old, is a short thick set fellow, is apt to get drunk when he gets liquor, he chews tobacco, has lived several years with JONATHAN WARD, at East Chester, in the State of New-York, he is a bold impudent looking fellow.
Run away from ABRAHAM EVERIT, in Carmel town, Dutchess county, a negro man named BOB, on the 9th of last Sept. he is 24 years old, very black, 5 feet 8 or 9 inches high, slim made and quick spoken, has a small scar on one foot.
Run away from SAMUEL LYONS, at Bedford, on the 14th of Dec. 1803, a negro man named BOB, he was about 20 years old when he left home, middling tall, yellowish complexion, he plays on the fife, he has a scar on the out side of his right leg, six inches above his ancle, that come by a burn,—also, a cut on the shin bone, near the same.
Run away from ISAAC PURDY, in North Salem two negro men, one of them named LEW, plays on the fiddle, is about 5 feet 10 inches high, slim made, yellowish complexion, he ran away on the 23d of last June, is 21 years old; the other named ANDREW, very black, 6 feet 1 inch high, ran away on the 14th of last Nov. is 19 years old. The above reward will be given for the said negroes, if delivered to ISAAC PURDY, North Salem, West Chester county and state of New-York, or 50 dollars for either of them.
Feb. 16, 1807.
95

The Connecticut Courant, *The Connecticut Historical Society Museum, Hartford, Connecticut*

When these runaway-slave ads were published in the late 1830s, more than 90,000 bales of Southern cotton were arriving in Boston annually for use in Northern mills, and the demand only continued to grow, as did the need for labor.

The Boston Associates were increasing their wealth and solidifying their influence in numerous spheres. The core group consisted of about 80 members, many related by blood or marriage. Three of the top men were Nathan Appleton, a distant cousin of Francis Cabot Lowell's, and brothers Abbott and Amos Lawrence, descendants of one of the first settlers of Groton, Massachusetts. By 1845, the group's 31 textile companies in Massachusetts, southern Maine, and New Hampshire could produce one-fifth of all U.S. textiles.

These "cotton lords" ruled over an expanding and increasingly interconnected empire. They invested in the new business of railroads, helping to develop lines such as the Boston & Lowell, in part to transport their cotton from warehouse to factory. They started banks, including the powerful Suffolk Bank, which helped standardize the currency of Massachusetts. Eventually, the Associates controlled 40 percent of banking capital in Boston, close to 40 percent of all insurance capital in Massachusetts, and 30 percent of the state's railroad mileage.

A banknote from the Sanford Bank in Maine is illustrated, most appropriately, with a power loom similar to those used in textile mills owned by members of the Boston Associates. The illustration nearly mirrors the one used on the labels of cloth produced by the Merrimack Manufacturing Company of Lowell, Massachusetts. Top: *Maine State Museum.* Bottom: *American Textile History Museum, Lowell, Massachusetts*

The influence of the Associates in the life of Bay State residents was broad and deep. This was not only because of their businesses, which employed tens of thousands of New Englanders, but also because of their extensive and generous charitable activities. Members helped found Massachusetts General Hospital and its famous McLean Asylum, and donated liberally to Harvard University and Williams College, among many, many other high-profile institutions. This gave them extraordinary political clout. A number of the Associates became significant, almost iconic, figures, leaving a permanent stamp on the American landscape.

Abbott Lawrence missed, by one vote, being nominated for vice president on the Whig ticket led by William Henry Harrison in 1840.

The city of Lawrence, Massachusetts, another prosperous manufacturing center, was named for Amos Lawrence. Lawrence, Kansas, site of the University of Kansas, was named for his son, Amos A. Lawrence, who paid groups of abolition-minded people from the East to settle the territory of Kansas.

Throughout the ascent and reign of the Associates, however, slavery was the complicating factor in virtually every important national issue, and none more so than that of whether slavery should be permitted in new territories and states that sought admission to the Union. Here, however, the textile manufacturers drew a line. They wouldn't oppose slavery where it already existed. After all, it was permitted under the Constitution. But slavery in new states? Unacceptable, despite the insistent campaigning of the South.

Northern industrialists did not necessarily approve of slavery. But eliminating it jeopardized everything they had. And given the South's continual threats of secession, slavery jeopardized the nation's very existence. Amos Lawrence may have said it best when he justified the vote by a Massachusetts congressman (and investor in textiles) for the hugely controversial Fugitive Slave Act. Lawrence noted that Samuel Eliot "loves the black race more than most men. . . . But he loves the perpetuity of this Government and the Union of these States . . . better."

The issue was even more complicated. Even if the Union could be preserved, the delicate balance of power in Washington could be upset by the addition of slave states. Northern and Southern economic interests often clashed. For example, Northern manufacturers favored high tariffs, to protect their products from competition from Europe, while Southern planters favored free trade, so they could import cheaper textiles from the countries to which they sold their cotton. A Congress dominated by men elected from slave states could be disastrous for the North. "Where will be the patronage and Executive power of the Government?" complained Abbott Lawrence in 1837. "Will it not be gone, forever departed, from the Free States?"

At the same time, textile manufacturers had to maintain good relations with the cotton states. Threats to the stability of the Union wreaked havoc with their industry and the national economy, and there were several periods of economic panic in the decades before the war that drove that terrifying point home to Northern businesses. So much of the energy of Massachusetts industrialists and their Whig Party was devoted to forging coalitions that Charles Sumner, a Bay State abolitionist, famously decried the alliance "between the cotton-planters and flesh-mongers of Louisiana and Mississippi and the cotton spinners and traffickers of New England—between the lords of the lash and the lords of the loom."

Philosopher Ralph Waldo Emerson agreed, wryly commenting at one point, "Cotton thread holds the union together; unites John C. Calhoun [the powerful South Carolina senator] and Abbott Lawrence. Patriotism for holidays and summer evenings, with music and rockets, but cotton thread is the Union."

As LATE AS 1850, THERE WERE SIGNS THAT THE CENTER COULD HOLD, that the Union could compromise its way to an agreement on slavery. Hope lay with a series of bills proposed by the elderly senator Henry Clay of Kentucky and endorsed by New England icon Senator Daniel Webster (who had "bent his supple knees anew to the Slave Power," the *Liberator*'s Garrison sneered). Webster was named secretary of state several months later, and he supervised the enforcement of the most controversial part of the Compromise of 1850, the resolution that helped turn the feelings of many in the North, including some of its business class, against slavery.

The Fugitive Slave Act gave the federal government jurisdiction over the capture of runaway slaves, allowing plantation owners and their agents to come north and apprehend their escaped "property" with the help of federal marshals. The law enraged abolitionists, but by and large it was accepted, if unenthusiastically, by leaders of the financial community, who insisted they had little choice. It also allowed them, once again, to show their solidarity with their Southern suppliers. And there was hope that the Compromise of 1850 had thwarted, once and for all, a national breach.

"Shall we stand by the laws or shall we nullify them? Shall we uphold the Union or shall we break it up?" Amos A. Lawrence asked rhetorically. The industrialist even offered his services to the U.S. marshal's office in Boston in enforcing the Fugitive Slave Act, to the utter disdain of abolitionist Wendell Phillips, who remarked cynically that the law would help determine whether "the mills of Abbott Lawrence make him worth two millions or one."

But others in Massachusetts and elsewhere in the North were furious at the idea of Southerners stomping through the Free States in pursuit of their human property.

Dramatic rescues of arrested fugitives took place in several Northern cities. In Boston, William and Ellen Craft, a married couple who had fled Georgia several years earlier, were smuggled onto a ship bound for Great Britain, and freedom. A waiter named Frederick Minkins, called Shadrach by his Virginia owner, was spirited away to Montreal.

The success of the federal government in shipping a skinny bricklayer back to Savannah shook many in the city. In the early morning of April 12, 1851, it took 300 policemen to march a weeping twenty-three-year-old Thomas Sims through the crowded streets of Boston onto a waiting ship at Long Wharf. A week later, Bostonians learned that upon arriving in Savannah, he'd received 39 lashes—a near-fatal beating—in a public square.

In the next three years, 98 fugitives from slavery were returned to their owners.

It took a proposal in Congress to start to change the minds of Boston's powerful mercantile class. A bill was offered by the man who would be Abraham Lincoln's opponent for the presidency in a few years. Illinois senator Stephen A. Douglas proposed that the territories of Kansas and Nebraska be admitted to the Union "with or without slavery." In a flash, Douglas had reopened the fight over the balance of political power. And despite the furious efforts by the textile manufacturers, who felt betrayed by this bald attempt to extend the "Cotton Kingdom"—and after all of their concessions to the South!—the Kansas-Nebraska Act was signed into law in May 1854 by Presi-

ELLEN CRAFT, A FUGITIVE SLAVE.—(SEE NEXT PAGE.)

The Crafts fled Georgia in 1848, the light-skinned Ellen chopping off her hair, donning green spectacles, and disguising herself as the master of her darker-skinned husband, William. They became popular speakers in Boston's abolitionist circles, but in October 1850, they were hunted by agents from Georgia. Antislavery supporters promised the Crafts that if the couple returned to Georgia, the abolitionists would purchase and then liberate them. But the Crafts refused to legitimize the new law, fleeing to Great Britain, and freedom. Illustrated London News *Picture Library*

As Anthony Burns began his journey back to Virginia and captivity on June 2, 1854, 50,000 people thronged the streets of Boston, and black crepe hung from the buildings. Burns had to be escorted by two companies of U.S. Marines onto a federal cutter. More than any other fugitive the pursuit of Anthony Burns galvanized many in the Bay State to support abolition.

The Man is Not Bought!

He is still in the SLAVE PEN in the COURT HOUSE!

The kidnapper agreed, both publicly and in writing, to sell him for $1200. The sum was raised by eminent Boston citizens and offered him. He then claimed more. The bargain was broken. The kidnapper breaks his agreement, though the United States Commissioner advised him to keep it.

Be on your guard against all LIES!

Watch the SLAVE PEN!

LET EVERY MAN ATTEND THE TRIAL.

dent Franklin Pierce, a native of New Hampshire.

As one sign of their fury, the merchants did an about-face on a fugitive slave case that had just erupted in Boston. But despite their best efforts—Amos Lawrence himself paid the legal bills—after an explosive week of legal and physical fights, which had led to the fatal shooting of one of hundreds of deputies hired to guard the courthouse, the slave, Anthony Burns, was sent back to Richmond. (Burns gained his freedom, however, when Boston's black community purchased him.)

The Burns case helped persuade Amos A. Lawrence to finance his campaign to settle the Kansas territory with antislavery settlers. It was a strife-filled campaign, in which Kansas was the locus of violence between proslavery and antislavery forces. It was made infamous by John Brown's massacre of five proslavery settlers. "Bleeding Kansas" was the prototype of what awaited the nation.

IN THOSE FINAL YEARS BEFORE WAR, THE COUNTRY'S MOST IMPORTANT financial centers continued to seek ways to compromise with the South, to reconcile, to form third parties to bridge differences, and to make peace. After an economic crisis in 1857 gave the industrial North a taste of what war could mean, as businesses closed and hundreds lost their jobs, the merchants redoubled their efforts. There were emotional meetings in Manhattan and almost pathetic accolades to Southerners at Faneuil Hall in Boston.

Representatives from 21 states attended one of the last-ditch efforts to avoid war. The Virginia legislature had called a Peace Conference, which met in February 1861 at Willard's Hotel in Washington, D.C. No one from the Deep South attended because all seven Deep South states had already seceded. Former U.S. president John Tyler, a Virginian, presided over the conference, at which more compromise proposals were discussed and voted on. Only one of the proposals was sent to Congress, which dutifully passed it, though only barely in the Senate. That sole "compromise" was to amend the Constitution to allow slavery to remain in any state where it then existed. The states never got a chance to consider ratification.

At one point, Abraham Lincoln, the president-elect, stopped by to chat with the attendees, who pushed him to tip his hand. Would he say anything in his inaugural address the next week to give them hope? New York merchant William E. Dodge was particularly blunt in his questions to Lincoln. "Then you will yield to the just demands of the South? . . . You will not go to war on account of slavery?"

"I do not know that I understand your meaning, Mr. Dodge," Lincoln replied, "nor do I know what acts or opinions may be in the future, beyond this." Lincoln would defend the Constitution "as it *is*," he said, "not the Constitution as I would like to have it."

Dodge had given an outstanding speech at the Peace Conference. The turmoil terrified him, he said. The United States must stay united. "I love my country; my heart is filled with sorrow as I witness the dangers by which it is surrounded," the Connecticut native declared.

"I regret that the gentlemen composing the committee did not approach these questions more in the manner of merchants or commercial men," Dodge said. "We would not have sacrificed our principles, but we would have agreed—have brought our minds together as far as we could; we would have left open as few questions as possible. Those we would have arranged by mutual concessions."

Inexplicably, some Northern merchants continued to be optimistic that concessions could, at that point, thwart civil war. In April, William Appleton left New York harbor aboard the steamer *Nashville* and headed south.

At seventy-five years old, Appleton, Amos Lawrence's cousin and Amos A. Lawrence's father-in-law, was a major investor in a dozen textile mills and related businesses. The Boston Associate was on his own private peace mission, hoping to use personal diplomacy to encourage some kind of compromise between North and South.

The *Nashville* arrived at Charleston on Thursday evening, April 11, 1861, and anchored just outside

"The Constitution will not be preserved and defended until it is enforced and obeyed in every part of every one of the United States," president-elect Lincoln told members of the Peace Convention in Washington, D.C., in 1861, shortly before the bombardment of Fort Sumter. Abraham Lincoln, *Alexander Gardner, National Portrait Gallery, Smithsonian Institution, Art Resource/New York*

the city's great harbor, waiting for the morning tide to bring her in. So Appleton and his fellow passengers were in an extraordinary position early the next morning to witness the shelling of Fort Sumter by the guns of South Carolina, and the destruction of any possibility of compromise over slavery.

*The Pride of the South was among the dozens
of models turned out by the New Haven carriage and buggy
factory that advertised itself as the world's largest.*

THE CARRIAGE TRADE

IN ITS 1860 SALES CATALOG, THE G. & D. COOK CARRIAGE COMPANY boasted that its factory in New Haven was the largest in the world, capable of building a vehicle an hour. It listed more than a hundred models, many pitched to buyers in the Cotton Kingdom.

Model No. 4, the Pride of the South, cost $145 to $180. "This is a very appropriate name for this Buggy, for with the Southern people it is a universal favorite, and is used in every section of the South," the catalog copy stated. A convertible, the Pride of the South came equipped with a "lever for raising and lowering the top from the inside; an acknowledged great improvement on the old way."

Model No. 16, the Georgia No Top, $80 to $100, was said to be "well-liked as a cheap durable buggy."

Model No. 33, the Mobile Top, $160 to $200, sported a "leather dash, stick seat, shifting top, [and] branch steps," and was said to be "well-liked and much in use in Southern cities."

Models No. 42 and No. 43, the Plantation No Top and Plantation Top, were "roomy, strong and convenient" buggies, identical except that one offered protection from the weather.

The catalog said that New Haven was home to more than 60 companies that made carriages or carriage accessories, and added, "It is rapidly coming to be felt that New Haven is to the carriage trade what Nantucket and New Bedford are to the whale fishery, Lynn to the shoe trade, and Lowell and Manchester to the trade in cotton goods."

In 1857, a peak year, New Haven produced more than 7,000 vehicles, valued at $1.6 million, chiefly for the Southern market. A city history credits Connecticut Yankee and *Mayflower* descendant

James Brewster with introducing New Haven carriages to the South in the 1830s.

Brewster subsequently invested in railroads, in canals, and in G. & D. Cook & Company. He opposed slavery but enjoyed cordial relations with his Southern customers. Revered as a city benefactor, Brewster gave a speech in 1857 advising his audience of ambitious young men to be "industrious and temperate in all things" and, most of all, to "LEARN TO CONFORM TO CIRCUMSTANCES."

Given its dependence on the cotton economy, the New Haven carriage industry ought to have been crippled by the Civil War. Some companies did close, but most rebounded even before the war ended. G. & D. Cook & Company in particular made a quick adjustment.

"Instead of the light and tasteful pleasure vehicles, for which it was a few months ago so famous, it is now fashioning large bars of iron and heavy oak into ponderous gun carriages; but the thorough finish of the latter is fully equal to the former," a contemporary observer reported proudly.

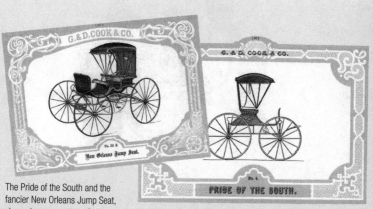

The Pride of the South and the fancier New Orleans Jump Seat, shown here, were two of many models G. & D. Cook & Company of New Haven pitched to the Southern market in its 1860 catalog. At the time, New Haven was a national center of carriage manufacture. The New Orleans Jump Seat was a midrange model, priced at $200 to $250. "Is fine and elegant in appearance, and generally liked," the Cook catalog promised. G. & D. Cook & Co.'s Illustrated Catalogue of Carriages and Special Business Advertiser, *1860, facsimile reprint, Dover Publications, 1970*

Horses and barrels, fish and flour—the North's earliest traffic in slave commerce ran from Plymouth Rock to the West Indies.

Two

FIRST FORTUNES

V IRGINIA MAY HAVE BEEN SETTLED FIRST, BUT THE UNITED STATES
was born in New England.

At the end of the twentieth century, the dean of colonial historians, Bernard Bailyn, noted that in the beginning, New England was an "unpromising, barely fertile region."

But John Winthrop, Puritan, founding governor of the Massachusetts Bay Colony and visionary, knew better. "We shall be as a City upon a Hill," he declared in 1630. "The eyes of all people are upon us." Winthrop was borrowing phrases from the Gospel of Matthew, and he was right. This "unpromising" area became America's moral womb, the philosophical and religious center of a new nation.

Yet New England, and indeed the rest of the northern region of this new land, became an entrepreneurial incubator, too. It just took a little time, and a radical switch in direction. The winds may have carried the first settlers west, but their first fortunes were to be found far to the south.

As early as 1627, when the Pilgrims were still clinging to Plymouth Rock, John Winthrop's son, Henry, landed on Barbados. One of that island's 74 original settlers, Henry hoped to become a planter, and he soon wrote home to ask his father, still in England, to please ship him a squad of indentured servants. People willing to sell themselves into years of labor were apparently in short supply, however, because the older Winthrop was able to recruit just two boys.

But the exchange between Henry and his father is most significant for what it reveals about the early English settlements in America. Religion aside, the first colonies were essentially start-up business ventures, scattered from Canada to South America, intended to make a profit.

At the same time that John Winthrop left England to establish his city on a hill, another group of Puritans left England for the Caribbean. While the New England colonists shipped beaver pelts, codfish, and timber back across the Atlantic, the West Indies group ended up on Providence Island raising tobacco and cotton, using slave labor. The warm Caribbean, not raw New England, was quickly taking shape as the area of real economic promise, and this promise was fulfilled when the English eventually struck the sweet mother lode of sugar.

Europeans already prized sugar. The English had tried growing it in Virginia and their privateers had seized it from Spanish ships. But sugar then was a luxury for the rich, or an ingredient in medicine.

The crop roared across the Caribbean like an agricultural hurricane. It denuded islands of their forests and siphoned hundreds of thousands of Africans into slavery to feed a boundless, addicted market. As early as 1643, an observer raved that Barbados was "the most flourishing Island in all those American parts, and I believe in all the world for the producing of sugar."

Governor John Winthrop of the Massachusetts Bay Colony led his followers to the "city upon a hill" that became Boston and to the West Indies trade that enabled the new colony to prosper. *Culver Pictures*

Growing all that sugar—"white gold"—required a huge supply of labor, which was available in Africa. Between 1640 and 1650, English ships delivered nearly 19,000 Africans to work the fields in Barbados. By 1700, the cumulative total had reached 134,000. The pattern was repeated on other islands. Jamaica, barely populated when the English invaded it in 1655, had absorbed 85,000 African slaves by 1700. The Leeward Islands, including Antigua, took 44,000.

In 1645, John Winthrop got a report from a nephew visiting Barbados that its planters that year had bought "a thousand Negroes; and the more they buy, the better able they are to buy, for in a year and half they will earn (with gods blessing) as much as they cost."

That same year a Boston ship made one of the earliest known New

The plantation labor system, shown in this 1849 illustration of field workers on a West Indies sugar plantation, was a New World invention. It consumed the lives of millions of African slaves. Those in the West Indies lived on a diet that often consisted of New England produce, meat, and fish. Illustrated London News *Picture Library*

Because sugarcane had to be processed within hours of harvest, plantation boiling houses functioned like factories operating round the clock. Rivers of molasses, a by-product of the cane juice, flowed northward to New England, where scores of distilleries turned it into rum. Illustrated London News *Picture Library*

England slave voyages to Africa, delivering its cargo to Barbados. The Puritans thought about using captive labor themselves. In 1645, Emanuel Downing, John Winthrop's brother-in-law, advised Winthrop, "I do not see how we can thrive until we get a stock of slaves sufficient to do all our business."

ALTHOUGH RESIDENTS OF NEW ENGLAND AND THE MIDDLE ATLANTIC States owned slaves and trafficked in slaves, they profited more from feeding the increasingly large numbers of Africans in the West Indies and providing the materials to operate the sugar plantations and mills.

As colonial historian Bailyn wrote, the main factor in New England's phenomenal economic success, "the key dynamic force," was slavery.

"New England was not a slave society. . . . But it was slavery nevertheless that made the commercial economy of New England possible and that drove it forward. Slavery was the ultimate source of the commercial economy of eighteenth-century New England," the Harvard professor wrote. "Only a few New England merchants actually engaged in the slave trade, but all of them profited by it, lived off it."

The flow of commerce between America, Africa, and the West Indies entered history as the Triangle Trade. In its classic shape, Northern colonies sent food, livestock, and wood (especially for barrels) to West Indian sugar plantations, where enslaved Africans harvested the cane that fed the refining mills. Sugar, and its by-product molasses, was then shipped back North, usually in barrels made of New England wood and

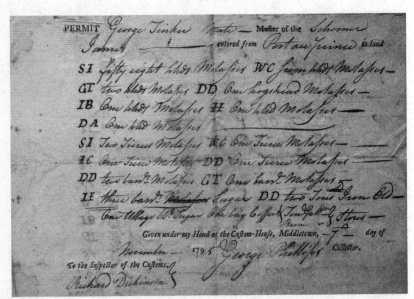

A 1795 manifest from the customshouse in Middletown, Connecticut, shows a cargo consisting almost entirely of molasses from the island now comprising Haiti and the Dominican Republic. The year before, Congress had passed the first U.S. anti-slave-trade law, partly in response to a slave rebellion on the French portion of the island, a volcanic event that threatened the entire plantation system. *Connecticut River Museum*

sometimes accompanied by slaves. Finally, scores of Northern distilleries turned the molasses into rum to trade in Africa for new slaves, who were, in turn, shipped to the sugar plantations.

The sugar planters imported most of what they needed from the Northern colonies and from Europe, because the planters devoted almost every acre of their land to the crop. As one Winthrop correspondent noted, the planters would "rather buy food at very dear rates than produce it by labor, so infinite is the profit of sugar." The nature of the sugar plant made the labor of slaves additionally precious. Because the cane had to be crushed within hours of harvest, the plantations operated like factories, with sugar-boiling houses running around the clock.

The scale of the trade from New England alone is astonishing. On the eve of the American Revolution, almost 80 percent of New England's overseas exports went to the British West Indies. From New England river towns to expanding cities like Boston, New York, and Philadelphia, a steady stream of flour, dried fish, corn, potatoes, onions, cattle, and horses as well as the fruits of Northern forests poured down to the Caribbean. And one needn't be a rich landowner or merchant to join the trade. Even a small farmer could sling a few bags of garden crops or bundles of winter-cut wood onto a dock and become part of this global venture.

One of Connecticut's first towns became famous for just one crop. Wethersfield's "onion maidens" cultivated the pungent crop in their

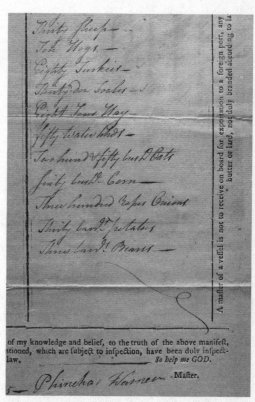

Most of the food listed on this 1795 manifest from the Connecticut brig *Matilda* probably fed slaves. Oats, corn, onions, potatoes, and beans were typical crops exported for almost two centuries from New England to the West Indies. *Connecticut River Museum*

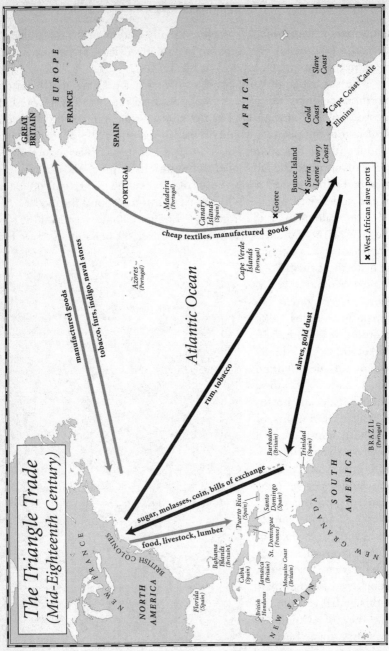

The classic outline of the eighteenth-century Triangle Trade was formed between New England, Africa, and the Caribbean Islands. But as the map shows, other trade routes departed from the triangle shape. Another major route for merchants from New England, New York, and Pennsylvania ran directly south along the Atlantic coast, supplying livestock, foodstuffs, and wood products, such as barrel staves, to island slave plantations. *Map © 2005 by David Lindroth*

backyard gardens. As late as 1800, the small town on the Connecticut River produced 100,000 five-pound ropes of onions, most destined for the West Indies.

The islands became so dependent upon Northern provisions that during the American Revolution, when colonial ships could not get through to the West Indies, famine swept the sugar islands. Between 1780 and 1787, some 15,000 slaves in Jamaica alone died of hunger

But the Caribbean market was critical to the North, too, and if it was important to the Middle Atlantic States, it literally shaped New England.

Colonists from Massachusetts migrated to the Connecticut River valley to find more land to raise livestock. Towns passed ordinances regulating when livestock could be let loose to forage, and they organized overland cattle drives to seaports. Ships that were designed to carry livestock were called "horse jockeys."

Transporting livestock down the Atlantic coast, incidentally, could be as dangerous as voyaging on the high seas. An account survives of a Barbuda-bound Connecticut vessel loaded with horses caught in a storm the winter of 1817, near the end of the West Indies trade. As waves swept the deck, the tethered horses began to slip and fall, and drown. The crew jettisoned bales of hay in hopes of balancing the ship, but could not lift the dead horses overboard. Desperate, the crew dismembered their carcasses on the pitching deck. The butchery saved the vessel and 20 horses.

Meanwhile, the Narragansett area of Rhode Island developed its own plantation system, using slave labor on huge estates dedicated to raising horses, cattle, and dairy cows. In their mid-eighteenth-century heyday, there were at least 10 Narragansett plantations in the tiny colony that ranged in size from 1,000 to 5,000 acres; each employed 10 to 20 slaves. Both in acreage and in numbers of slaves, they matched the plantations of Virginia's famed Tidewater region in the same period.

Connecticut, too, experimented with slave plantations. In New London County, on Connecticut's border with Rhode Island, archaeologists are surveying a long-lost plantation that covered at least 4,000 acres at the time of the Revolution and may have employed as many as 60 slaves. It was owned by a wealthy Salem, Massachusetts, family involved in the West Indian trade.

The owners of small plots and farms in New Jersey and throughout rural areas of New York—including Long Island, Westchester, and Staten Island—also used slaves to grow crops to supply the sugar plantations.

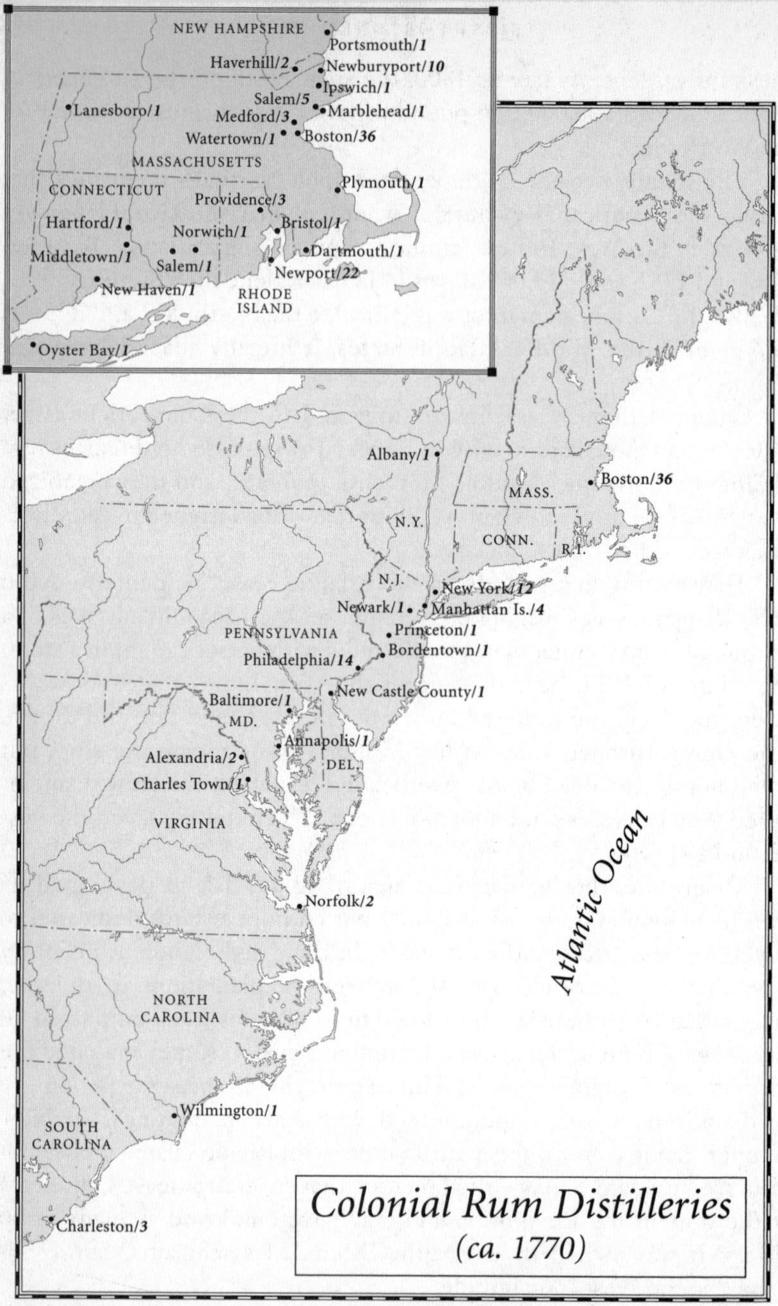
NEW HAMPSHIRE
Portsmouth/1
Haverhill/2
Newburyport/10
Ipswich/1
Salem/5
Marblehead/1
Lanesboro/1
Medford/3
Watertown/1
Boston/36
MASSACHUSETTS
CONNECTICUT
Plymouth/1
Providence/3
Hartford/1
Bristol/1
Norwich/1
Middletown/1
Salem/1
Dartmouth/1
Newport/22
New Haven/1
RHODE ISLAND
Oyster Bay/1
Albany/1
Boston/36
MASS.
N.Y.
CONN.
R.I.
N.J.
New York/12
Newark/1
Manhattan Is./4
PENNSYLVANIA
Princeton/1
Bordentown/1
Philadelphia/14
New Castle County/1
Baltimore/1
MD.
Annapolis/1
Alexandria/2
DEL.
Charles Town/1
VIRGINIA
Norfolk/2
Atlantic Ocean
NORTH CAROLINA
Wilmington/1
SOUTH CAROLINA
Charleston/3
Colonial Rum Distilleries
(ca. 1770)

Rum distilleries concentrated in New England and New York depended on molasses imported from West Indian slave plantations and are a measure of the importance of the colonial trade between the two regions. *From John J. McCusker and Russell R. Menard,* The Economy of British America, 1607–1789, *2d edition (Chapel Hill, NC: 1991). Originally drawn by Richard J. Stinely. Courtesy of the Omohundro Institute of Early American History and Culture. Redrawn by David Lindroth.*

Lewis Morris, a signer of the Declaration of Independence, was the third and final lord of Morrisania, a 1,900-acre operation in what is now the Bronx, on which staple crops like wheat and corn were grown, livestock was raised, and timber was cut, all for transport to the Caribbean. Over the decades, dozens of slaves were put to work in Morrisania's fields and other businesses.

The Van Cortlandts—who, in 1889, donated their home and hundreds of acres of land in the northwest Bronx to New York as a public park—were also major West Indies and transatlantic traders. As late as 1810, Augustus Van Cortlandt ran a large-scale farming operation that used slave labor. His will freed his slave Dinah in 1823, in gratitude for the care she had given his wife, Catharine, who'd died after a long illness 15 years earlier.

IT'S DIFFICULT TO OVERSTATE THE IMPORTANCE OF MOLASSES, OR, MORE specifically, of rum, particularly to the New England economy.

At various times, Massachusetts and Rhode Island together had nearly 70 distilleries for rum, and New York City had more than a dozen. The Africa trade, however, took only a fraction of the rivers of molasses and rum flowing into and out of the North.

In 1770, Massachusetts and Rhode Island together imported 3.5 million gallons of molasses, which their distilleries turned into 2.8 million gallons of rum. New Englanders drank up most of the rum themselves, but 1.3 million gallons was reexported up and down the Atlantic coast, from Newfoundland to the Deep South. New England distilled more rum than all the rest of North America. The volume drunk was astonishing—an average of 1.5 quarts a week for every adult male. So was the amount of molasses smuggled past customs agents—probably more than 1.5 million gallons in 1770.

Like almost everything the North traded in, the hogsheads of molasses and rum were transported by water, and the revenue from shipping rivaled the value of West Indian exports. Shipbuilding became a major industry both in New York City and in New England. John Winthrop himself financed the construction of the Massachusetts Bay Colony's first ship, the *Blessing of the Bay*, launched in 1631. By 1700, Boston and nearby towns were turning out 70 ships a year—the most in number and tonnage in the Western Hemisphere.

The industry employed hundreds of shipwrights, carpenters, sailmakers, and ironworkers, not to mention lumbermen. Two thousand trees, mainly oak and pine, were cut to build a single decent-sized ship.

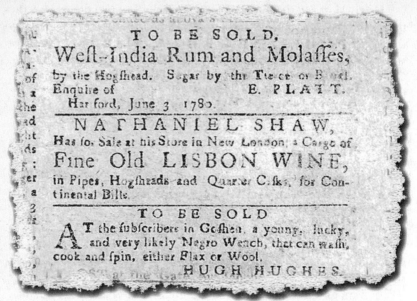

This advertisement from the June 6, 1780, *The Connecticut Courant and The Weekly Intelligencer* (a predecessor of today's *Hartford Courant*) shows the shape of colonial trade in a nutshell. New England imported molasses, and rum and sugar in lesser amounts, from the West Indies. The Lisbon wine often was exchanged for New England fish. The "negro wench" for sale may not have been bought in Africa with New England rum, but her ancestors likely were. In 1780, slavery had been practiced in Connecticut for more than a century and the state's slave population had grown to about 5,000. The Connecticut Courant and The Weekly Intelligencer

The ships were sold, often to West Indian buyers, or kept for Massachusetts's own fleet. In the early 1700s, Boston's adult male population had risen to only about 1,800. Incredibly, though, nearly one-third of Boston's men owned shares in at least one oceangoing vessel.

Given the risk of shipwreck or seizure, every voyage was in itself a business venture. The trade—legal or illegal—shifted with the tides of war and taxation.

Trade also bound fortunes and families together. A social register of New England families and families from elsewhere in the North that derived their wealth from the West Indies slave islands would include hundreds or thousands of names, depending on where the qualifying bar is set. In the eighteenth century, Boston merchant Peter Faneuil (endower of Faneuil Hall) had a plantation on French St. Domingue. Before its slaves rebelled, Sainte-Domingue (now Haiti) had supplanted Barbados and Jamaica as the world's richest colony. And, of course, the Winthrop family did very well. John Winthrop's youngest son, Samuel, eventually acquired a plantation on Antigua and became president of its ruling council. A Winthrop cousin named Turner owned a 400-acre plantation on Barbados.

Plantation slavery created tremendous wealth in the New World and the Old. It was the engine of the colonial Atlantic economy.

The evidence that New England, the cradle of American civilization, was rocked by this slave economy had been there from the start, provided by John Winthrop as early as 1648.

A single entry from the Puritan's journal revealed the origins of New England's wealth and that of much of the rest of the North. In between reporting interruptions to the beaver and fish trade and complaining about New England's reputation as a "poor, barren place," Winthrop gave the real news:

"It pleased the Lord to open us a trade to Barbados and other islands in the West Indies."

The Nathaniel Russell House in Charleston, South Carolina, is a 200-year-old landmark, built by one of the many New Englanders who moved south to make their fortunes. Russell began to make his in 1765 as an importer of New England rum, cheese, and fish, and soon, African slaves.

TRANSPLANTED YANKEES

THE MAIN FOYER OF NATHANIEL RUSSELL'S HANDSOME HOUSE, WITH one of the most stunning stairways in America, has been painted a color called "Russell Gold."

Rhode Islander Russell went to Charleston, South Carolina, in 1765, and gold is what he found. By the time he died in 1820, this son of New England was known as "the King of the Yankees," and though not the only Northern transplant to make his fortune in the slave trade, he set the benchmark for success.

Russell held on to his New England roots and became the center of a circle of Northerners, even while transforming himself into a true Southern magnate.

Born in the coastal town of Bristol, he was the son of a lawyer who became Rhode Island's chief justice. The same year Joseph Russell was named to the high court, his son moved to Charleston to sell, as an agent for Providence merchants, New England–distilled rum, and cheese, and shad in barrels on one of the city's bustling wharves.

Russell moved quickly to the merchandising of rice, cotton, indigo, and captured Africans. By 1769, just four years after arriving in Charleston, he was the head of a firm owning the ship *Lilly*, which carried slaves from Africa to Charleston. In the following years he expanded his fleet.

In those decades, an estimated 55,000 Africans were brought into Charleston harbor. The city's thriving weekly, the *South Carolina Gazette*, trumpets, in column after column, "Prime Negro Slaves Fresh from the Windward Coast," and the shipping news shows traffic to and from Africa and the sugar islands.

Rhode Islander Nathaniel Russell treasured his New England roots, even as he became a Southern business magnate and slave dealer. *Miniature of Nathaniel Russell by Charles Fraser, 1818. Historic Charleston Foundation*

In July 1772, Russell wrote to merchant Aaron Lopez of Newport, Rhode Island, that "their [*sic*] has been a Great many Negroes imported here this summer and many more expected; they continue at very Great Prices."

In 1788, he married the daughter of a prominent Charleston

Nathaniel Russell's spectacular Robert Adam–style mansion on Charleston's fabled Meeting Street was considered one of the most beautiful houses in the city, and included this "flying" cantilevered staircase, one of the most remarkable in America. © Rick Rhodes

rice and indigo merchant. He was fifty, and Sarah Hopton, described in one early document as "a wealthy spinster," was thirty-five.

In 1795, the Rhode Islander was listed as the top merchant in Charleston. By then, he controlled a network of commercial and

trade interests, and he was a compatriot of the city's aristocrats—
South Carolina Governor William Bull willed him his gold-headed
cane and a diamond buckle—and a philanthropist. He was also active in state politics. In surviving portraits, he is bald with a fringe
of white hair, rather like John Adams, and has bushy eyebrows. He
looks solemn but not displeased.

In the earliest years of the nineteenth century, Nathaniel and
Sarah built a grand brick mansion on Charleston's landmark-rich
Meeting Street and took up residence with their two daughters and
18 African slaves.

Russell's connections to New England never faltered, however, and he maintained deep business and family relationships in
Rhode Island in particular.

He was a founder and first president of the New England
Society of Charleston, a social and philanthropic group devoted to
the ideals of Yankee independence and industry, and the courage
shown by the members' *Mayflower* ancestors. Yankees in need in
Charleston found help at the New England Society, where raised
glasses of steaming punch and hearty fellowship were part of the
agenda.

In 1955, the Historic Charleston Foundation bought Russell's
house to serve as a museum and the foundation's headquarters, and
some 70,000 visitors view its grand furnishings every year.
Charleston Style, a popular coffee-table book about Charleston interior design, by Susan Sully, displays on its cover not the homes of
Southern aristocrats, but the oval drawing room of New Englander
Nathaniel Russell.

Venture Smith was captured in Africa, shipped to Rhode Island, and bought, beaten, and sold in colonial Connecticut, where there were 5,000 others like him.

Three

A CONNECTICUT SLAVE

SCREAMS AND CURSES POURED FROM THE OLD HOUSE ACROSS THE farmyard. The young black man, working in the barn, recognized the sobbing shrieks as his wife's and the torrent of abuse as coming from their mistress. He flew across the yard into the house. In the low-ceilinged kitchen before a great hearth, he tried to shield Meg from Elizabeth Stanton's fists.

As the man begged his wife to apologize, Elizabeth Stanton turned her fury on him, seizing her horsewhip.

"I reached out my great black hand, raised it up and received the blows of the whip on it which were designed for my head," Venture Smith recalled many years later in his life story. He yanked the leather whip from the furious woman and hurled it into the fire.

By the 1750s, when Meg and Venture Smith were fighting with their owner's wife, New England and the other Northern colonies were already becoming wealthy feeding slaves on the sugar plantations that covered the islands of the West Indies. The trade system that swept those Africans into permanent bondage also carried thousands of other Africans into forced labor in the American colonies.

In the collection of the Stratford, Connecticut, historical society is a paper silhouette of a nineteen-year-old woman named Flora. The silhouette, showing Flora's spiky hair and blunt young profile, was drawn in 1796 when Margaret Dwight of Milford sold her to Asa Benjamin—and "his Heirs & Assigns forever"—for about $150 in today's currency. It is tempting to see Flora's silhouette as a metaphor for Northern slav-

When "a certain Negro Wench named Flora" was purchased in Connecticut, the 1796 transaction included a profile of her along with the bill of sale. *Stratford Historical Society, Stratford, Connecticut*

ery: the thousands of enslaved people who lived in the North remain in the shadows.

In the years before the signing of the Declaration of Independence, there were tens of thousands of people in bondage in the Northern United States. Although precise figures are impossible to obtain, in 1760 there were at least 41,000 Africans enslaved in the North. This includes New England and the Middle Atlantic States of New York, New Jersey, Pennsylvania, and Delaware.

After the American Revolution, the numbers of slaves in the North dropped. George Washington had freed many Africans who fought for America because the British had promised freedom to blacks who joined the Loyalist cause. But in the 1790s, when Flora was sold to Asa Benjamin, Connecticut and Rhode Island together still had more than 6,000 people in bondage; Pennsylvania had 3,700; and New York had more than 20,000.

Despite these numbers, it didn't take long for an idealized notion of slavery to take root in the North. It soon became accepted as fact that Northern slavery was benign, loosely defined, more like a mutually agreed-upon indenture. Two centuries of human bondage was recast as a paternalistic, "family-style" arrangement, as beneficial to the slave as to the owner.

Missing from this rosy view was, among other things, the fact that owners had, in effect, the power of life and death over their "property." In Connecticut, for example, the colony's public records first mention a slave in 1639, reporting that a Hartford man had killed African Louis Berbice. Yet historian Bernard Steiner could write late in the nineteenth century that "Connecticut had little to apologize for in her treatment of the Negro," a statement most Northern citizens would have echoed comfortably.

But the actual experience of slaves was often closer to that of Cato, Newport, and Adam. In 1758, Jonathan Trumbull, the future governor of Connecticut, sentenced the three "to be publicly whipped on the naked body for nightwalking after nine in the evening without an order from their masters."

Or that of the New York husband and wife sold by their master in 1765 for having too many children.

Or that of the eleven-year-old boy put up for sale in New London County, Connecticut, in 1760 by the family of Benedict Arnold, the nation's most infamous traitor. The advertisement for the child's sale said he was accustomed to work.

A respected study of the lives of slaves in coastal Narragansett, Rhode Island, where Venture Smith lived as a child, found that captives were routinely subjected to denigration, harsh corporal punishment, and the fear tactics inherent in a system of oppression.

Slaves in the North, like those in the South, served at the whim of their owners and could be sold or traded. They were housed in unheated attics and basements, in outbuildings and barns. They often slept on the floor, wrapped in coarse blankets. They lived under a harsh system of "black codes" that controlled their movements, prohibited their education, and limited their social contacts. Laws governing the rights and behaviors of slaves varied slightly from colony to colony, but they were updated in reaction to each new real or perceived threat. The two defining assumptions of all the codes were that blacks were dangerous in groups and that they were, at a basic human level, inferior.

VENTURE SMITH PROVIDED A WINDOW INTO NORTHERN SLAVERY WITH his life story, which he dictated to Elisha Niles, a schoolteacher and Revolutionary War soldier. Published in New London, Connecticut, in 1798, it's one of only a handful of surviving black narratives encompassing life in Africa and colonial enslavement. The 31-page document is harrowing.

Venture was raised as Broteer Furro in the west of Africa, the first son of a rich and indulgent father. Two centuries of the slave trade had made that part of Africa a battleground, with thousands kidnapped and sold into slavery every year. Black armies had been plundering communities on the continent's rich west coast since the sixteenth century, when Africans were first stolen to provide labor in the New World. Lining the coast were about 40 "slave castles," or "slave factories," that

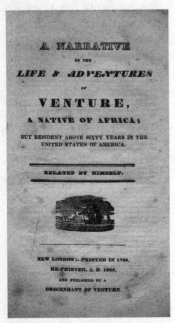

A NARRATIVE

OF THE

LIFE & ADVENTURES

OF

VENTURE,

A NATIVE OF AFRICA;

BUT RESIDENT ABOVE SIXTY YEARS IN THE
UNITED STATES OF AMERICA.

RELATED BY HIMSELF.

NEW LONDON:—PRINTED IN 1798.
RE-PRINTED, A. D. 1835.
AND PUBLISHED BY A
DESCENDANT OF VENTURE

Venture Smith dictated his life's story to a Revolutionary War soldier, and his account, originally published in 1798, is one of the few surviving narratives to encompass life in Africa, enslavement in colonial America, and freedom. *Title page to* A Narrative of the Life and Adventures of Venture, *1835 ed., The Connecticut Historical Society Museum, Hartford, Connecticut*

were, in effect, warehouses, established largely by Europeans, where traders from Europe and the colonies could select and buy captive human beings.

Believed to have been born about 1729, Venture was about eight when he and his family were captured and force-marched to the coast of present-day Ghana. Though his father, Saungm Furro, had initially offered protection from the marauding army to a neighboring tribe, he and his community were quickly overrun as they tried to escape the slave-gathering dragnet.

"The very first salute I had from [the soldiers] was a violent blow on the head with the fore part of a gun, and at the same time a grasp round the neck," Venture said. "I then had a rope put about my neck, as had all the women in the thicket with me, and were immediately led to my father."

The soldiers wanted Saungm Furro's money, "but he gave them no account of it," his son said. So, his family watching, they tortured Saungm Furro until he died. "The shocking scene is to this day fresh in my mind, and I have often been overcome while thinking on it." The old chief was spared seeing his wives and children dragged hundreds of miles to a coastal factory, where Broteer and many others were held for sale.

John Atkins, a British surgeon aboard a slave trade ship in the decade before Broteer was taken, described the captives at Cape Coast Castle, an infamous slave fortress 15 miles from where Broteer and his family were held: "In the Area of this Quadrangle, are large Vaults, with an iron Grate at the Surface to let in Light and Air on those poor

Wretches, the Slaves, who are chained and confined there till a Demand comes. They are all marked with a burning Iron upon the right Breast." Atkins went on to remark upon the castle's "pleasant Prospect to the Sea," which allowed traders to watch for arriving ships sailing down the coast.

Venture was about to fall into the hands of a Rhode Island family whose name figures prominently in eighteenth-century New England. The Mumfords were quintessential Triangle Trade entrepreneurs: they commanded slave trade ships, owned farms where enslaved blacks worked, and sold captives in the West Indies and American colonies. On Africa's Gold Coast, about 40 miles from where Broteer was imprisoned, there was a city called Mumford.

Venture remembered being seated in a canoe and rowed out to a vessel bound for Barbados. Once on board, he was purchased by Robertson Mumford, the ship's steward, for a piece of calico cloth and four gallons of rum. He was named "Venture," because he was Mumford's private investment, and in that moment, he lost his name, his country, and his freedom.

The Middle Passage, the sea voyage from Africa into enslavement, ended Venture's childhood. The mortality rate among the captives, pinioned cheek by jowl with the dead and dying, could be 15 to 20 percent at that time. On Venture's voyage the rate was even higher: of the 260 taken aboard in Africa, 60 died in an outbreak of smallpox.

Cape Coast Castle, a slave-trading compound not far from where Venture and his family were held, was described as "ye largest, strongest & most beautifull castle" belonging to the Royal African Company. *The Mariners' Museum, Newport News, Virginia*

Most of the survivors were sold in Barbados. Only Venture and three others made the last part of the voyage to Rhode Island, to the Mumfords' dairy and stock farms in the Narragansett region. Within a year or two, Venture was moved to New York, to live with another branch of the family on Fishers Island in Long Island Sound. He spent his days carding wool and performing other household tasks. Then, because he was big and strong, he was set to work pounding corn for animal feed. He regularly labored far into the night, and was punished if his work was not done well. But the hardest part was the abuse by his master's son.

"[James] would order me to do this and that business different from what my master directed me," Venture recalled. One day, when Venture refused to set aside his assigned tasks, James tried to beat him with a pitchfork. Venture fought back and sent James crying to his mother.

Venture may have been more than James's equal physically, but he was also a slave, and in colonial America in the late 1730s, he was nobody's equal. Venture allowed himself to be bound and carried to James for punishment. "He took me to a gallows made for the purpose of hanging cattle on, and suspended me on it," said Venture. Probably slung up by a rope bound around his wrists, the boy hung there for an hour.

VENTURE'S STORY AND THE ACCOUNTS OF OTHER ENSLAVED BLACK Northerners share a leitmotif of abuse. Beatings and the threat of beatings were constant. Children were whipped and saw their parents and siblings whipped.

One of the most famous freedom fighters of the nineteenth century was born a slave in 1797 in Ulster County, New York. The property of Colonel Johannes Hardenburgh and later of his son, Charles Hardenburgh, she was christened Isabella, but history knows her by the name she gave herself, Sojourner Truth. She left a record of her nearly 30 years in captivity.

She and her family lived in the dark cellar of the Hardenburghs' house. After Charles Hardenburgh's death, a neighbor bought her, and some sheep, for $100. She was nine years old.

"They gave her plenty to eat," she recalled in her third-person narrative, "and also plenty of whippings." One Sunday morning, Sojourner's owner beat the child severely, until blood streamed from her wounds. " 'And now,' she says, 'when I hear 'em tell of whipping women on the bare flesh, it makes my flesh crawl, and my very hair rise on my head! Oh! My God!' "

I SELL THE SHADOW TO SUPPORT THE SUBSTANCE.
SOJOURNER TRUTH.

Freedom fighter Sojourner Truth was sold, beaten, and abused in New York, and she saw her parents die of hunger and cold there. *Library of Congress, Prints and Photographs Division [LC-USZ62-119343]*

Killing a slave at the time of Sojourner Truth's severe beating was taken more seriously than when Venture Smith was young in the mid-1700s. In Venture's youth, the black codes almost demanded harsh punishment, and it was not considered a capital crime to kill an enslaved man, woman, or child in the course of "correcting" him or her. Corporal punishment was advocated as necessary for the "good regulating and ordering" of slaves. The assumption was that an owner would never deliberately destroy his own property. Since a whip or a cane was not necessarily a lethal weapon, it was difficult to prove that a master, in his rage, had intended to kill a disobedient slave.

Joshua Hempstead, whose diary documents a half century of life in eighteenth-century New London, wrote of the time in 1751 when a husband and wife were questioned about the beating death of their slave girl: "In the aftern I was att Capt Danll Coits to hear the Examination of Mr. Nicholas Letchmere & his wife upon accot of the Sudden Death of their Servt Zeno a female about 6 or 7 year old who Died a Sund night about 2 in ye morning." The child's body was examined, and her death was attributed to the severity of the beating. Hempstead's last reference to Zeno's fatal punishment was that there was a well-attended public hearing into the incident, and that the child was buried.

VENTURE LIVED WITH HIS OWNERS IN A FRAGILE TRUCE THAT WAS frequently interrupted by open warfare. As he matured, he grew into the kind of captive who pushed back—though slavery scholars agree that most captives resisted in some way. Passive resistance included doing work slowly or poorly, breaking or stealing tools and objects from the household, pretending not to understand instructions, truancy, and a kind of mild noncompliance that tested an owner's will. More overt forms of resistance included fighting back when beaten or abused, appealing to the legal system for justice, and running away. The more active the captive's resistance, the more punishment and dislocation he or she tended to suffer.

Despite its risks and poor odds for success, running away was one of the clearest statements a captive could make, and it baffled most slave owners, who believed blacks, as inferior and passive, were naturally suited to slavery.

Venture was in his early twenties when he ran away from the Mumfords' Fishers Island property with two other enslaved black men and a white indentured servant named Joseph Heday, who had devised the plan. Detailed information about their getaway survives in Venture's narrative: "We privately collected out of our master's store, six great old cheeses, two firkins of butter, and one whole batch of new bread. When we had gathered all our own clothes and some more, we took them all about midnight, and went to the water side. We stole our master's boat, embarked, and then directed our course for the Mississippi river." (In his later life in freedom, Venture became a skilled mariner, but his seamanship at this time was murky.)

In an April 1754 advertisement in the weekly *New-York Gazette* seeking the return of his runaways, George Mumford offered the modern-day equivalent of about $1,000, an unusually large reward, for the return of the men or his two-masted boat and white pine canoe. The ad also gives scholars the only existing description of Venture. He is described as "a very tall fellow, 6 feet 2 inches high, thick square shoulders, large bon'd, mark'd in the face, or scar'd with a knife in his own country."

The most accurate description of Venture Smith survives in an advertisement placed by his owner when Venture, two other slaves, and a white indentured servant fled their captivity in 1754. *Rare Books Division, The New York Public Library, Astor, Lenox and Tilden Foundations*

Some of the most dramatic moments described in Venture Smith's narrative—such as his grabbing the whip from his owner's wife and throwing it into the kitchen fire—occurred in this house, which still stands. *Library of Congress, Prints and Photographs Division, Historic American Buildings Survey (HABS, CONN, 6-STONI, 4-2)*

The men got as far as the eastern end of Long Island. Though the four had promised to stick together, Heday stole everyone's gear from the boat while Venture was looking for water, and the other two slaves, Fortune and Isaac, were cooking. The three blacks pursued Heday and caught up with him a few miles away, but Venture, hoping to minimize the damage to his eventual chances for freedom, decided they should return and confess.

The white man was punished for his role as ringleader. Venture's punishment was to be sold, the price rebellious slaves often paid. Purchased by Thomas Stanton of Stonington, Connecticut, Venture had to leave behind Meg and their month-old daughter, Hannah.

About a year and a half later, probably sometime in 1758, Stanton bought Venture's family, too. The house, where Meg and her mistress fought, still stands. Meg and Venture may have lived in the attic. The stairs leading to it rise a few steps, then turn sharply to the attic's main floor, with its steeply pitched roof and small windows. On the first step, just where Venture and Meg would have turned for the sharp climb, a smooth hollow has been worn into the stair.

The wide door at the front of the house overlooks fields of tall grass, and at the back of the gray-shingled house is a small, weathered doorway to the kitchen. Family descendants who own the property still call it "the slave door."

Thomas Stanton was a short man, and Venture's strength was already legendary. While a captive on Fishers Island, he had won a dare by carrying a 42-gallon barrel filled with salt nearly 50 feet. But the balance of power in this master/slave relationship rested with Stanton, who had been hunting on Long Island when Venture grabbed the whip from Elizabeth Stanton and threw it into the fire. This kind of resistance, a direct threat to the authority of the slaveholder, could not go unpunished. Stanton waited a few days before responding, and then had surprise on his side.

"In the morning as I was putting a log in the fire-place, not suspecting harm from any one, I received a most violent stroke on the crown of my head with a club two feet long and as large round as a chair-post," Venture recalled. "The first blow made me have my wits about me you may suppose, for as soon as he went to renew it, I snatched the club out of his hands."

As he continued to resist, Venture made life harder for himself. Yet he refused to give in.

Carrying the bloody club, Venture went to a neighboring justice of the peace to complain about his treatment. Furious, Thomas Stanton and his brother, Robert, jumped on horses and tracked the slave to the justice's home, only to receive a humiliating rebuke for their cruelty. But the justice counseled Venture to be patient and await another incident of abuse before complaining again.

The mood on the trip home was frosty, until the three came to a secluded place and the two white men dismounted and began beating Venture. His reaction, predictably, was rage. He threw both men to the ground and, he said, "laid one of them across the other, and stamped both with my feet what I would." The two managed to get control over him and hauled him to a blacksmith, who put him in handcuffs. When Elizabeth Stanton gloated over his constraints, Venture thanked her merrily, and for his insolence was draped in heavy chains. Robert Stanton had borrowed money from Venture that the slave had earned doing extra jobs. Robert did not intend to repay the loan, which may have been part of the reason he advised his brother to sell the slave.

After several days of silent treatment for Venture from the Stantons, Hempstead Miner, another Stonington resident, offered to buy him. (Miner secretly counseled him to appear especially truculent and miserable, which drove down the purchase price.) So, at the age of thirty, for the third time in his life, Venture was sold, and for a price that reflected the fact that the Stantons just wanted to be rid of him.

Despite the high quality of his work, Venture was breaking all of slavery's rules, and in getting physically violent with the Stantons he had crossed every boundary except the last one: murdering his owner.

Incidents of slaves' trying to kill their owners jump from colonial records. As early as 1708, a New York couple and their three children were murdered by the family's two slaves. In New Jersey, a slave struck off his owner's head with an axe, and in Newport, Rhode Island, a black man murdered the white woman who had beaten him. Connecticut's colonial diarist Joshua Hempstead wrote of the New London slave who slipped ratsbane into the family "coffy." Other poisonings or attempts to poison owners appear frequently in records.

IF THE FIRST HALF OF VENTURE'S LIFE DEMONSTRATES THE PHYSICAL and psychological violence that was a consistent feature in slavery's landscape, the next period, his final years as a captive, offers the even broader lesson of how indispensable slavery was for the North. Southern captives were overwhelmingly agricultural workers, usually laboring in groups. But the North had a different ecosystem and a different style of slavery, and captives had to adapt to the diverse requirements of their owner's household, or farm, or other business. Slaves in the North worked in agriculture and in the maritime trades, but they also had tasks as varied as operating printing presses, shoeing horses, and constructing houses and barns.

Hempstead's longtime slave, Adam, who worked on his land in New London and Stonington for 40 years, labored all day, every day. Hempstead mentions Adam's threshing hay and wheat, tending livestock, building and repairing stone walls, cutting wood, harvesting apples and other crops, fixing broken wagons and farm equipment, and carting loads of seaweed.

Newspaper advertisements for runaway slaves are a testament to the variety and skill level of their work, and they indicate, further, how valuable the slaves were to their owners. Eighteenth-century ads for runaways in New York and New Jersey, for example, contain descriptive phrases such as "shipwright by trade," "a carpenter and a cooper by trade," "understands all sorts of Husbandry Work, and something of the Trade of a Black-Smith," "a very good cooper, speaks English, French and Dutch and can read and Write," "can bleed and draw Teeth, Pretending to be a great doctor," "a Chimney-sweeper," and "a very good shoemaker." These were just a few of the many trades and professions mentioned.

Enslaved black women in the North were maids and household servants. They were spinners, weavers, cooks, and cleaners. They grew food, hauled wood and water, watched the children, tended the sick, made medicines, and helped with the family business. They were seamstresses, soap makers, dyers, and laundresses.

John Adams, one of the few Founding Fathers who refused to own black people, said he paid handsomely for his principles because captive labor (in New England) was widespread, very skilled, and cheap.

Venture Smith had the diverse skills of many Northern captives. His work experiences including farming, fishing, logging, woodworking, and shipping. Like any mid-eighteenth-century countryman, he could fell a tree, build a house, and roast a raccoon. He was also, at one point during his enslavement, a household servant. He was the kind of slave described in sales advertisements as "fit for town or country work."

Hempstead Miner, Venture's new owner, removed the slave's chains and said he would not oppose Venture's saving for his eventual freedom. But there was a snag. Miner, who later ended up in debtor's prison, may never have intended to keep Venture for his own service, and he immediately took him from coastal Stonington up to Hartford and pawned him for £10 to a lawyer named Daniel Edwards. The black man became Edwards's house servant, his "cupbearer" and waiter.

The Hartford man liked and trusted Venture, and asked him why Miner had wished to part with him. The black man answered with a candor that shows how well he understood his position in chattel bondage: "I replied that I could not give him the reason, unless it was to convert me into cash, and speculate with me as with other commodities." Edwards must have been moved by the reply, because he gave Venture a horse to return to Stonington to see his wife and children at Thomas Stanton's farm. (Venture notes wryly, "My old master appeared much ruffled at my being there.")

Miner worked out an arrangement whereby Colonel Oliver Smith, also of Stonington, would assume ownership of Venture, by then thirty-one. Smith owned a new, handsome, gambrel-roofed house in Stonington Borough, a waterfront pocket settled by merchants, shipowners, and sea captains. Smith, a big, good-looking man, was a shipbuilder and a personal friend of George Washington's. He was involved in trade with the West Indies and owned several slaves besides Venture. He was also receptive to Venture's plan to earn the money for his freedom, a goal Venture pursued aggressively, although it took him nearly a half-dozen years to achieve.

Venture worked on Fishers Island and on tiny Ram Island, cutting wood, threshing grain, and performing other agricultural tasks. He bought nothing he could live without, sleeping on a cold hearth with one blanket over him and one under. A quarter of his earnings went to his owner.

A man saving to buy his freedom was subject to various forms of deceit. The owner could set a price, then change his mind once the agreed-upon sum was saved. Or he could take the money and refuse to free the slave. Even for Venture, who had the physical and mental stamina to resist the soul-crushing effects of American slavery, the system was filled with uncertainty and fraught with risks.

After several years, Venture went to Oliver Smith with close to the price they had agreed upon, £71. It was a large sum—a man could buy hundreds of acres for that amount—but the colonel had said he wanted to have enough money to cover Venture's care in case his health broke down. Increasingly, towns were turning to former owners for help in supporting freed slaves who became indigent.

Sojourner Truth of New York describes the broken health of her enslaved parents, and their owner's decision to free them both so that her mother could take care of her blind, lame father. But her mother did not live long, and her father died of hunger and cold in a filthy shed. "What a compensation for a life of toil, of patient submission to repeated robberies of the most aggravated kind, and, also, far more than murderous neglect," their daughter wrote bitterly.

"Being thirty-six years old, I left Col. Smith once for all," Venture said. "I had already been sold three times, made considerable money with seemingly nothing to derive [from it], . . . lost much by misfortunes, and paid an enormous sum for my freedom."

He called himself Venture Smith.

Years later, he said, "My freedom is a privilege nothing else can equal."

ASSEMBLING HIS FAMILY IN FREEDOM TOOK 10 MORE YEARS AND THE modern-day equivalent of $1,500 dollars. Venture first bought his sons Solomon and Cuff, Hannah's younger brothers, so they would help him earn the money to buy their mother and sister. To his father's grief, Solomon went to sea at seventeen with a Rhode Island man to learn whaling and died of scurvy on his first voyage. Cuff, who later fought on the side of the colonists in the American Revolution, worked with his father on Long Island, farming, chopping wood, fishing for eels and lobsters, and making a homestead. They owned a 30-ton sloop and used it to ferry wood to Rhode Island; this was one of Venture's most lucrative endeavors.

Venture eventually owned several dwellings and boats, and had substantial landholdings. "My temporal affairs were in a pretty prosperous condition," he said. He was in his midforties when he and Meg had another son, whom they named Solomon, after their lost child. In 1776, they left their Long Island village and moved to Haddam Neck on the Connecticut River, establishing a homestead on 100 riverfront acres. Venture made enough money farming, fishing, and shipping wood to buy several other black men, expecting that they would repay their purchase price and then begin their own lives in freedom.

And although he prospered, the injustice that dominated the first half of his life was never far from his experience. In 1780, a hogshead of

Venture Smith is buried in the cemetery of a Congregational church not far from where he lived and prospered after becoming a free man. *Joanne HoYoung Lee,* The Hartford Courant

molasses that was being shipped to a wealthy merchant on one of Venture's boats was lost overboard. Though not on board at the time of the loss, Venture was held liable and advised to settle up, since the rich man planned to sue until he recovered the price of the molasses. Venture paid the £10 to the merchant, Elisha Hart, who later taunted him repeatedly over the mishap.

In Africa, Venture wrote, such a proceeding "would have been branded as a crime equal to highway robbery. But Captain Hart was a white gentleman and I a poor African, therefore it was all right, and good enough for the black dog."

Venture died in 1805. He was in his midseventies, almost blind, his huge body broken by hard work. He and Meg are buried in the cemetery next to a tall white church in East Haddam, Connecticut, near soldiers of the American Revolution and local merchants and landowners. His headstone is made of a reddish-brown stone quarried locally, and carved with an angel.

The inscription reads: "Sacred to the Memory of Venture Smith, African. Tho the son of a King he was kidnapped and sold as a slave but by his industry he acquired Money to Purchase his Freedom."

In the last few sentences of his narrative, Venture took his own measure. Chief among his consolations he cited Meg, "the wife of my youth, whom I married for love and bought with my money," and his freedom.

He outlived the three men who owned him, but not slavery itself. By the Civil War, more than a half century after Venture died, America's enslaved population was close to 4 million, more than five times what it had been when he was a slave.

The record Venture Smith left of his singular life shows the burden of suffering that all slaves bore. When he was carried to his grave by his pallbearers, two white men and two enslaved black men, they complained of his weight.

The fires of 1741 taught New Yorkers

that their slaves hated bondage as much

as blacks did in the South,

and that they were just as willing to

strike back at their masters.

Four

REBELLION IN MANHATTAN

MORE THAN A CENTURY OLD, FORT GEORGE DOMINATED LOWER Manhattan. Now it was throwing off huge billows of black smoke. Flames blew across the wooden roofs of the governor's residence and barracks, and the fire roared as a fierce March wind whipped the blaze from building to building.

At the first alarm, sounded just after noon, men from throughout the city rushed to the waterfront. They threw buckets of water onto the flames, which the wind blew right back at them. Just one man, a soldier, died in the inferno, but by three that afternoon, only the outer stone walls of the fort, which had been the heart of the city, remained.

In the following days, as spring unfolded in an increasingly tense New York, residents asked how the fire could have taken hold in so many places before it was detected. Some asked whether sparks from a workman's fire-pot could have blown onto the shingles of the governor's house, but by the time the alarm sounded, smoke already hovered over the roof of the residence, indicating an interior fire.

"No one imagined it was done on purpose," said the man who was to become the brutal prosecutor in a months-long conspiracy trial that became known as the "Great Negro Plot" of 1741.

But the fire at Fort George was indeed arson. And it was just the first of nearly a dozen that led to the jailing of 200 black men, the execution of 35 people—31 blacks and 4 whites—and the deportation of 72 slaves to certain death by labor on plantations throughout the hemisphere.

The catalyst of the conflict, the true spark, was the anger of captive blacks. The scope of the subsequent trials—their ferocity and their extraordinary conviction rate—is without parallel in the nation's early history.

FROM THE MOMENT THEIR ENSLAVEMENT BEGAN, AFRICANS FOUGHT BACK.

When they could, they revolted on the ships that carried them across the Atlantic to a life of slavery in the New World. At times their resistance was more passive, more self-directed: the newly enslaved would refuse to eat or would attempt suicide.

They fought back early and fiercely in the West Indies in the 1600s. Then, for three weeks during the summer of 1791, the horizon of Sainte-Domingue, now known as Haiti, became "a wall of fire" as 100,000 slaves torched plantations. It was just the beginning, as the re-

In 1813, an elderly New Yorker named David Grim drew an extraordinarily detailed map of the city he remembered from his childhood in the early 1740s. He remembered seeing two black men burned alive, and another black man whose dead body was hanging in chains, and he noted these on his map. *Plan of the City and Environs of New York as they were 1742–1744, map by David Grim, 1813; [detail] negative #3046, Collection of the New-York Historical Society*

volts jumped to other Caribbean islands. Over the next dozen years, Francois Dominique Toussaint L'Ouverture, a "model slave" and carriage driver, became a storied general in Haiti, leading tens of thousands of slaves in extended revolt against slavery.

They also resisted in the colonial South. Slaves performed substandard work, stole, ran away, and poisoned their owners. And they fought even more violently, as in Virginia in 1831, in a rebellion led by the slave Nat Turner, in Stono, South Carolina, and in many lesser-known revolts.

Slaves fought back fiercely in the North, too.

There was an uprising in 1657 in Hartford, Connecticut.

In 1706, New York's governor, in response to reports of slaves behaving "in a riotous manner" in Brooklyn, ordered the arrest of blacks who assembled illegally. "If any of them refuse to submit, then fire upon them, kill or destroy them, if they cannot otherwise be taken," he said.

And in 1708, on Long Island, an Indian slave and three Africans murdered an entire family—the man who owned them, his pregnant wife, and their five children. When captured, the men were hanged and the woman slave was burned alive.

Despite the likelihood of terrible punishment, rebellion continued throughout the eighteenth century and into the nineteenth until the decade before the Civil War. In a sampling from the North alone, just in the 1700s:

- An unrelated, two-year spate of arsons occurred in New Haven, Connecticut, and in Boston, Massachusetts, between 1721 and 1723. In Boston, it led to the execution of a slave charged with burning down a house.

- Sentencing an African after a similar arson in Philadelphia, Pennsylvania, in 1737, the judge called for the city to pass stronger laws because of slaves' recent hostile behavior.

- In Hackensack, New Jersey, in 1741, two slaves convicted of arson were sentenced to be burned alive. The same punishment was ordered in Perth Amboy, New Jersey, in 1750, for two slaves convicted of murder and attempted murder.

But New York City holds a singular place in the chronicle of Northern slave revolts: two of the most violent uprisings in early colonial America happened there. The first, in 1712, set the stage for the arsons, and then the panic, that seized the city twenty-nine years later.

BY 1712, NEW YORK CITY WAS ALREADY BEGINNING ITS ECONOMIC AS-cendancy. Much of the traffic at its busy port consisted of ships heading south to the Caribbean carrying pork, beef, lumber, corn, and flour (New York's flour was then considered the finest in the colonies). An equal number of vessels were returning laden with sugar, molasses, and other island products such as cocoa, indigo, and Madeira and port.

Census figures from earlier in the century show a population of about 4,000 whites and about 600 blacks; most of the latter were slaves. In the decades that followed, particularly as commerce with the Caribbean increased, the percentage of the enslaved would grow. But by 1712, slave ownership had already permeated the culture of the New York colony.

Wealthy merchants like Adolphus Philipse owned slaves, but so did tradesmen such as baker Gysbert Vaninburgh, bricklayer Thomas Stoutenburgh, and carpenter Captain William Walton. Slavery was the bedrock of the city's developing economy, and the labor of Africans who hauled wood and water, who worked on the waterfront, in warehouses, in bakeries, and in cooperages, making barrels and casks, was helping the young colony prosper.

Several hours after midnight on April 6, 1712, two dozen black men, many of whom had recently arrived from Africa, gathered in an orchard a few blocks from the East River. Most were Coromantees, named for the slave fortress at Coromantine on the west coast of Africa, in what is now Ghana. Regarded as exceptional workers, considered brave and warlike, Coromantees were more in demand than other slaves. On this evening, they were living up to their reputation and preparing for battle.

They had sworn an oath in blood, dusted their clothes with a con-jurer's magic powder, and armed themselves with axes, hatchets, guns, and pistols. As the others watched, two set fire to an outhouse that be-longed to the baker who owned one of them. The plan was to cut down the white men who came out to fight the fire, and then flee the city to freedom.

As the white men rushed out, eight were slaughtered almost in-stantly—one man was killed when his slave drove a knife into his chest—and seven were wounded. Outnumbered, the Coromantees fled into the neighboring forests. They thought the witch doctor's dust would make them invisible, but within a day, most were captured. Rather than be taken, six Africans killed themselves, one Coromantee leader cutting his wife's throat before he cut his own.

The city was in a panic. Seventy black men were arrested immediately, and the *Boston Weekly News-Letter* reported that the uprising had put the "whole town . . . under arms."

Governor Robert Hunter suggested that the men had revolted against their masters in retaliation for "some hard usage." He could think of no other reason. Of the 39 men who were indicted, 23 were convicted, and 19 of those convicted were executed. None of the 39 received legal counsel.

The usual sentence for capital crimes was hanging, but because a slave insurrection—or even an act of rebellion by one or two enslaved people—posed such a threat to the social order, courts had almost unlimited latitude in deciding punishment. Hunter knew that the colony could not let the rebels off lightly; the consequences of these acts had to serve as a warning to other slaves.

In a report that June, Governor Hunter assured the Lords of Trade, his supervising authority in London, "There has been the most exemplary punishment inflicted that could possibly be thought of."

Three slaves, Clause, Robin, and Quaco, were found guilty of murdering Adrian Hoghlandt, Robin's master. Clause was tied to a wheel and, over a period of hours, his bones were smashed, one by one, with a crowbar, until he died. Robin was chained, strung up, and kept hanging without food or water until he died. Quaco was burned alive. Another slave, owned by Nicholas Roosevelt, was also burned alive—in a slow fire so that his death took hours.

Satisfied that justice had been served, the governor reprieved some of the other conspirators. "I am informed that in the West Indies where their laws against their slaves are most severe," he wrote to the Lords of Trade, "that in case of a conspiracy in which many are engaged a few only are executed for an example."

And although he was a man of his time and had not flinched from inflicting gruesome punishments, Hunter understood that the central problem of 1712 was not the slaves' rebellion but slavery itself. "The Late Hellish Attempt of yor Slaves," he warned the colonists, showed they needed to stop importing Africans and build a broader white working class. New York would contend with black revolts for as long as it had black slaves, he predicted.

LIKE MOST OF THE OTHER COLONIES, NEW YORK HAD LIVED WITH slaves from its earliest settlement. Fort George, called Fort Amsterdam when the city was a Dutch colony, was built in the late 1620s with the labor of some of the first slaves who were brought to the colony.

In the background of a seventeenth-century engraving of early Manhattan, half-clothed black workers carry heavy burdens on their heads. Many of the skeletons excavated from the city's African Burial Ground show back and shoulder injuries congruent with carrying heavy loads. *I. N. Phelps Stokes Collection, Miriam and Ira D. Wallach Division of Art, Prints, and Photographs, The New York Public Library, Astor, Lenox and Tilden Foundations*

Between 1712 and 1741, the number of slaves living in New York more than doubled, and the laws curtailing their freedom got tougher. Family members were routinely separated. Acts of brutality against blacks became more common and more acceptable. In 1735, when a slave who violated his curfew was horsewhipped to death by his owner, an all-white jury declared that the cause of death was not the beating, but "Visitation by God."

New slave markets, named after prominent city slave traders, sprang up on Wall Street near the East River. New York was building a contract with slavery. By 1741, one-fifth of the city's population consisted of black slaves—nearly 1,800 amid a total population of about 10,000. Blacks were one-third of the city's workforce; they were rapidly replacing its white indentured servants.

At the same time that the already-strict black codes severely limited slaves' lives, black men continued to gather, illegally, at taverns and "tippling houses," during their few leisure hours. The size of New

York's black population made it impossible for the city's tiny constabulary to enforce the codes more than sporadically.

IN THE TWO WEEKS AFTER THE MARCH 1741 TORCHING OF FORT George, there were eight more fires. Most of them were contained, yet they showed evidence of arson. Men found burning embers placed between two straw mattresses in a slave's quarters. Bales of hay were stacked right up against the rafters of a stable, glowing coals at their base. Hunks of burning hemp were tucked underneath roof shingles.

Although fire was always a serious threat in colonial times—burgeoning urban centers in the North were made up of wooden structures built close together—the timing of the New York arsons couldn't have been worse.

The old histories call the winter of 1740–1741 simply "the hard winter," and it was the worst in living memory. Intense cold and heavy snow had begun in mid-November, and by the new year, the Hudson River was frozen solid for 50 miles. Newspaper publisher John Peter Zenger said it was so cold the ink froze in his pen. Ships could neither leave nor enter the harbor. The week between Christmas Day and New Year's became known as "the Great Snow," as 10 feet fell in seven days. Residents were housebound for weeks with little to eat and no firewood.

That March, as winter began to wane, the single most important symbol of the city's military security was reduced to a smoking, ruined shell. The destruction of Fort George was a blow to the British colony, and not just because it was such a familiar landmark within the city. The three great European powers of Great Britain, Spain, and France were embroiled in intense struggles over trade, and the loss of the fort made the city vulnerable. Colonial authorities were hearing rumors of a possible attack by Spain, and the British captured a Spanish sloop that spring and brought it to New York harbor.

When the fires started, an already-stressed citizenry quickly noted that they occurred in or near areas where black people worked—on the waterfront, in bakeries, in cooperages, and in blacksmith workshops, places where fire was a daily tool.

On a Sunday morning in early April, Abigail Earle looked out the window of her home on Broadway and saw three black men walking by. They were laughing and she heard one of them chant, "Fire, Fire, Scorch, Scorch, A LITTLE, damn it, BY AND BY." She shrank back from the window, then ran to a neighbor, who recognized the speaker as Quaco, a slave belonging to a former assemblyman.

The next day, as flames raced along the roof of a timber storehouse belonging to Adolphus Philipse, New York's wealthiest merchant, Cuffee, one of his young slaves, was seen leaping from a storehouse window. He was captured immediately, and in the streets of New York was heard the cry "The Negroes are rising!" Dozens of black men were jailed and questioned about the fires, but when no evidence emerged, most were released.

At about the same time that anxious New Yorkers were distracted by the fires, a separate but parallel drama began, at the center of which was an already-notorious slave.

Caesar Vaarck, or "Vaarck's negro," as he appears in trial accounts, was a slave who refused to behave like one. He lived and thought independently, sometimes dangerously so. When he was not firing ovens for his owner, baker John Vaarck, he was an accomplished thief. Publicly flogged for stealing casks of gin, he insouciantly founded a drinking club named Geneva, after *jenever*, the Dutch word for gin. He fenced his stolen goods to whites and had a beautiful white mistress with red hair.

Peggy Kerry had several aliases and a murky past. She had immigrated from Ireland and claimed to have a husband, but by the spring of 1741, "Negro Peg" was living at Hughson's tavern, the rough hostelry on the Hudson where Caesar and others brought

96   JOURNAL OF THE PROCEEDINGS

taken; that the same mischief which you have contrived for others, and have in part executed, is at length fallen upon your own pates, whereby the sentence which I am now to pronounce will be justified against ye; which is,

"That you and each of you be carried from hence to the place from whence you came, and from thence to the place of execution, where you and each of you shall be chained to a stake, and burnt to death; and the lord have mercy upon your poor, wretched souls."

Ordered, that the execution of the said Quack and Cuffee be on Saturday the 30th of this instant, between the hours of one and seven o'clock in the afternoon of the same day.

The court adjourned till Tuesday the 2d of June next, ten o'clock in the morning.

SATURDAY, MAY 30.

This day Quack and Cuffee were executed at the stake according to sentence.

The spectators at this execution were very numerous; about three o'clock the criminals were brought to the stake, surrounded with piles of wood ready for setting fire to, which the people were very impatient to have done, their resentment being raised to the utmost pitch against them, and no wonder. The criminals shewed great terror in their countenances, and looked as if they would gladly have discovered all they knew of this accursed scheme, could they have had any encouragement to hope for a reprieve. But as the case was, they might flatter themselves with hopes: they both seemed inclinable to make some confession; the only difficulty between them at last being, who should speak first. Mr. Moore, the deputy secretary, undertook singly to examine them both, endeavouring to persuade them to confess their guilt, and all they knew of the matter, without effect; till at length Mr. Roosevelt came up to him, and said he would undertake Quack, whilst Mr. Moore examined Cuffee; but before they could proceed to the purpose, each of them, was obliged to flatter his respective criminal that his fellow sufferer had begun, which stratagem prevailed: Mr. Roosevelt stuck to Quack altogether, and Mr. Moore took Cuff's confession, and sometimes also minutes of what each said; and afterwards upon drawing up their confessions in form from their minutes, they therefore intermixed what came from each.

Quack Roosevelt and Cuffe Philipse were the first black men convicted of conspiracy to commit arson in the New York slave revolt of 1741, and an angry court sentenced them to a ferocious fate: The two men, who had not had any legal defense and whose trial lasted less than a day, were burned alive. The New-York Conspiracy, or a History of the Negro Plot, with the Journal of the Proceedings Against the Conspirators at New-York in the Years 1741–2, Daniel Horsmanden, Esq., Southwick & Pelsue, New York, 1810, Library of Congress

their stolen merchandise. The previous fall she had given birth to Caesar's child.

The drama began shortly after Caesar and his accomplice, a slave named Prince, stole silver candlesticks, coins, and some fancy cloth from a shop belonging to Robert and Rebecca Hogg. Caesar gave Peggy a few of the coins and a length of speckled linen.

City authorities knew that tavern owner John Hughson and his wife, Sarah, frequently violated the black codes by serving food and drink to slaves. They also knew that Hughson, a tall man with a mild appearance and a tough cookie for a wife, often served as a fence for Caesar and other black men.

When Rebecca Hogg entered her shop the next morning and discovered the theft, she spread word among the other shopkeepers, prompting one, Anne Kannady, to question sixteen-year-old Mary Burton, an indentured servant who worked for the Hughsons. In a society where unfree labor was commonplace, Kannady knew just what to say to the young servant. If Mary could provide information about the theft, Kannady promised she would arrange for her indenture to end. Mary hedged, but just briefly, and in short order Caesar was arrested, as was Peggy Kerry. The Hughsons were taken into custody but released on bail.

Caesar's situation was bad, but not hopeless. As a repeat offender, he faced at least a beating and probably banishment from the colony. But then, while he was still in prison, the fires began, and with them, a grimmer outcome for Caesar was almost guaranteed.

AGAINST THE CONSPIRATORS AT NEW-YORK.   123

The prisoners being called up to judgment upon their conviction for the conspiracy, and placed at the bar, the second justice proceeded to pass sentence, as followeth.

John Hughson, and you the rest of the prisoners at the bar.

" You are now brought before this court to receive that sentence which the law has appointed for your offences; though I cannot say the punishment is adequate to the horrid crimes of which you stand convicted. The Roman commonwealth was established some hundred years before any law was made against parricide, they not thinking any person capable of so atrocious a crime; yours are indeed as singular, and unheard of before, they are such as one would scarce believe any man capable of committing, especially any one who had heard of a God and a future state; for people who have been brought up and always lived in a christian country, and also called themselves christians, to be guilty not only of making negro slaves their equals, but even their superiors, by waiting upon, keeping with, and entertaining them with meat, drink and lodging, and what is much more amazing, to plot, conspire, consult, abet and encourage these black seed of Cain, to burn this city, and to kill and destroy us all. Good God! when I reflect on the disorders, confusion, desolation and havock, which the effect of your most wicked, most detestable and diabolical councils might have produced (had not the hand of our great and good God interposed) it shocks me! for you, who would have burnt and destroyed without mercy, ought to be served in like manner; and although each of you have with an uncommon assurance, denied the fact, and audaciously called upon God as a witness of your innocence; yet it hath pleased him, out of his unbounded goodness and mercy to us, to confound your devices, and cause your malicious and wicked machinations and intentions to be laid open and clear before us, not only to the satisfaction and conviction of the court, the grand and petty jury, but likewise to every one else that has heard the evidence against you: all are satisfied the just judgment of God has overtaken you, and that you justly merit a more severe death than is intended for you, having, in my opinion, been much worse than the negroes: however, though your crimes deserve it, yet we must not act contrary to law.

" And now I do most earnestly exhort you, and each of you, to a serious and diligent improvement of the little time you have yet to live on this side of eternity, duly and heartily to weigh and consider your past wicked and ill-spent lives, by bewailing, confessing and sincerely repenting of your sins; that thereby you may obtain mercy and forgiveness from our great and just

John Hughson was well known to city authorities as an obliging fence for black thieves, but his real offense may have been his willingness to entertain black men at his tavern on the Hudson River and to allow them to conspire under his roof. The New-York Conspiracy, or a History of the Negro Plot, with the Journal of the Proceedings Against the Conspirators at New-York in the Years 1741–2, *Daniel Horsmanden, Esq., Southwick & Pelsue, New York, 1810, Library of Congress*

As Caesar and Peggy sat in City Hall's dank cells, New York's residents grew more panicked with each new arson. By mid-April, there had been a dozen fires of unexplained origin, and when the colony's supreme court opened its spring session on April 21, Justice Frederick Philipse II, nephew of the wealthy merchant, summed up the fears of the other colonists when he asked, "Who can say he is safe or tell where it will end?"

No one had died except that first soldier at Fort George, but the destruction and threatened destruction of property had been substantial. A grand jury—which included the owner of a warehouse that had been burned—was impaneled to investigate the fires and the thefts.

Only circumstantial evidence linked black men to the fires, but the court decided that the unlawful gatherings of blacks in taverns was worth pursuing. "How this notion of its being lawful to sell a penny dram, or a pennyworth of rum to a slave, without the consent or direction of his master, has prevailed, I know not," said Justice Philipse, suggesting that slaves' drinking might have led to their plotting.

The grand jury quickly focused their attention on John Hughson's tavern, the notorious haven for black thieves and a site of "caballing" by slaves. They called maidservant Mary Burton to testify. Burton grudgingly agreed to "acquaint them with what she knew relating to the goods stolen from Mr. Hogg's, but would say nothing about the fires."

The *fires?*

This was more than the grand jury had hoped for.

As a servant in a tavern house where black men caroused over trenchers of mutton and bowls of strong punch, Burton was privy to every illegality, from Caesar's going upstairs with his white lover, to the slaves' dancing and drinking, to the Hughsons' hiding of stolen merchandise. In the following months, her spectacular testimony dovetailed perfectly with the ambitions and racial hatred of the most powerful lawyer in New York.

Son of an English minister, Justice Daniel Horsmanden was trained for the law in England. He presided over the months of trials with two other men, and recorded the day-to-day proceedings of the tribunal. His loathing of the black defendants—revealed consistently in remarks about their demeanor and way of speaking—and his certainty of their guilt leaps undimmed from his account, now more than two and a half centuries old.

Horsmanden's bias appears in other ways as well. He described defendant Peggy Kerry as "a person of infamous character, a notorious

A

JOURNAL

OF THE

PROCEEDINGS

IN

The Detection of the Conspiracy

FORMED BY

Some *White* People, in Conjunction with *Negro* and other *Slaves*,

FOR

Burning the City of *NEW-YORK* in AMERICA,

And Murdering the Inhabitants.

Which Conspiracy was partly put in Execution, by Burning His Majesty's House in Fort GEORGE, within the said City, on Wednesday the Eighteenth of *March*, 1741. and setting Fire to several Dwelling and other Houses there, within a few Days succeeding. And by another Attempt made in Prosecution of the same infernal Scheme, by putting Fire between two other Dwelling-Houses within the said City, on the Fifteenth Day of *February*, 1742; which was accidentally and timely discovered and extinguished.

CONTAINING,

I. A NARRATIVE of the Trials, Condemnations, Executions, and Behaviour of the several Criminals, at the Gallows and Stake, with their *Speeches* and *Confessions*; with Notes, Observations and Reflections occasionally interspersed throughout the Whole.

II. AN APPENDIX, wherein is set forth some additional Evidence concerning the said Conspiracy and Conspirators, which has come to Light since their Trials and Executions.

III. LISTS of the several Persons (Whites and Blacks) committed on Account of the Conspiracy; and of the several Criminals executed; and of those transported, with the Places whereto.

By the Recorder of the City of NEW-YORK.

Quid facient Domini, audent cum talia Fures? Virg. Ecl.

NEW-YORK:

Printed by *James Parker*, at the New Printing-Office, 1744.

In lawyer Daniel Horsmanden, the "Great Negro Plot" found a man who served as stenographer for the proceedings, as well as a judge and chief inquisitor. His detailed and hate-filled record of the conspiracy trials is the only contemporary account to survive. © Bettmann/CORBIS

prostitute, and also of the worst sort, a prostitute to Negroes." Hughson was equally despicable in his eyes, and for the same reason. "That any white people should become so abandoned as to confederate with slaves in such an execrable and detestable purpose," Horsmanden wrote, "could not but be very amazing to every one that heard it."

Mary Burton had a lot to say. She told the judge that Caesar, Prince, and Cuffee had often talked about burning the fort and then the town, and that the Hughsons had promised to help. What's more, said the sixteen-year-old, she had once heard Cuffee say that "a great many people had too much, and others too little," and he wanted to change that. She was making it clear that Hughson's tavern, already recognized as a center for thieves, was also the war room of a plot to burn down the city.

Prince and Caesar were already in jail, and Cuffee, the accused conspirator, found himself there before day's end. A jailhouse informant gave the frightened slave a sympathetic hearing "over a bowl or a tankard of punch" and extracted from him the name of the man who set fire to the fort. Quack Roosevelt, who was owned by a prominent builder, was arrested that day, and charged, as was Cuff, with arson and conspiracy.

Quack, enraged by having been denied permission to visit his wife, Barbara, a slave who was the governor's cook, had set the Fort George fire.

The informant later said that after revealing Quack's name, Cuffee refused to speak further, and sat in his cell, weeping.

It took only a day to convict Caesar and Prince of stealing from the Hoggs and another merchant. It was their bad luck to be tried for theft at a time of acute public hysteria and at the beginning of what would become a huge conspiracy trial. They were without counsel and, in any case, every lawyer in the city had already agreed to assist the prosecution. Although Caesar and Prince were allowed to call witnesses, the two men seem to have said nothing. They must have known they were doomed.

The men were quickly sentenced to hang. Because Caesar was perceived to be the leader in the thefts, his body was to hang in chains until it rotted. Sounding resentful, Horsmanden recorded that the two "died very stubbornly," without confessing anything about the conspiracy, "although the proof against them was strong and clear concerning their guilt for that also."

ALTHOUGH CAESAR AND PRINCE WERE THE FIRST TO BE CONVICTED AND executed in the 1741 events, the trial of Cuffee and Quack, tried together for conspiring to "kill and murder" city residents, set the tone in terms of the ferocity of the proceedings.

Mary Burton's testimony was the engine for the tribunal, and the plan for the prosecution was elegant in its simplicity. Men suspected of involvement in the arsons would be arrested and brought in for questioning. In the hope of avoiding trial, conviction, and death, they would name coconspirators, who would then name others.

As the court began to collect names and confessions, a teenage slave, Niblet's Sandy, dropped a bombshell: the plan had been to burn the property of white men, then kill the whites as they tried to put down the fires. Sandy also claimed that Hughson was to become king, Caesar governor, and the black men were to take the murdered white men's wives as their own.

This was a substantial escalation of what the grand jury had understood to be a plot by a handful of black men to destroy some city buildings. This was "murther and rapine," and a dramatic overturning of society's structure. For Horsmanden, every word confirmed the existence of a grand plot, and a spectacular case affirming his deepest belief: slaves were, above all, a danger to the community.

It is not surprising that the conviction rate for the many men who stood trial in the case was 100 percent, a figure without precedent in colonial jury trials.

The powerful language of the trial—of the justices, the witnesses—and even that of onlookers in the streets reveals more than the fears of a city under siege; it speaks to the white society's distrust of a growing population its members depended upon for labor. Slaves were referred to as "black devils" and "sable fiends" who had hatched "a hellish project in the cabinets of Hell."

In addition, the hundreds of slave-owning families in New York thought of themselves largely as benefactors, and of their system of forced labor as an improvement for blacks over life in Africa. Prosecutors' statements about the "ingratitude" of the slaves certainly echoed more widespread feelings.

In Horsmanden's lengthy account of Cuffee and Quack's trial, the only reference to testimony by the slaves was their statements that they were not guilty.

Other testimony reveals the tension between society's need for the work of an enslaved population and its divided feelings toward the people who provided it. Cuffee's owner, Adolphus Philipse, testified that on the day the storehouse burned, he had left his slave sewing a sail for his boat, but he refused to testify about Cuffee's character. Quack's owner testified that on the day the fort burned, the slave had been "cutting away the ice out of the yard" the entire morning, and was out of his sight only when he ate breakfast. Another man told the court he had hired Quack to help build the city's new battery, and that Quack had been a good worker and "minded his business very well."

Character references had little impact on the brief trial anyway. By the end of the day, the prosecution was already wrapping up its case. The summation, made by attorney William Smith, was long, dramatic, and calculated to make New Yorkers feel good about their legal system, which had kept them safe from this "wicked and foolish plot."

"Gentlemen, no scheme more monstrous could have been invented. . . . That the white men should all be killed, and the women become a prey to the rapacious lust of these villains!" He concluded with a warm paean to slavery. They are indeed slaves, Smith noted, "but under the protection of the law."

The jury found the defendants guilty in just a few minutes and sentenced them to be burned at the stake the next afternoon. Quack and Cuffee's trial, conviction, and sentencing had taken less than a day.

The next afternoon, a great crowd gathered on the public commons, a low-lying marshy area just beyond the city gates. At about three, the two slaves were led to the stake. Upon seeing the huge piles of wood to be burned, the slaves "showed great terror in their countenances," Horsmanden noted. John Roosevelt, who had stood by his slave as far as the law allowed and spoken up for him at his trial, stood by Quack at the

EXECUTING NEGROES IN NEW YORK.

At least 17 enslaved black men were hanged for their part in the 1741 slave revolt, but 13 others faced the agonizing punishment of death at the stake—a death sentence that was not common in the American colonies except when the convicted people were slaves. *Culver Pictures*

stake. Cuffee was alone. Terrified and chained back-to-back at the stake, the condemned prisoners made separate confessions about their parts in the plot. Both named other men who had known of the conspiracy and had promised to destroy property. John Hughson was the "contriver" of the plot to murder and plunder New Yorkers, they said.

They hoped to be spared death. Even Horsmanden thought the detailed confessions merited a reprieve, possibly even a pardon. The lieutenant governor approved a provisional stay of execution, and the government secretary raced back toward the commons with the news. But the huge crowd grew restive when it appeared they might be cheated out of seeing the black men suffer their sentence, and officials feared a riot.

"For these reasons," Horsmanden wrote coolly, "the execution proceeded."

Quack's dying words were that his wife, Barbara, knew nothing of his plan to burn Fort George.

BEFORE MORE BLACK MEN—THE "CONSPIRATORS" NAMED BY CUFFEE and Quack—could be tried, the travails of John and Sarah Hughson and Peggy Kerry drew to a close. Hughson was vital to the prosecution because it was inconceivable to the judges that a group of slaves had devised this elaborate plot without white leadership. The tavern keeper, with his generous meals and open-door policy for blacks, was also a danger to the established social order. The court wanted to send a powerful message to white people who treated blacks as equals.

In his summation, William Smith said Hughson's crimes made him "blacker than a Negro" and a scandal to his "complexion." The judge dispatched the jury with a cheery exhortation to be sure to find the defendants guilty, calling the evidence against them "so ample, so full, so clear and satisfactory."

The Hughsons and Peggy Kerry were hanged a stone's throw from the East River. At the last moment on the gallows, Peggy started to speak, but Sarah Hughson gave her a sharp shove and she fell silent.

THE ORIGINAL GOAL OF THE INVESTIGATIONS HAD BEEN TO FIND THE ringleaders of the plot to burn Fort George and a few other city properties, not to surrender a large part of the city's skilled workforce. But the escalation of the trials resulted not only in the deaths of slaves but also in financial losses to their owners.

Gerardus Comfort, a cooper with a business near Hughson's on the

Hudson River, lost two slaves in the events of 1741, one to the stake and another to banishment, despite his insistence in court that he'd seen "nothing amiss" at Hughson's tavern.

Meanwhile, the jail cells at City Hall, then located on Wall Street, were crowded with black men, and the justices decided to suspend all other court business until they could get to the bottom of "Hughson's Plot." An offer of a pardon to all who would confess and tell what they knew pulled in droves of fearful black men. So many wanted to confess that the deadline for the pardon had to be extended. The harried court justices became "virtual scriveners."

"The trouble of examining criminals in general, may be easily guessed at," Horsmanden complained, "but the fatigue in that of Negroes, is not to be conceived, but by those that have undergone the drudgery."

By the end of the first week in July, 11 black men had been burned at the stake, and 10 blacks and 3 whites had been hanged. By the end of the month, 7 more black men would die.

By that point, the plot was turning in new directions and encompassing different prejudices.

Charges were brought against five Spanish blacks who had been part of the crew of the Spanish sloop brought into New York harbor earlier in the year. And Horsmanden got ready to continue his prosecution, focusing next on the Irish soldiers who had been garrisoned at Fort George, as well as on other suspicious characters about the city.

Hughson tavern regular John Ury, thought to have helped black men in the plot and suspected of being a Catholic priest, made an eloquent self-defense, but was hanged in late August.

But the court was ready to bring this spectacular series of trials to a close, and not only because public hysteria was dying down. When star witness Mary Burton, the "obscure drudge" with the prodigious memory, started to identify influential New Yorkers as plotters, even Horsmanden hesitated, then moved quickly to suppress her testimony.

The questionings and detentions of black men continued for some months, but the tribunal was losing momentum. The last death was that of Mrs. Bradt's Tom, convicted of setting fire to an outhouse. He was hanged on March 13, 1742. Horsmanden wanted to burn Tom, but the other justices seem to have said "Enough."

THE GREAT NEGRO PLOT TERRIFIED AND BAFFLED WHITE NEW YORKers, who failed to understand their slaves' hatred of bondage, and so made 1741 a tale of black evil.

By the early nineteenth century, when the American North had a growing population of free blacks and greater awareness of their human rights, the events were recast as an overreaction to the fires and general hard times. After the Civil War, amid the racism that outlived slavery, the outbreak was regarded as limited in scope because slaves weren't thought capable of organizing a plot so potentially lethal.

But Daniel Horsmanden, his race hatred aside, may have been right all along. He believed the slaves' plot to destroy city property was comprehensive, well-planned, and known to many men. Modern scholars tend to agree.

The plot might have had at least a chance to succeed had an enraged Quack Roosevelt not set fire to Fort George earlier than planned. The wrongfully enslaved Spanish blacks, some of whom were trained in the use of incendiary materials, knew that hostile Spain would have five ships off the East Coast in May. With the British colony's defenses in ruins, Spanish bombardment on top of a city in flames could have meant a different ending for the slaves' revolt.

In the end, Horsmanden's detailed trial accounts proved one thing: During the cold, early months of 1741, blacks talked constantly about freedom. In the taverns willing to serve them, when they fetched water for their masters, when they traveled around the city doing their work, they talked ceaselessly of how to end their bondage.

Horsmanden's accounts reflect slaves' bottomless anger. Jamaica, a young fiddler owned by a Thomas Ellison, said he "would dance over [the white people] while they were roasting in the flames." He had been a slave long enough, the boy said. Though at first sentenced to hang, Jamaica was banished to the Portuguese island of Madeira.

City fathers in 1741 were convinced that New York's problem was not enslavement but the slaves themselves. They reacted to the fires in the same narrow way they had responded to the rebellion in 1712.

Believing that slaves had hatched their plot when fetching water for their owners' tea from springs around the city, authorities in the colony decided to further limit opportunities for the slaves to gather. After the trials, after the deaths and deportations of more than 100 people, slaves were no longer permitted to draw fresh water from city wells. Instead, great municipal wagons were hauled around the city, dispensing water. A visitor later noted that New York water tasted brackish and hard.

And to better meet any future threat of arson, the city bought 100 new fire buckets.

*In the eighteenth century, Rhode Island
captains paid for slaves by the barrel and,
on the deadly Middle Passage from Africa to
market, hoped that enough of their human
cargo would survive to sell at a profit.*

Five

NEWPORT RUM, AFRICAN SLAVES

AMONG THE THIRTEEN ORIGINAL STATES, ONLY ONE PLUNGED INTO the African slave trade in a big way—little Rhode Island.

In the century before Congress voted to ban the slave trade beginning in 1808, Rhode Island launched nearly 1,000 voyages to Africa, carrying at least 100,000 slaves back across the Atlantic.

In sheer volume, U.S. participation in the trade may be seen as insignificant. European ships transported nearly all the estimated 11.5 million Africans sold over three centuries into New World slavery, including the approximately 645,000 sent to the American colonies.

On this side of the Atlantic, however, Rhode Island had no rival. At the outbreak of the American Revolution, it controlled two-thirds or more of the colonies' slave trade with Africa. When the trade resumed after the war, Rhode Island seized a virtual monopoly, shipping nearly 50,000 new slaves in less than twenty years.

Perhaps more than anything, Rhode Island's deep and direct involvement in what ranks as one of the most momentous and cruel forced migrations in history shows the extent to which slavery penetrated the New World. While Rhode Island's neighbors, and Rhode Island itself, found ways to profit by trading first with the slave plantations of the West Indies and later with the cotton plantations of the American South, this smallest of states went even further, competing with European powers in

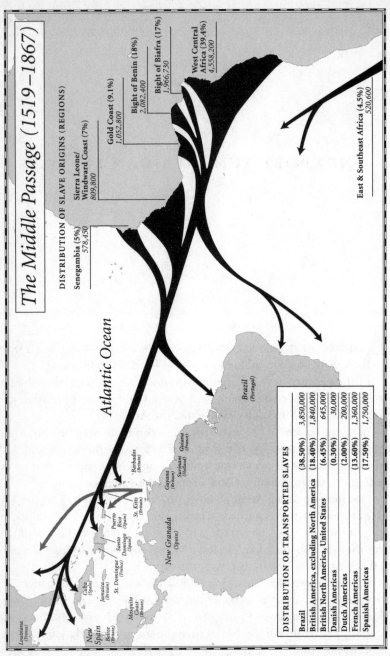

The Middle Passage (1519–1867)

DISTRIBUTION OF SLAVE ORIGINS (REGIONS)

Senegambia (5%)
578,450

Sierra Leone/
Windward Coast (7%)
809,800

Gold Coast (9.1%)
1,052,800

Bight of Benin (18%)
2,082,400

Bight of Biafra (17%)
1,966,730

West Central
Africa (39.4%)
4,558,200

East & Southeast Africa (4.5%)
520,600

Atlantic Ocean

Brazil
(Portugal)

New Granada
(Spain)

New
Spain

Louisiana
(France)

Belize
(Britain)

Mosquito
Coast
(Britain)

St. Domingue
(France)

Jamaica
(Britain)

Cuba
(Spain)

Santo
Domingo
(Spain)

Puerto
Rico
(Spain)

St. Kitts
(Britain)

Barbados
(Britain)

Guyana
(Britain)

Surinam
(Holland)

Guiana
(France)

DISTRIBUTION OF TRANSPORTED SLAVES

Brazil	(38.50%)	3,850,000
British America, excluding North America	(18.40%)	1,840,000
British North America, United States	(6.45%)	645,000
Danish Americas	(0.30%)	30,000
Dutch Americas	(2.00%)	200,000
French Americas	(13.60%)	1,360,000
Spanish Americas	(17.50%)	1,750,000

During the three and a half centuries the transatlantic slave trade lasted, nearly 12 million Africans were transported to South America, North America, and the Caribbean islands. The partial figures for each region shown here are estimates derived from a database of more than 27,000 slave-ship voyages, developed at the W. E. B. DuBois Institute for Afro-American Research at Harvard University. Map © 2005 by David Lindroth

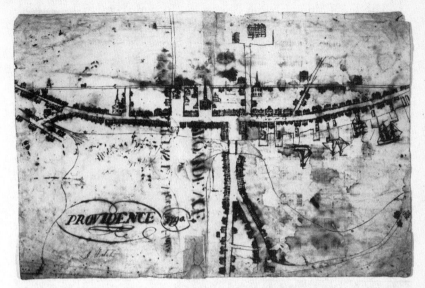

The large structure at the top of this 1790 map of the Providence waterfront is in the proximate location of Brown University, then called Rhode Island College and later renamed for a family that traced part of its fortune to the slave trade. *Map of East Side of Providence drawn by student John Fitch, 1790, Brown University Library*

The Redwood Library is one of several Newport architectural legacies left by philanthropic merchants who earned their wealth in the slave trade or in trading with West Indies plantations. *Pierre du Simitiere, 1768, Library Company of Philadelphia*

the slave trade itself. Remote as it was, Rhode Island transported more slaves than any other of the original 13 states—North or South.

Elegant Newport dominated the first and longest period of the state's slave trade. Its legacy can still be seen in architectural treasures such as the Francis Malbone mansion, now a lovely inn, and the library founded by Abraham Redwood.

Malbone and Redwood were just two among a host of slave merchants in a town where commerce was a family affair.

The reputation of Aaron Lopez and his father-in-law Jacob Rodriguez Rivera as wealthy and supremely honorable Jewish businessmen spread far beyond Rhode Island. Lopez, a "merchant prince" who prospered in the Triangle Trade, was a founder of Touro Synagogue in Newport, the oldest synagogue in America and a site on the National Historic Register. The Wanton family produced four colonial governors and also launched slave voyages. Two of Newport's most active traders, the Vernon brothers, Samuel and William, found a steady customer in Henry Laurens, the leading slave merchant in Charleston, South Carolina. During the Revolution, Laurens was a president of the Continental Congress.

In Charleston, South Carolina, Henry Laurens dealt regularly with Newport's Africa merchants. During the American Revolution, Laurens served as president of the Continental Congress. Later captured on a diplomatic mission to Europe, he was held prisoner for a year in the Tower of London. Henry Laurens, *John Singleton Copley, 1782. National Portrait Gallery, Smithsonian Institution/Art Resource, New York*

The rich Newport traders rarely sailed slave ships; they owned or bankrolled them. A slave ship was a hugely risky investment, but a successful voyage could bring ten times the profit of an ordinary New England trading voyage to the West Indies.

Nor did Newport's slave traders traffic only in Africans. As always, the successful merchants diversified their wares. Rhode Islanders became closely identified, however, with one other product in particular: rum. At slave depots on the African coast, Rhode Island vessels were known, and welcomed, as "rum-men." When the Newport trade first reached a peak just before the Revolution, its vessels were carrying 200,000 gallons a year to Africa, where ship captains bartered for slaves by the barrel. An African man in his prime could be bought for about 150 gallons.

Two dozen distilleries operated in Newport alone. In 1772, merchants who owned slaving vessels, who traded in molasses and rum, or who operated distilleries occupied 8 of the top 10 positions on Newport's tax rolls. Some, like the Malbone brothers, Evan and Francis, did all three.

In those pre-Revolution years, Newport launched 70 percent of all American slave voyages.

Slave trade commerce ushered the town into its first golden age. The rich and famous from distant colonies spent summers there. Prosperous ship captains formed the charitable Fellowship Club that had rules against cursing, gambling, and drunkenness.

TO BE SOLD, on board the Ship *Bance-Island*, on tuesday the 6th of *May* next, at *Ashley-Ferry*; a choice cargo of about 250 fine healthy **NEGROES**, just arrived from the Windward & Rice Coast. —The utmost care has already been taken, and shall be continued, to keep them free from the least danger of being infected with the SMALL-POX, no boat having been on board, and all other communication with people from *Charles-Town* prevented.

Austin, Laurens, & Appleby.

N. B. Full one Half of the above Negroes have had the SMALL-POX in their own Country.

Bance (or Bunce) Island, an African slave depot for which the ship in this advertisement was named, and Charleston, South Carolina, where the ad appeared in 1760, were favored ports of call for New England slave traders. The dealer Laurens mentioned in the ad was the wealthy merchant and patriot Henry Laurens. *Library of Congress, Prints and Photographs Division*

On Sundays, when not on voyages, many of these captains sat in pews at Trinity Church. Elite Anglicans like the Malbones and Wantons welcomed the upwardly mobile captains into their church, and, by marriage, into their families. A brood of three Wanton sisters married slave captains.

The orders that Jacob Rivera and Aaron Lopez gave to one of their slave captains as he embarked in 1772 suggest the businesslike attitude with which Newporters conducted the perilous trade. "Lying any considerable time on the [African] coast is not only attended with very heavy expense, but also great risk of the slaves you have on board. We therefore would recommend to you dispatch, even if you are obliged to give a few gallons more or less on each slave," they wrote.

They then advised the captain to brand one lot of 40 slaves already acquired to keep them separate from the slaves still to be purchased. "To these slaves we desire you'll put some particular mark that may distinguish them from those of the cargo, so that their sales in the West Indies may be kept by itself, for the insurance on these is not blended with the cargo."

The Reverend Samuel Hopkins, one of his era's foremost theologians, was one of the few who dared to preach against the slave trade. Looking

Upon purchase in Africa, slaves routinely were branded. Their owner's mark might be sketched with a hot iron, as shown in this 1857 illustration, or by monogrammed irons like these that probably belonged to English slave traders.

Wilberforce House, Hull City Museums and Art Galleries, United Kingdom/The Bridgeman Art Library

Branding a Negress, *engraved by Whitney, Jocelyn & Annin/The Bridgeman Art Library*

back after the Revolution, Hopkins condemned his own state: "The inhabitants of Rhode Island, especially those of Newport, have had by far the greater share of this traffic, of all these United States. This trade in human species has been the first wheel of commerce in Newport, on which every other movement in business has chiefly depended."

THE AMERICAN REVOLUTION CREATED THE FIRST SERIOUS STIRRINGS of abolitionist sentiment, and also mothballed Newport's slave fleet. The town hadn't undergone a change of conscience; it had been occupied by the British. But war merely interrupted the slave trade, which had dwindled from a prewar peak of several thousand slaves a year to a few hundred.

That trade was about to rebound with a vengeance.

Before the Revolution the rich West Indies sugar islands had been the main ports of call for Rhode Island slave ships. With the advent of the cotton gin at the end of the eighteenth century, though, the states of the Deep South hungered for workers for their burgeoning cotton plantations.

In the last frenzied years of the legal slave trade—the federal law banning the importation of African slaves took effect on January 1, 1808—the previously minor port of Bristol, a few hours' sail north on Narragansett Bay, outstripped Newport.

During the Bristol era, two of America's most audacious slave merchants, John Brown of Providence and Captain James DeWolf of Bristol, joined forces to protect the trade. Though Brown was a generation older than DeWolf, they might have been twins. Both were physically imposing men. In his maturity, Brown, called "the Providence Colossus," grew so large that he filled a whole carriage seat. The leaner DeWolf had the thick hands of a sailor.

Brown, perhaps the richest man in Providence, shared a business empire with three brothers. DeWolf, once reputed to be the richest man in America, may have used the Browns as the model for the business empire he shared with seven brothers. Both Brown and DeWolf morphed into plutocrats, at odds with and above the law.

Brown entered Congress in 1799, a few years after he became the first American indicted for violating the federal government's earliest attempt to restrict the slave trade. DeWolf served a term in the Senate,

HON. JAMES DE WOLF (25).
BRISTOL, R. I.
BORN MARCH 18, 1764; DIED DEC. 21, 1837.

Above left: Probably the richest and most audacious slave trader in U.S. history, James DeWolf of Bristol, Rhode Island, personally captained or financed almost two dozen African voyages. *Milstein Division of United States History, Local History & Genealogy, The New York Public Library, Astor, Lenox and Tilden Foundations*

Above right: As a fiery colonial patriot, John Brown of Rhode Island led one of the first violent acts of rebellion, the 1772 attack on the British customs schooner *Gaspee* that patrolled Narragansett Bay. *Brown University Library*

even though, during his years as a slave ship captain, he had been accused of drowning a female slave infected with smallpox.

Brown was acquitted and DeWolf was never even arrested for what
were considered ordinary crimes. Slave merchants generally viewed
laws as annoyances made to be broken. Captains routinely ordered sick
slaves thrown overboard, almost as a matter of hygiene, to keep them
from contaminating the whole ship.

But DeWolf had a reputation for being especially callous. His
African victim was tied to a chair when he threw her overboard, and he
was said to regret losing the chair. The incident lent credence to rumors
that one of his captains cut off the hands of two sick slaves who were
clinging to his ship's railing.

Brown, at one point, discouraged DeWolf from running for the state
legislature, worried that his reputation would harm slave merchants' interests.

Yet if either man retains the stigma of slave trader, it would be
Brown. The family name is preserved in Brown University. The Brown
brothers helped found the school. John himself laid the cornerstone of
its first building. His still-standing home on the Brown campus in Providence was once described as "the most magnificent and elegant private
mansion" in America.

Most of the Brown family's early wealth came from ordinary West
Indian commerce, privateering (basically, legalized pirating), an iron
foundry, and the manufacture of spermaceti candles. Their pig iron and
candles found their way into the holds of Newport slave ships. The
Browns, including John, really only dabbled in the trade itself.

Brown's father, James, and uncle, Obediah, first tested the African
market in 1736. It appears that Obediah captained their vessel, the
Mary, because James wrote him while he was at sea that their mother
had passed away. "She died about two months after you sailed, and I
hope that she is now more happy than either of us are, we being bur-
thened with the world and she at rest as I hope," James wrote. The letter, short on sentiment, mostly dwelt on business. In closing, James
wrote, "If you cannot sell all your slaves . . . bring some home. I believe
they will sell well. Get molasses if you can and if you cannot, come without it."

Two decades later, a second Brown slave ship was lost to a French
privateer. A third try, by the *Sally*, met such awful luck that it soured
Moses and his brothers John and Joseph on the trade once and for all.
Failed voyages drove many slave traders out of the business. The ill-
fated *Sally* is special because the records from her voyage, from Septem-

ber 1764 to October 1765, are among the fullest left behind from any American slave ship. They expose the trade's perils, its routines, and the tangled roots of Rhode Island's slave-trading families.

The first captain the Browns tried to engage for the *Sally* was already working for Simeon Potter, described by a family biographer as "the Satan emeritus" of Bristol. A plundering privateer in his youth, Potter was young James DeWolf's uncle and the family's guide in the slave trade. (His advice to "wort'r down yr rum and measure it short" is quoted in several histories.)

The Browns next considered Joseph Wanton of Newport as captain, but finally chose Esek Hopkins, who'd commanded Brown privateers during the Seven Years' War between Britain and France.

In the summer of 1764, three of the Brown brothers personally went to Newport to arrange for the *Sally* to be outfitted and then loaded with 17,000 gallons of rum. The rest of the cargo comprised the necessary provisions: goods to barter, including crates of spermaceti candles; a small armory of muskets and cutlasses; and 40 sets of manacles and shackles. If the *Sally* returned with 140 slaves, the Browns would make a profit.

Hopkins, like many captains, worked on commission. The Browns promised he could have 10 "privilege" slaves to sell himself, 4 more

Sea Captains Carousing in Surinam contains more history than meets the eye. The artist, John Greenwood, actually visited the Dutch colony on the northeast coast of South America, where Rhode Island merchants frequently traded. The real captains Greenwood depicted include Esek Hopkins, seated at the center of the table in a black hat. Standing just to the right is his brother Stephen, later a Rhode Island governor, who pours rum on a sleeping Jonas Wanton. At far right, the man bending to have his shoulder dubbed by a sword is thought to be Godfrey Malbone Jr., who belonged to another Newport slave trading family. Greenwood showed himself in the right rear, exiting with a candle. His 1758 tavern scene is thought to be the earliest American "genre" painting, drawn from everyday life. *Saint Louis Art Museum, Museum Purchase*

HOPKINS,
'omman^{dt} en Chef la flotte Américaine

In the early years of the American Revolution, Esek Hopkins commanded the Continental Navy, flying a "Don't Tread on Me" flag as his ensign. Before the war, he commanded privateers as well as the slave ship *Sally*, owned by the Browns of Providence. *U.S. Naval Historical Center*

slaves for every 100 he delivered to market, and 5 percent of the gross sales. From Africa, Hopkins was to take his cargo to Barbados first, but if the market there was depressed, to try others in the West Indies or go to the South. The Browns also ordered Hopkins to set aside, if available, 4 healthy young slaves "about 15 years old" for their own use.

Hopkins's privateering experience didn't help him much in Africa, where even seasoned slave captains needed several months to acquire a full cargo. Rhode Island ships, always smaller than their European rivals, poked into river villages and shopped at the slave "factories," or warehouses, strung along nearly 2,000 miles of coast. At each stop, bribes or gifts had to be dispensed before the real bargaining for slaves could begin.

Hopkins reached Africa in mid-November 1764. Within a few days he managed to buy a boy and a girl for 156 gallons of rum and a barrel of flour. But by early January, Hopkins had gotten only 32 slaves aboard the *Sally*. Three months later, he still had fewer than 100 Africans.

Slave captains tried to escape the coast before hot weather set in, raising the risk of disease. Hopkins lingered. On May 1, he recorded the first death of a slave, a boy. A few weeks later, a woman slave hanged herself below deck. Another 20 slaves died, presumably of natural causes, before Hopkins finally escaped the coast in late August with a cargo of about 170 Africans.

A few days out to sea, the captives revolted. Captains knew from experience that the danger of revolt was greatest when the ship was close to the coast and slaves still hoped they could regain their homeland. Hopkins's account of the revolt on the *Sally* was terse and semiliterate.

"Slaves rose on us was obliged [to] fire on them and destroyed 8 and several more wounded badly 1 thye & ones ribs broke," he wrote. Two of the wounded later died. Evidently, none of his small crew was injured. Slave captains always expected to lose some of their cargo, and Hopkins probably hoped the *Sally* would still turn a profit. But her human cargo perished steadily during the Middle Passage. In October, when Hopkins landed at Antigua after stopping at Barbados, he reported that half his slaves had died. He believed the failed revolt led some to drown themselves in despair and others to starve. The 90 Africans who survived were described as being in a "very sickly & disordered manner."

The *Sally*'s records do not reveal how much the damaged slaves sold for, but it wasn't nearly enough to cover the Browns' investment. One sympathetic friend wrote that the voyage was the most disastrous he'd ever heard of by a Providence vessel. The Browns did not blame Hopkins, perhaps because they had been prepared for worse. At one point, they'd gotten word from Africa that the *Sally*'s entire crew had been lost. Hopkins's safe return, Nicholas Brown wrote, was solace for the brothers' "heavy loss." Hopkins went on to command the Continental Navy for a time during the American Revolution.

As detailed as Hopkins's log was, it omitted many of the trade's most appalling practices, indiscernible in the familiar diagrams that show a cargo of stick figures packed in neat rows aboard a slave ship. Slaves did spend long hours chained on shallow platforms. None would have survived to be sold, however, if left continuously in such claustrophobic bondage.

From beginning to end, a slaving voyage rode on the brink of disaster. Insurance policies identified at least some of the hazards.

In 1770, John Brown, informing an insurer that he had armed his ship the *Sultan* with 6 swivel guns, 2 carriage guns, 4 blunderbusses, and 14 or 15 small arms, suggested he'd lowered the risk of insurrection. A policy written for a DeWolf ship covered losses from "risks of the Seas, Men of War, Fires, Enemies, Pirates, Rovers, Thieves, Jettisons ... Captures at Sea by American cruisers and Insurrection of slaves but not of common mortality." Insurers knew revolts were usually suppressed with minimal loss of life. Deaths from natural causes or accident at that point, however, averaged 10 percent or more.

Slave ships did not dock at wharves in Africa to have newly purchased captives marched aboard. Instead, the ships waited at anchor for small boats to ferry their cargoes from shore. The loading process could be brutal and dangerous. Africans who balked on the beach might be

Top: The claustrophobic sleeping platforms aboard slave ships are suggested in this painting based on the dictated biography of Mahommah Gardo Baquaqua, whose Middle Passage took him to Brazil in the mid-1800s. Sheol, *Rod Brown, 1993. Artwork courtesy of the "Journey to Freedom" education series. Private collection of Dr. Velma Laws-Clay and Vivian Laws Ritter, Battle Creek, Michigan, and Washington, D.C., respectively*

Bottom: Aboard ship, slaves suffered in suffocating heat, deprived of room to either stand or move. Engraving of Slave Quarters Aboard Ship *from A History of the Amistad Captives, John Warner Barber, c. 1840. MSS #119, Whitney Library, New Haven Colony Historical Society*

whipped. Slaves and captors alike drowned in heavy surf that capsized the ferries.

In his old age, a slave brought to Bristol on a DeWolf ship said that he remembered being snatched from his mother's arms on the beach and that she ran into the ocean after him, begging to be taken, too.

Once on board, slaves might be stripped of their clothing and branded if they hadn't already been. They had to be brought above deck to eat, and even that could be frightening. Meals were cooked in enormous vats that fueled a common African fear: many had heard that white people were cannibals.

In his famous Middle Passage memoir, the slave Olaudah Equaino said he fainted when he first saw dejected black people chained near a "large furnace of copper boiling." Equaino regained consciousness uneaten, but was later beaten for refusing to eat.

(An incidence of actual cannibalism—and a revolt—on a slave ship was reported in the *New-York Gazette* in May 1766. The crew and slave cargo of a sloop bound for North Carolina began to starve after the ship lost its sails and drifted for six weeks. "In want of provisions, they were put to the necessity of eating one of the dead negro children, which so exasperated the negroes on board that they fell on the crew." Two crew members died, the *Gazette* reported.)

Disease—smallpox, dysentery, malaria, ophthalmia (an infection that caused blindness)—was a constant threat. Crewmen referred to the African coast as "the White Man's Grave." To keep disease in check, slaves were bathed regularly, with vinegar or some other strong solution.

Slaves became so depressed they had to be forced to exercise and sometimes even to eat. Their aerobics in chains became a ritual "dance" practiced to the very end of the slave trade. Cultural historians believe the slave dance evolved into the Caribbean limbo. Those who tried to

This illustration of slaves being marched in a coffle is disturbing for its chains and wooden yokes, and its apelike depiction of the captive Africans. *Illustration from* Old Times in the Colonies, *Charles Carleton Coffin, 1880. The Mariners' Museum, Newport News, Virginia*

starve themselves were force-fed, their mouths pried open with a speculum oris—a plierslike instrument.

Such practices underscore the essential difference between slave traders and slave masters. For better or worse, the lord of a plantation had to coexist with his slaves. The slave trader had only to deliver them. Until recently, historians were inclined to pardon the trader and master as morally blind men who merely did what their times condoned. If so, they had to be willfully blind.

When Thomas Jefferson drafted the Declaration of Independence, he included the slave trade in his list of grievances against the British crown. Jefferson wrote that the king had "waged cruel war against human nature itself, violating it's [*sic*] most sacred rights of life and liberty in the persons of a distant people who never offended him, captivating and carrying them into slavery in another hemisphere, or to incur

Above: During the weeks-long Middle Passage, slaves were brought on deck to be fed and to be exercised. Exercise took the form of a forced dance, depicted in this 1837 illustration. *Illustration from* La France Maritime, *1837–1842. The Mariners' Museum, Newport News, Virginia*

Right: On slave ships, males spent hours shackled or handcuffed together. Those who refused to eat might be punished with thumbscrews, center left, or have their jaws pried open with a speculum oris, center right. *Engraving from* The History of the Rise, Progress and Accomplishment of the Abolition of the African Slave-Trade by the British Parliament, *Thomas Clarkson, 1808. The Mariners' Museum, Newport News, Virginia*

Slave shackles, ca. eighteenth to nineteenth centuries. Courtesy of the Amistad Foundation of the Wadsworth Atheneum of Art, Hartford, Connecticut. Purchase of the Simpson Collection. Photograph by Stephen Dunn, The Hartford Courant

miserable death in their transportation thither." Jefferson's now-forgotten indictment was deleted, in deference to proponents of slavery.

Rhode Island slave traders certainly could not have pleaded ignorance. From Samuel Hopkins onward, credible voices denounced the trade. In the case of John Brown, the voice belonged to his own brother.

The voyage of the *Sally* repulsed Moses, the youngest Brown. In 1768, Moses Brown freed the six slaves in his own household and soon converted to the Quaker faith. Years later, he confessed in a letter that his personal ownership of slaves had denied him the clean conscience he needed to oppose his brothers in sending the *Sally* to Africa. "I have many times since thought that if I had known the sentiments of others . . . I should have been preserved from an evil which has given me the most uneasiness and has left the greatest impression and stain upon my own mind of any, if not all my other conduct, in life," Moses wrote.

Moses became one of the new nation's most outspoken abolitionists. He favored gradual emancipation for

Moses Brown of Providence became an ardent abolitionist, opposed to his brother John. *Brown University Library*

the children of slaves, argued against ratifying the Constitution because it supported slavery, and backed a law prohibiting Rhode Islanders from engaging in the slave trade. Usually, Moses faced an opposing faction led by his brother John. Their running argument filled pages of Providence newspapers.

John Brown's real significance as a slave merchant was political. Although he sponsored only six slave voyages, so far as is known, John Brown was a shameless advocate for the trade. Writing as "a citizen" in a Providence newspaper, he said that in his opinion, "there was no more crime in bringing off a cargo of slaves than in bringing off a cargo of jack-asses."

Defending the trade in Congress in 1800, he further revealed his utter pragmatism. He argued that U.S. citizens had as much right as Europeans to the "benefits of the trade" and that barring U.S. ships would not stop a single slave from being exported from Africa. "We might as well therefore enjoy that trade as leave it wholly to others," Brown said.

He further argued that the trade fed the U.S. Treasury and that other industries—rum in particular—depended on it. Congressional notes, referring to Brown, read: "Mr. B. said our distilleries and manufactories were all lying idle for want of extended commerce. He had been well-informed that on those [African] coasts New England rum was much preferred to the best Jamaica spirits, and would fetch a better price. Why then should it not be sent there, and a profitable return be made?"

John Brown's economic reasoning was correct. As long as there was a market for slaves, someone would serve it. Economics were already betraying even Moses Brown's good intentions. In 1790, in the quest for new industry, Moses had hired Englishman Samuel Slater to design better machinery for a textile mill he had invested in. Slater turned the mill into a profitable operation at about the same time Eli Whitney perfected the cotton gin. By 1800, the cotton gin and Slater's machines were transforming Southern agriculture and Northern industry.

The conscience-stricken Moses had done more to perpetuate slavery than his avaricious big brother. Still, John's support of the slave trade had tangible results, especially for Bristol, Rhode Island, and the De-Wolfs.

THROUGHOUT THE 1790s, THE DEWOLFS HAD TO CONTEND WITH THE man George Washington had installed as customs collector for the Newport district, which then included Bristol. The man was a signer of the

Declaration of Independence named William Ellery, who knew that the DeWolfs were cheating the new government out of badly needed revenue.

In 1799, Ellery ordered the DeWolfs' schooner, the *Lucy*, auctioned off as a suspected slave ship. John Brown came down from Providence to intervene. He pressured Ellery's bidder to withdraw from the auction. The bidder tried to oblige, but Ellery would not allow it. On the day of the auction, men dressed as Indians waylaid the bidder and rowed him miles away. When the auctioneer finally banged his gavel down, the *Lucy* had been sold for a pittance to a DeWolf agent.

The DeWolfs managed a greater coup a few years later, with Congressman Brown's vital help. In early 1801, Brown got a bill passed creating a separate customs district for Bristol. The change eliminated their nemesis Ellery. But the DeWolfs were frustrated when, as one of his last acts, outgoing president John Adams appointed an unfriendly collector to the new Bristol district. They had to wait to get free rein of the port until 1804, when they persuaded their Republican ally, President Thomas Jefferson, to expel Adams's collector. In his place Jefferson appointed Charles Collins, who was—though Jefferson might not have known this—a veteran captain of DeWolf slave ships.

Collins remained the Bristol collector for almost two decades. During that time his lax enforcement helped the DeWolfs cement a unique legacy. "Theirs was one of the few fortunes that truly rested on rum and slaves," declared the premier historian of the Rhode Island slave merchants. "In the annals of the American slave trade, the deWolfs are without peer."

The sheer number of DeWolf voyages is in itself remarkable. The DeWolfs launched 88 slave voyages between 1784 and 1807, four times more than their closest Rhode Island rivals. DeWolfs personally commanded many of these voyages. Captain James DeWolf is supposed to have made a farewell voyage in 1807 aboard the *Andromache*, the pride of the DeWolf fleet.

Furthermore, the DeWolfs ran an integrated business, shipping molasses from their Cuban sugar plantations to their distilleries in Bristol. They even established a bank and an insurance company dedicated to supporting the Bristol trade.

When the Charleston slave market reopened in 1804, they dispatched a young DeWolf to set up an office there. After Congress voted to close the trade, the DeWolfs rushed 18 ships filled with Africans to South Carolina alone in just seven months. The traffic became so heavy that Charleston newspapers ran articles worrying about the health threat from dead slaves floating in the harbor.

The DeWolf shipments, combined with those of other Bristol and Newport slave merchants, would haunt the North in the coming national fight over slavery.

In 1820, when the trade had been illegal for more than a decade and when Missouri's admission to the Union was being debated, James De-Wolf, newly elected to the Senate, had to listen to Senator William Smith of South Carolina mock him in a speech attacking Northern hypocrisy. "The people of Rhode Island have lately shown bitterness against slaveholders, and especially against the admission of Missouri," Smith said. "This, however, cannot, I believe, be the temper or opinion of the majority, from the late election of James deWolf as a member of this house, as he has accumulated an immense fortune in the slave trade."

After Smith was interrupted for impugning a senator by name, he made a more veiled accusation. "I dare not ask whether citizens of Rhode Island have trafficked in slaves since such traffic became illegal—that were indeed out of order," Smith said, "but [I] would show the Senate that those people who most deprecate the evils of slavery and traffic in human flesh, when a profitable market can be found, can sell human flesh with as easy a conscience as they sell other articles."

In conjunction with his speech, Smith submitted records he'd collected from the Charleston customshouse for the years 1804 to 1808. The "black catalog," as he called it, showed that of 12,000 slaves imported on U.S. ships, nearly 8,000 were shipped on Rhode Island vessels. Smith's argument that New England followed Britain in foisting slavery on the South eventually would become a secessionist shout.

Senator DeWolf could not himself be accused of hypocrisy. He is supposed to have traveled to Washington in an elegant horse-drawn coach with one of his favorite slaves serving as groom.

DeWolf's most important act as a senator was in amending a new treaty that allowed the British and U.S. navies to jointly patrol the African coast for illegal slave ships. His amendment, which denied the British the right to search American vessels, had little immediate impact. By 1860, however, the fact that the British could not board U.S. ships helped give New York City the freedom to become the criminal headquarters of a massive illegal slave trade to markets in Brazil and Cuba.

In the colonial era even the most respectable New England merchants had been prolific smugglers, ignoring loosely enforced British trade rules. But Rhode Islanders were masters. Later, ignoring early federal laws that prohibited U.S. citizens from transporting slaves to foreign countries, they anticipated many of the illegal slave traders' methods. They disguised their ships with foreign flags and landed illicit cargoes in remote coves. They bought back confiscated ships for a fraction of their value. Simeon Potter, the old privateer, suggested that his nephew James could evade federal laws by landing slaves in Georgia and then smuggling them to Cuba, where they could be sold for a higher price. "This is my advice you can take or leave as you please, but it must be kept a profound secret," Potter wrote.

And Senator Smith of South Carolina was right when he implied that Rhode Island kept up the trade after it became illegal in 1808.

James DeWolf insisted he had retired from the trade. But he sold at least three of his slave ships to his nephew George DeWolf, and by 1810 George could afford to build a $60,000 mansion in Bristol. George also acquired a Cuban plantation he named "Noah's Ark." He probably smuggled surplus slaves from Noah's Ark to the South.

The Bristol slave trade was nearing its end, however, in 1820 when Senator Smith reproached the town. That same year, Congress passed a law mandating the death penalty for those trafficking in African slaves. The economy of Bristol itself, which depended so much on the trade, collapsed in 1825 when George DeWolf suddenly went bankrupt.

Like Bristol, Newport also failed to adapt to the end of the slave trade. Years earlier, customs collector Ellery had written to Moses Brown, "An Ethiopian could as soon change his skin as a Newport merchant could be induced to change so lucrative a trade."

The ruins on Bunce Island hold at least two secrets. The slave factory there sent more Africans to America than any other. And New England slave ships sailed from Connecticut, too.

HELL'S GATE

ON THE AFTERNOON OF JANUARY 18, 1757, A FAST, TWO-MASTED SHIP called the *Africa* sailed from New London harbor under a northwest wind. The day, a Tuesday, had dawned fair and clear as the ship headed briefly west, around Fishers Island in Long Island Sound, and then east, out to open sea.

Samuel Gould, the second in command, noted that it was "very could [*sic*]"—his first entry in an extraordinary ship's log that the Connecticut man kept for 18 months on three voyages, taken on three different vessels. Each trip had the same purpose: to buy and sell slaves.

Rhode Island's leading role in the transatlantic slave trade is well documented, but the role of neighboring Connecticut on the front lines of the slave trade has been buried. The recent resurfacing of Sam Gould's log, tucked away in the Connecticut State Library for 80 years, is changing that history.

The lack of research into Connecticut and the slave trade is, at least in part, the fault of the United States' most infamous traitor.

Benedict Arnold was born and raised just up-river from New London

When the two-masted ship the *Africa* left New London in January 1757, Captain John Easton and his crew were headed for the west coast of Africa and Sierra Leone, to buy slaves. *State Archives, Connecticut State Library, photograph by Tom Brown,* The Hartford Courant

African slaves had been sold from Bunce Island since the 1670s, but when Richard Oswald and his London partners bought the operation in 1748—the year this survey was made—they developed the island into a true focal point of the slave trade and reaped fortunes. *The National Archives of the UK (PRO): ref. CO 700/SIERRA LEONE 1A*

and was already a turncoat when, during the American Revolution, he led 800 British soldiers on a raid of the port city in 1781 and nearly destroyed it. About 150 structures were burned, including the New London customshouse, with its decades of shipping records.

Connecticut's highly profitable involvement in the West Indies trade, particularly as a shipper of livestock, is recognized. But Gould's log reveals that men from the colony were regularly in Africa buying men, women, and children. During the latter half of the eighteenth century, New London–based ships worked the coast of Africa alongside competitors from Rhode Island and Europe, transporting captives to the West Indies and back to the American colonies.

By the early 1600s, European nations were establishing slave-trading centers—slave warehouses that were often called "castles"—along the west coast of Africa. By about 1700, there were an estimated 40 such castles along nearly 2,000 miles of coast, from Senegal's Gorée Island, south to Ghana's Cape Coast Castle and the infamous Portuguese stronghold Elmina (from *el mina*, "the mine").

By the time Sam Gould and the *Africa* sailed into the mouth of the Sierra Leone River, Bunce Island, one of the most successful slaving businesses on the coast, was in operation. Bunce, then called Bence, or Bance, has largely been forgotten, but four separate entries on a single page of Gould's log for April 1757 indicate that slaves were purchased there.

Although the majority of Africans were brought to the Western Hemisphere through private traders, the castle system was a critical conduit. And there is no equivalent to Bunce Island, which, unlike many other fortresses, was built specifically to hold slaves. During the long history of the slave trade, an estimated 645,000 Africans were forced into slavery in the American colonies. More Africans—perhaps as many as 12,000—came here through Bunce than through any other African fortress.

Twenty miles from the point of land later established as Freetown, now the capital of Sierra Leone, tiny Bunce was rapidly emerging in the 1750s as the source of the American colonies' most desirable slaves. In the 1740s, the colonists of South Carolina and Georgia were starting to grow rice, turning over thousands of acres

The ruins of a major slave-trading fortress still stand on Bunce Island in the mouth of the Sierra Leone River. Agents from England lived in the upper story of this building, which overlooked an open yard where slaves were held for sale. *Tom Brown*, The Hartford Courant

to raising the crop, and they needed the rice-growing farmers from Sierra Leone for their knowledge as well as their labor.

Thousands of Africans from the "Rice Coast," which included parts of Senegal and Liberia as well as Sierra Leone, saw home for the last time from the jetty at Bunce Island.

Gould's log records the daily realities of life aboard a slave ship and the known horrors of the Middle Passage. On May 5, 1757, for example, ten days after leaving Bunce for the West Indies, Gould wrote from aboard the sloop *Good Hope*, "This 24 hours Died three Small Slaves with the Flux—165 Slaves Remain living on Board." In the first 19 days of the voyage, a dozen captives, 10 of them children, died, apparently of "the flux," or amoebic dysentery, which was common. On some days, Gould notes the gender of the dead children. On others, the children are, simply, "small slaves."

The ruins of the last slave fortress on Bunce—the island may have had six different castles between 1670 and the 1790s—are nearly swallowed up by equatorial jungle. Yet the functioning and daily operations of this slaving center are evident.

The second-story windows of what once was Bunce Island House, a stone building where the company agent lived, now frame views of sky and tall vegetation growing amid the ruins. These windows also overlooked the open slave yard, and visitors would have looked down upon the hundreds of chained captives.

The double doorways still stand where black workers entered the slave enclosures with food and water. The outer door was locked before the inner door was opened, and one can still see where an armed guard stood.

New England and British commanders made their trade arrangements in the captain's office, with its fireplace evocative of cold weather and home. Of the fireplace, designed without a flue and simply for show, only a mantel survives on a wall now exposed to sun and rain.

Cannons bearing the elaborately curling monogram of King George III still point toward the Atlantic, and the gravel path where captive people were forced down to the waiting ships still curves toward the jetty. Though the island ceased to be a trading center

Bunce Island's caretaker holds eighteenth-century objects collected from the beach next to the jetty where slaves were loaded onto waiting ships. China from England, bits of pipe stems, remnants of ancient bottles, and beads used in trade for human beings still litter the beach. *Tom Brown,* The Hartford Courant

two centuries ago, the beaches nearest the jetty are still littered with the Venetian glass beads of deep blue, wine red, and dark green taken in trade for the Africans.

Manned largely by free black workers called "grommetos," Bunce offered for sale captive people taken from as far as 100 miles inland and 600 miles of coast. New England ships like Gould's could drop anchor for trade and find, on neighboring islands, ample supplies of fresh water, produce, and wood.

"On board the Good Hope Lying at Bence Island Taking in Slaves and Stores [supplies]," Sam Gould wrote on April 15, 1757, adding that he "Din'd and Sup'd at the factory with Capt. John Stephens." Stephens was then the ranking English agent at Bunce.

Bunce's ready supplies of slaves allowed traders to assemble their human cargo quickly and avoid lengthy exposure to the malarial climate of coastal Africa.

Some of the surviving slave castles on Africa's western coast have become destinations for African Americans longing to explore personal history, but Bunce—reachable only by boat—is too remote to encourage modern visitors. Now, green monkeys chatter in the treetops around the ruins, and insects hum in the stillness. One's face and body run with sweat in the equatorial heat, which is thick and muffles sound. Despite the water surrounding the island, there is no breeze and the tall, canopy palms are motionless in the dead air.

The island once had a resident caretaker who lived in a two-room shed, but he died and his ancient widow, nearly blind from cataracts, lives on neighboring Tasso Island in a community of fishermen and farmers. No one lives on Bunce now. The Temne caretaker who carefully maintains a scrapbook of signatures of visitors to the island lives with his family on another island.

From a small point of land beyond the tower that once housed company offices, human remains have begun to surface, as if the island were trying to speak, to say what happened here. On the broken gravestone of a long-ago company agent named Thomas Knight, only the word "memory" is perfectly legible.

Sam Gould didn't know that his 80-page log would one day provide a penetrating glimpse into the heart of the transatlantic slave trade. When this mariner lived and sailed, the trade was legal, and it would remain legal for nearly a half century more.

In the log's last voyage, Gould is serving aboard a ship called the *Fox*, under Captain William Taylor, another Connecticut native. The ship had sailed from New London in late March 1758, and the captain was buying slaves on the coast of Ghana in July when a large ship was sighted to windward. Gould thought at first that it was an English warship, but that sail in the distance proved to be a French man-of-war carrying 60 guns. Colonial rivals England and France were then constantly skirmishing, and the *Count Florentine* made prisoners of the men aboard the *Fox*.

But the French must have let the men go, because two weeks later the *Fox* departed from Fort Coromantine, a notorious slave fortress in Ghana, and headed, under "small winds and pleasant weather," for New England and home.

Saturday 16. April 1757.
Lying at Bence Island Taking in Slaves & Water

A slave ship log in the Connecticut State Library states, in the barest possible terms, that the ship was anchored at Bence Island and taking on board supplies of food and water, probably from neighboring Tasso Island, and buying enslaved people. The slaves were destined for St. Christopher, a sugar island in the West Indies today better known as St. Kitts. *State Archives, Connecticut State Library. Photograph by Tom Brown, The Hartford Courant*

After Congress outlawed the importation of slaves,

ship captains began to hide their boxes of shackles.

But little else about the slave trade changed, except

that its center shifted to Manhattan, and its

conditions became even more horrific.

Six

NEW YORK'S SLAVE PIRATES

IN AUGUST 1860, A U.S. NAVY STEAMER PATROLLING THE AFRICAN coast intercepted a ship that was sailing suspiciously close to the mouth of the Congo. The *Erie* was flying an American flag as proof of her nationality and innocence. But when naval officers boarded her, they found her crammed with nearly 900 newly purchased Africans.

Half were children, and even though their "middle passage" had just begun, they already stank with their own filth. Running sores ate at their flesh. Stripped naked and packed like cattle, the Africans almost stampeded when their rescuers tried to give them water. Even under U.S. Navy care, 30 would die in the 15 days it took to deliver them to Liberia, sanctuary and dumping ground for slavery's refugees.

The *Erie* and her crew were sent to New York City, where their voyage had begun, and where ships like theirs were well known. By 1860, New York was notorious as the hub of an international illegal slave trade that, like the latter-day traffic in drugs, was too lucrative and too corrupt to stop.

Ships destined to carry slaves were built and sold in New York. There they were outfitted for their African voyages, sometimes complete with crates of shackles and the supersized water tanks needed for their human cargo. Customs agents, uncaring or bribed, looked the other way as slave ships sailed from New York harbor under the flimsiest of disguises. The traffickers relied on fake owners, forged documents, and, most shamefully, the American flag's guarantee of immunity from seizure by foreign nations.

The illegal slave trade was carried on so flagrantly that New York newspapers reported the names of ships leaving for slave voyages. The barely clandestine trade flourished for 20 years. During peak years in 1859 and 1860, at least two slave ships left from New York every month, according to one cautious estimate. Most could hold between 600 and 1,000 slaves. So in each of those years, New York ships might have carried as many as 20,000 new Africans into bondage.

At that point, most were sold in Spanish-controlled Cuba, one of the last open slave markets in the Western Hemisphere. In the summer of 1860, the traffic from Africa was so heavy that the U.S. Navy actually seized a second slave ship in sight of the *Erie*. The *Storm King* carried about 620 Africans, half of them children. The next month the *Cora*, loaded with 700 Africans, was captured. All three were New York ships.

The slave ship captains, too, usually hailed from the North, especially New England, which had dominated American shipping since colonial times. The *Erie*'s captain, Nathaniel Gordon, was the son of a Portland, Maine, sea captain and a seasoned slave trader.

DRAWN BY W. TABER.　　　THE CHASE.　　　ENGRAVED BY HENRY WOLF.

By 1894, when *Century* magazine ran this illustration of a U.S. Navy vessel chasing the slave ship *Cora* toward the horizon, the slave trade was remembered with the gloss of adventure. But only on the verge of the Civil War did the U.S. Navy's Africa squadron begin to pursue illegal slavers aggressively. Century: A Popular Quarterly, *vol. 48, no. 1, May 1894,* Capture of the Slave-Ship "Cora" *by Wilburn Hall, p. 115. Courtesy of Cornell University Library, Making of America Digital Collection*

EXECUTION OF GORDON THE SLAVE-TRADER, NEW YORK, FEBRUARY 21, 1862.—[See Page 155.]

The hanging of Captain Nathaniel Gordon on February 21, 1862, marked the end of an era in which New York City was home port to illegal slave ships. His ship, the *Erie,* was captured in August 1860 loaded with nearly 900 new slaves. *Illustration from* Harper's Weekly, March 8, 1862. *Photographs and Prints Division, Schomburg Center for Research in Black Culture, The New York Public Library, Astor, Lenox and Tilden Foundations*

Earlier, in 1853, when the coffee plantations of Brazil were a market for slaves, U.S. diplomats reported that Gordon had landed 500 slaves near Rio de Janeiro, then burned his ship to escape capture. Few slave ship captains had such long careers. Their gravest risk was not capture but dying from fever on the African coast or being killed in a slave revolt. For captives, captain, and crew, slave ships fully deserved the epithet Brazilians gave them, *tombeiros,* "bearers to the tomb."

Captain Gordon, however, met a fate that neither he nor the New Yorkers of his day could have expected. The federal government had passed the first law regulating the transatlantic slave trade even before it outlawed the importation of slaves in 1808. And in 1820, trafficking in slaves was made an act of piracy and a capital crime for U.S. citizens, though the law was hardly a deterrent. For the next four decades, prosecutions for piracy were rare, and convictions were nonexistent.

Gordon himself almost got off. His first trial ended with a split jury. But his second trial, in November 1861, took place in a less forgiving atmosphere. The North and South had gone to war and the new Republican administration was less tolerant of slavery. Gordon was convicted and sentenced to death. Abraham Lincoln twice refused pleas to spare Gordon, despite a petition for mercy signed by 11,000 sympathetic New Yorkers.

The night of his scheduled hanging, Gordon tried to poison himself by smoking cigars laced with strychnine. On February 21, 1862, while a U.S. Marine guard stood by to prevent a rumored rescue, the Yankee sea captain became the first and only American ever executed for participating in the African slave trade.

THE ILLEGAL NEW YORK SLAVE TRADE OF THE MID-NINETEENTH CENtury amounted to an intercontinental shell game. From voyage to voyage, a ship might switch from legitimate merchant vessel to slave ship and back again. Crossing the Atlantic, they would carry duplicate sets of ownership papers, and even duplicate captains and crews—one American and one foreign.

New York emerged as the hub of the illegal trade partly because slave ships blended easily with the port's enormous fleet of legitimate merchant ships and partly because of official indifference.

One longtime federal judge in New York, Samuel Rossiter Betts, later lauded as the father of U.S. admiralty law, set a standard of proof so high that slave trade convictions were rare and severe punishment even rarer. Betts once ordered a slave ship captain released on bail so he could go to Rio to gather information for his defense. The captain never returned and was reported to have bragged to his cohorts, "You don't have to worry about facing trial in New York City. . . . I can get any man off in New York for $1,000."

No amount of disguise and neglect could have made New York safe for slave traders, however, without the national complicity that protected slave ships flying the American flag from the British, since Britain was the world power most dedicated to stopping the slave traffic.

After abolishing slavery in its colonies in 1833, Britain had begun to negotiate treaties that gave its vaunted navy the right to police the slave trade. By the 1850s, the only holdout that mattered was the United States. Jealous of the sovereignty of its ships at sea, resentful of Britain's former domination, the U.S. government insisted that only its navy could detain American ships.

The U.S. Navy did muster a squadron, but it was tiny, with five ships at most assigned to patrol hundreds of miles of African coastline. In the two decades before the *Erie* was seized, the U.S. Africa squadron had caught exactly two ships actually loaded with slaves. British commanders complained that their U.S. counterparts let blatant slave ships pass unchallenged. The two navies did not cooperate fully until 1862, when President Lincoln reluctantly signed a treaty permitting the

British to board ships flying the American flag. The Senate approved the agreement in secret, fearing a public backlash.

No nation, however, could entirely shed the slave trade's taint. In the eighteenth century, Britain itself was a major slave carrier. In the nineteenth century, defensive U.S. diplomats complained that Britain allowed its own merchants to export goods to Africa that they knew supported the slave economy.

"It is worse than idle," wrote Henry Wise, U.S. ambassador to Brazil in the 1840s, "for Great Britain to reproach the United States for permitting their flag and their vessels to be common [slave] carriers, as long as British manufacturers, merchants, brokers and capitalists are allowed to furnish the very pabulum of the slave trade."

Even Britain's efforts to suppress the slave trade were not entirely humanitarian. Squeezing the slave pipeline gave Britain leverage over African kingdoms and helped it regain the competitive balance it lost after abolishing slavery in its colonies. What's more, when its navy captured slave ships, Britain didn't always return the "liberated" slaves to Africa. Often it delivered them to years of indentured labor on plantations in its Caribbean colonies.

In the 1840s, when the illegal trade went mostly to Brazil, New Yorkers were front men for foreigners based in Manhattan. An entity known as the Portuguese Company that arranged slave voyages kept several offices. One carried on a legal wine-importing business. At another, the man in charge was John Albert Machado, a naturalized American citizen from the Azores whose fleet of illegal slavers included New England whaling ships. In June 1860, one of Machado's whalers, the *Thomas Watson*, aroused such suspicion while outfitting for an African voyage in New London, Connecticut, that customs officials there denied it clearance. So the *Thomas Watson* sailed to New York and left from there. Months later it landed 800 slaves in Cuba.

BEFORE IT FINALLY DISAPPEARED DURING THE CIVIL WAR, A NOT-QUITE-underground industry supported New York's illegal slave trade. It included ship fitters, suppliers, recruiters of crews, and bribed marshals and customs agents. Ship owners and captains accused of violating slave trade laws often were defended by Beebe, Dean & Donohue, leading admiralty lawyers with offices at 76 Wall Street.

When it appeared that Nathaniel Gordon might go free after his first trial in June 1861, the *New-York Daily Tribune* complained in an editorial that "the slave-traders in this city have matured their arrangements so thoroughly that they almost invariably manage to elude the meshes of the law. Now they bribe a jury, another time their counsel or agents spirit away a vital witness. . . . Fortunately, however, a new class of men [Lincoln appointees] now have direction of affairs, and a stop will be put to this iniquitous complicity with crime. . . . To effect this it will be necessary to purge the courts and offices of these pimps of piracy, who are well known, and at the proper time will receive their desserts."

By 1861, the illegal trade had grown so brazen that anyone who read a New York newspaper would have known how it worked.

New York ships sailed to Rio de Janeiro or, later, Havana, where they might take aboard a second captain and crew. For the crossing to Africa, the U.S. ship would list the foreigners as "passengers." Then, on the African coast, came a sudden switch in nationality. Just before or even while slaves were being loaded, the foreigners would declare themselves owners and commanders of what—moments before—had been a U.S. vessel. The American captain and crew sometimes made the return voyage as working passengers on the now-foreign slave ship. More often they returned safe from arrest on an "innocent" tender that was the slave ship's accomplice.

In its final years, as abolition threatened entire national economies that were still dependent on slave labor, the illegal slave trade became more profitable and, if possible, more horrific. Ships grew larger, able to stow close to 1,000 Africans chained in pairs between their narrow decks. Some traders ordered steamships built that could cross the Atlantic more quickly. But those new vessels led to new kinds of suffering on the centuries-old Middle Passage. The hot boilers could cause skin ulcers. Water-distilling machines that malfunctioned could poison an entire cargo of slaves.

Meanwhile, the older wooden vessels became so disposable that slave captains routinely burned them once they had delivered their cargoes. Burning avoided the filthy work of decontaminating a befouled ship and kept it from being seized as evidence. Like bribes paid to harbor agents, the ship's loss was just another cost of doing business.

In 1861, a British diplomat estimated that a single successful voyage might yield a 250 percent profit to the owners of an average slave ship. The asking price for slaves in Africa at that point was about $50, while the selling price in Cuba was more than $1,000. The diplomat's calculations included deductions for bribes fixed at $120 per slave, $25,000 for the vessel, and $30,000 for the crew. Captains were probably paid close to $4,000, enough to make a man rich.

The death of slaves during the Middle Passage was another predictable cost of doing business. For accounting purposes, the diplomat figured 10 percent of the slaves originally embarked in Africa would die. The actual rate, of course, could be much higher. On its way to Cuba in 1857, one of the largest New York slave ships, the *Haidee*, lost 200 of its 1,100 slaves.

TODAY, THE MOST FAMOUS SHIP THAT CARRIED SLAVES MAY BE THE *Amistad*. Even before Steven Spielberg made his 1997 movie, the *Amistad* remained afloat in popular memory because its story has foreign villains and American heroes. The *Amistad* was a Spanish schooner recovered by the U.S. Navy, its rebellious slaves eventually declared free by U.S. courts.

But the *Amistad* was an anomaly.

In November 1841, while the *Amistad* survivors were on their way back to Africa, slaves revolted on the American *Creole*, killing or wounding some of the crew. The *Creole* had been carrying slaves from Richmond to New Orleans. The rebels managed to bring the *Creole* into British-controlled Nassau harbor where it became a cause célèbre equal to the *Amistad*. The revolt's hero, Madison Washington, was a fugitive American slave who'd been recaptured while trying to steal his wife from a Virginia plantation.

Three years later, while the international dispute still swirled around the *Creole*, a worse crisis erupted in Rio de Janeiro over a virtual

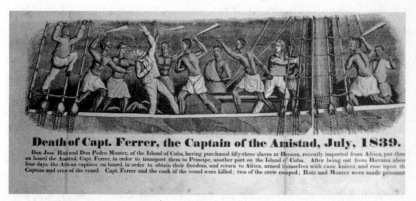

Death of Capt. Ferrer, the Captain of the Amistad, July, 1839.

Don Jose Ruiz and Don Pedro Montez, of the Island of Cuba, having purchased fifty-three slaves at Havana, recently imported from Africa, put them on board the Amistad, Capt. Ferrer, in order to transport them to Principe, another port on the Island of Cuba. After being out from Havana about four days, the African captives on board, in order to obtain their freedom, and return to Africa, armed themselves with cane knives, and rose upon the Captain and crew of the vessel. Capt. Ferrer and the cook of the vessel were killed; two of the crew escaped; Ruiz and Montez were made prisoners.

The rebellion aboard the Spanish vessel *Amistad*, depicted here, is remembered as a victory in America's fight against slavery. The *Amistad* incident, however, occurred at almost the same time as a similar revolt on the *Creole*, a U.S. vessel transporting slaves from Virginia to Louisiana. Death of Capt. Ferrer, the Captain of the Amistad, July 1839, *The Connecticut Historical Society Museum, Hartford, Connecticut*

flotilla of illegal slave ships from the United States. All were from the North. One, a New York brig named the *Kentucky*, arrived in Brazil drenched in blood from one of the most gruesome revolts ever recorded.

The ugly crisis began when the *Kentucky*'s accomplice ship, the *Porpoise*, sailed into Rio with two child slaves on board, both boys branded on the chest with the mark of their Brazilian owner. The *Porpoise*, of Maine, was a widely suspected slave tender. The ship had already been to Africa in 1843 with two other American slave ships.

One of those ships, the *Hope*, of New York, had carried the kind of cargo that made ships subject to seizure whether or not they were carrying slaves at the time. On board were rum casks filled with huge quantities of water. Lumber to build a temporary slave deck was listed as material for a frame house. A crate marked HATS carried an unassembled boiler for cooking food for large quantities of people. And boxes marked SOAP were filled with manacles.

Such deceptions easily fooled customs agents and U.S. Navy officers, especially if they wanted an excuse to look the other way. But any authorities willing to seize an obvious slave vessel such as the *Hope* were thwarted in court by a maze of owners. The *Porpoise*, for example, though registered in Maine, had been turned over to Maxwell, Wright & Company, U.S. coffee traders in Rio who chartered her out, through an English broker, to one of Rio's wealthiest slave merchants, Manoel Pinto da Fonseca.

In January 1844, Fonseca acquired control of the *Kentucky* when it arrived from New York. Two months later, he sent it to the east coast of Africa to rendezvous with the *Porpoise*. Together, the *Kentucky* and the *Porpoise* provide a blueprint of the manner and depth of U.S. involvement in the illegal slave trade.

The part-owner of the *Kentucky* had delivered her from New York to Rio. From Rio, she'd sailed for Africa under Captain George Douglass of Philadelphia. Meanwhile, Captain Cyrus Libby of Portland, Maine, had commanded the *Porpoise*.

Both ships spent most of the summer of 1844 sailing from one place to another in the vicinity of Mozambique, trying to acquire a full cargo of slaves. In late August, with slaves in short supply, Fonseca's agent settled for 500.

Then, working quickly, the two crews began to build a slave deck in the hold of the *Kentucky*. The *Porpoise* was moored so close to the *Kentucky* that Captain Douglass slept aboard the *Porpoise* and worked days aboard the *Kentucky*. In early September, boats from the *Porpoise* helped ferry captured Africans from the shore onto the *Kentucky*.

Months later the second mate of the *Kentucky*, Thomas Boyle of Boston, testified that Douglass purposely left the American colors behind when the two ships left Africa. Boyle himself helped paint out KENTUCKY OF NEW YORK from her stern; he said he later recognized the vessel, renamed the *Franklyn of Salem*, in Rio harbor. The *Franklyn*, previously the *Kentucky*, had delivered its cargo of slaves and escaped seizure.

The voyage had hardly been a complete success, though. The Portuguese captain who took over the command of the *Kentucky/Franklyn* told Boyle that while waiting for a favorable wind on the African coast, he'd had to put down a slave revolt. The captain led Boyle to believe that 27 rebels had been killed in the fight, a very high number for a failed revolt. But Boyle said another crewman told him not only that the death toll was much higher, but that the rebel Africans had not been killed in self-defense. They'd been executed.

William Page, an English sailor on the *Kentucky*, confirmed the carnage in a detailed deposition. He reported that, in fact, no slave had been killed during the brief, failed revolt. However, in the days after the revolt, 46 men and a woman had been strung from the yardarms, shot, and thrown overboard. If one of the rebels happened to be shackled to a slave whom the crew wanted to save, the execution was especially gruesome:

> *If only one of two that were ironed together was to be hung, a rope was put round his neck and he was drawn up clear of the deck, beside the bulwarks, and his leg laid across the rail and chopped off, to save the irons and release him from his companion. . . . The bleeding negro was then drawn up, shot in the breast, and thrown overboard.*
>
> *The legs of about one dozen were chopped off in this way. When the feet fell on deck, they were picked up by the Brazilian crew and thrown overboard, and sometimes at the body, while it still hung living; and all kinds of sport were made of the business. When two that were chained together were both to be hung, they were hung up together by their necks, shot and thrown overboard, irons and all.*
>
> *When the woman was hung up and shot, the ball did not take effect and she was thrown overboard living, and was seen to struggle some in the water before she sunk.*

Page also described the vicious flogging ordered as punishment for other *Kentucky* rebels, who were stretched flat on the deck and tied hand and foot:

They were then whipped by two men at a time, by the one with a stick about two feet long, with five or six strands of rawhide secured to the end of it . . . and by the other with a piece of hide . . . as thick as one's finger, or thicker, and hard as whalebone, but more flexible.

Page said the floggings were so prolonged that the Brazilian crew got tired and forced him and another English crewman to team up in beating 4 of the slaves. The 20 men whipped survived in agony, but all 6 of the women who were whipped soon died.

Most of Page's deposition focused on the partnership between the *Kentucky* and the *Porpoise* and their duplicate sets of captains.

The mate of the *Porpoise,* John Ulrick from Portland, Maine, bought at least two slaves, a boy about ten and a young woman about twenty, whom Page saw branded with a *U.*

Meanwhile, Captain Douglass, the Philadelphian, rushed from the *Porpoise* to the *Kentucky* whenever he needed to shield the latter vessel from being searched:

The understanding was so good between the Portuguese captain of the Kentucky and Capt. Douglass . . . that the Portuguese captain would only have to hold up his finger, and Douglass would go on board in a minute.

Page said the American flags that Douglass left on the *Kentucky* flew constantly. Such testimony prompted the U.S. ambassador to Brazil, Henry Wise, to comment, "Without the aid of our citizens and our flag, [the slave trade] could not be carried on with success at all."

British diplomats in Rio included Page's testimony in their annual report on the illegal trade. They noted that 43 vessels of various nations had brought 16,200 new slaves to Brazil, and that the most successful slave voyages were those of ships that flew the American flag.

The British identified one of the wealthiest and boldest slave dealers as Manoel Pinto da Fonseca, whose fleet included the *Porpoise* and the *Kentucky*. Fonseca had a mansion in the center of Rio, and he bought the friendship of government officials by lending them money. The government itself was controlled by coffee planters, who needed slaves to supply the world's growing addiction to their crop. In 1848, a peak year, Brazil exported 134,000 tons of coffee, much of it to the United States, and imported 60,000 African slaves.

"Brazil is coffee and coffee is the Negro," a Brazilian senator is said to have declared.

THE TRUE SCALE AND HORROR OF THE ILLEGAL SLAVE TRADE CAN ONLY be estimated. The trade was, after all, a criminal enterprise designed to evade detection. Moreover, storms, disease, and African resistance must have scuttled a significant number of voyages.

One of the last slave ships known to try to reach Brazil was the *Mary E. Smith*, a schooner that began its voyage in Boston in August 1855. As it left, a deputy U.S. marshal tried to arrest its defiant owners, who gave him a choice: Get off the ship, or go to Africa. He got off the ship. Months later the *Mary E. Smith* was seized cruising the Brazilian coast loaded with Africans dying of thirst and hunger. She had been unable to find a safe harbor to land her cargo.

Though the trade to Brazil had been technically illegal for decades, it remained effectively open until 1851, when the Brazilian government itself started to crack down on its powerful slave merchants. With the Brazilian market finally shut, the illegal trade shifted mainly to the sugar plantations of Cuba and even, briefly, to the cotton-producing South.

In June 1858, the single most notorious slave ship in the history of the U.S. trade left New York harbor for what government agents knew could only be Africa. The *Wanderer*, a racing yacht built on Long Island, was now outfitted with 15,000-gallon water tanks. Her owners were Southern members of the New York Yacht Club allied with Charles A. L. Lamar, a Georgia firebrand who publicly boasted that he intended to reopen the slave trade to the United States.

The *Wanderer's* mission was so well known that she was welcomed with a cannon salute when she stopped in Charleston, South Carolina, on the way to Africa. Newspapers reported her progress, and the British boarded her when she reached the Congo River in mid-September. No navy seized her, though.

In late November she landed a cargo of about 400 Africans, most of them teenage boys, on a private island off the coast of Georgia. As many as 80 other Africans had died during the Middle Passage on the giant yacht. The survivors vanished into slavery. Lamar and the *Wanderer* commanders went through a series of sensational trials that ended without convictions. A special prosecutor appointed to the cases later claimed the entire voyage was a conspiracy organized in New York.

Among the last Cuba-bound ships was the *Nightingale*, a yacht bigger and more exotic than the *Wanderer*. In April 1861, days before the bombardment of Fort Sumter and the start of the Civil War, a U.S. Navy vessel patrolling a section of the West African coast visited for centuries by slave ships seized the *Nightingale* with nearly 1,000 Africans on board and another 600 waiting on the beach.

Named for the Swedish singing sensation Jenny Lind, the *Nightingale* had been built a decade before in Maine, across the Piscataqua River from Portsmouth, New Hampshire, with no expense spared. Its speed soon made it a celebrity in the clipper ship China trade. Its glory days ended abruptly in January 1860 when it was sold in New York to a mysterious foreign buyer who hired an American captain, Francis Bowen, known as "the Prince of Slavers," to take her to Africa.

The capture of the *Nightingale* and Captain Nathaniel Gordon's death sentence together marked the closing of the illegal trade, but not its end. In November 1861, the same month Gordon was convicted, a deadlocked jury freed the *Nightingale*'s third mate, Minthorne Westervelt, a young man from of one New York's wealthiest families.

In February 1862, the week Gordon was hanged, the U.S. consul in Havana wrote a memo to Washington warning that the *Ocilla*, out of Mystic, Connecticut, had left on a suspected slave voyage. Despite the alert, the *Ocilla* was not caught. In December, the consul sent a more detailed memo reporting that the *Ocilla* had landed an unknown number of slaves in Cuba, and estimating that 2,000 slaves had been brought in illegally in the space of a month. One of the *Ocilla*'s crew, tracked to a Havana hospital, identified himself and the *Ocilla*'s captain as Philadelphians.

In May 1864, an even more tragic dispatch from Havana reported that the *Huntress* of New York, owned by a New Yorker and a New Bedford, Massachusetts, native, was found burned after landing 500 slaves. A captured crew member from New York said the voyage to Cuba from near the mouth of the Congo had taken so long—almost three months—that the ship began to run out of water. Some 250 Africans died. As usual, to protect the health of rest of the cargo, their bodies were thrown overboard.

THE *OCILLA* AND THE *HUNTRESS* WERE THE FINAL 2 OF MORE THAN 100 slave ship voyages documented by W.E.B. Du Bois in his still-authoritative *The Suppression of the African Slave Trade to the United States of America, 1638–1870.* In his book, originally published in 1896, Du Bois posed a question about the slave trade that each generation must answer: How should those who sanctioned or abetted it be judged?

"One cannot, to be sure, demand of whole nations exceptional moral foresight and heroism; but a certain hard common sense . . . must be expected in every progressive people," Du Bois wrote. "In some respects we as a nation seem to lack this; we have the somewhat inchoate idea that we are not destined to be harassed with great social questions, and that even if we are, and fail to answer them, the fault is with the question and not with us."

When his classic was reissued a half-century later, on the eve of the civil rights movement, Du Bois wrote that he wished he'd looked more closely at the economics driving the slave trade rather than the laws governing it. Laws codify morality; economics ignore both.

The illegal slave trade catered to an international plantation economy. As for its morality, the words spoken to Nathaniel Gordon in a New York courtroom at his sentencing in November 1861 sound correct even now. The judge, William Shipman, sent down from a court in Hartford, Connecticut, urged the slave captain from Maine to think about his crime, and the many who shared it during the slave trade's long history.

"Do not imagine that because others shared in the guilt of this enterprise yours is thereby diminished," Shipman said, "but remember the awful admonition of the Bible, 'though hand join in hand, the wicked shall not go unpunished.' "

These rare photos taken in late 1868 aboard the British ship *Daphne* show two groups of newly rescued slaves. The larger group on deck look reasonably healthy. But the youths in the smaller group appear near starvation. *The National Archives of the UK (PRO): ref. FO84/1310*

When Southerners tried to reopen the slave trade, they sent the Wanderer
*from New York to Africa. In 1858, it successfully smuggled almost 400
young Africans into the country. A few survived to tell their stories.*

LAST SURVIVORS

OF THE TENS OF THOUSANDS of Africans transported on illegal U.S.
slave ships before the Civil War, almost all vanished on foreign coffee and sugar plantations. There is information, however, about the
fate of some of the 400 young Africans who endured the Middle
Passage and were smuggled into the United States by the slave
yacht *Wanderer* in late 1858. They were spirited to plantations on
the Georgia mainland and ultimately scattered across the doomed
Cotton Kingdom.

Fast enough to outrun U.S. Navy steamers, the Long Island–built *Wanderer* was sent to Africa by a
group of Southerners intent on reopening the slave trade. *The Slaveship* Wanderer, *The Historical Society
of Greater Port Jefferson*

Fifty years after being smuggled into the United States as slaves, survivors of the *Wanderer* were photographed and interviewed by an anthropologist. The trio shown here are, from left, Ward Lee, originally named Cilucangy; Tucker Henderson, originally named Pucka Geata; and Romeo, originally named Tahro. Lee, who was found in South Carolina, still spoke fluently in his native language. He'd once handed out a circular asking for help to go back to Africa. "I will be glad of whatever you will give me," the circular said in part. "I am bound for my old home if God be with me white or black yellow or the red I am an old African." *American Anthropologist, Vol. 10, 1908*

A page from the 1900 South Carolina census shows that *Wanderer* survivor Ward Lee was born in 1846. Thus he would have been about fourteen when he endured the Middle Passage in 1858. *United States Census, 1900*

In 1998, descendants of Ward Lee had a unique family reunion on Long Island, where many lived and where the slave yacht *Wanderer* was built in 1857. At the time of the reunion, the late Ethel Lee Mitchell, in sweatshirt, and Ocea Lee Barnes were the former slave's oldest and youngest living granddaughters. Two of Lee's great-great-granddaughters, Sharon Sansaverino, left, and her sister Sheryl Valenti, had become the first black Doublemint gum twins. © 1998 Newsday, Inc. Used with permission.

Nearly 50 years later, an anthropologist named Charles Montgomery managed to track down and photograph a few of the survivors.

In a paper published in *American Anthropology* in 1908, Montgomery reported he found two of the *Wanderer* slaves on the South Carolina plantation of U.S. Senator Benjamin R. Tillman, "Pitchfork Ben." He found another in a rest home outside Augusta, Georgia.

All had been given new names in America. Some remembered the villages where they were born; others did not.

One survivor, Tom Johnson, born Zow Uncola, said he doubted that he would return to Africa even if he had the chance. "I'm gittin' so old, I'm 'fraid I couldn't git back," he told Montgomery.

Besides, Johnson/Uncola no longer knew exactly where home was. He said it was a part of the African coast where the sun rises, suggesting that it was the east coast, where the *Wanderer* had sailed, up and down the coast, looking for human cargo.

The old slave tried to be more specific. "Where I come from, you can see the water just drippin' out o' the sun."

For 50 years, kidnappers

prowled the streets of Northern

cities, abducting free blacks

to sell into slavery. Too few

tried to stop them.

Seven

THE OTHER UNDERGROUND RAILROAD

T HE KIDNAPPING OF FREE BLACKS FROM THE NORTH WAS SO RAM-
pant before the Civil War that abolitionists decried it as a slave
trade unto itself.

Abolitionists claimed the abductions boosted the South's slave population by the thousands each decade. They may have exaggerated, but
the traffic persisted for so long that modern historians have likened it to
an underground railroad, running in the wrong direction. Its most notorious conductors were organized gangs who, like outlaws from the Old
West, became legends in their own time.

The most unlikely gang leader was a woman named Patty Cannon,
said to be so strong she could jerk a 300-pound sack of grain to her shoulder, or a grown man off his feet. Her chief confederate was her son-in-
law, identified by a contemporary newspaper as "the celebrated Joseph
Johnson, negro trader."

The Cannon gang's territory extended from the Delmarva Penin-
sula of Maryland and Delaware, both slave states, to free Pennsylvania,
where the Philadelphia waterfront was one of their favorite hunting
grounds. During the summer of 1825 alone, the gang plucked at least a
dozen young victims from the City of Brotherly Love.

When they found it necessary, kidnappers, like slave ship captains,
resorted to murder to ensure the success of their enterprise. In April
1829, the skeletons of one adult and three children were discovered on
a farm that Patty Cannon had occupied. One of the children, thought to
be about seven years old, had a crushed skull. A former gang member

In 1817, illustrator and author Jesse Torrey Jr. published the first extended description of the United States inter-state slave trade that included abductions of free blacks as pictured here. *"Kidnapping," Jesse Torrey Jr.,* Portraiture of Domestic Slavery in the U.S., *1817. Beinecke Rare Book and Manuscript Library, Yale University*

later testified that he'd seen Cannon club the child to death in an effort to get rid of incriminating evidence.

No Northern city could guarantee the safety of its black residents, whether they were free people who had never been slaves or runaways who had established free lives in the North.

In November 1829, a New York newspaper warned that a kidnapping ring was snatching a black child a day from city streets. By 1835, the continued threat of kidnappings in New York led to the creation of the first important black self-defense association. Its leader, David Ruggles, also started a short-lived journal that exposed New York officials who worked with kidnappers. Ruggles even threatened to publish a separate "slaveholders directory" for New York City and Brooklyn listing the conspirators' names and addresses.

In 1838, Ruggles provided shelter for the most famous fugitive slave in American history, Frederick Douglass. In the 1855 expanded edition of his autobiography, Douglass paid homage to Ruggles and described the dread he'd felt before finding sanctuary with him. "New York, seventeen years ago, was

In 1830s New York City, David Ruggles publicly confronted slave catchers, hid the fugitive Frederick Douglass and published the first African American magazine. *David Ruggles, n.d., Amistad Research Center at Tulane University, New Orleans, Louisiana*

less a place of safety for a runaway than now," he wrote, "and all know how unsafe it now is, under the new fugitive slave law."

THE HARSH FUGITIVE SLAVE ACT, ADOPTED AS PART OF THE HISTORIC Compromise of 1850, terrified free blacks all over the North, and with good reason. A concession to the South, it gave new federal protections to slave catchers and, by extension, better cover to kidnappers posing as slave catchers.

Black communities reacted swiftly to the new law. In Pittsburgh, black hotel waiters fled en masse to Canada. One group of 300 went armed with pistols and bowie knives. A black church in Rochester, New York, reported that all but 2 of its 114 members crossed to Canada. Black congregations in Buffalo also abandoned their homes.

And in Lancaster County, Pennsylvania, where the vigilante "Gap Gang" had terrorized free blacks for years, the new law led indirectly to a battle in 1851 known as the Christiana Riot.

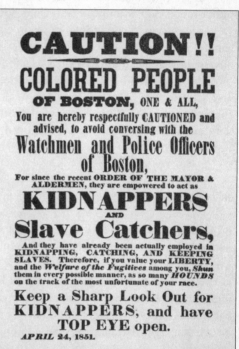

The passage of the Fugitive Slave Act of 1850 led to broadside warnings, like the one shown here, that even free blacks living in the North were not safe from being abducted into slavery. *Library of Congress, Rare Book and Special Collections Division*

The fight was sparked by the arrival in Christiana of a Maryland slave owner and a federal posse intent on retrieving four alleged runaway slaves. Free blacks in the area responded like minutemen, driving off the posse in a brief pitched battle that left the slave owner and three blacks dead.

The leader of the resistance was William Parker, an escaped slave who had been living in Pennsylvania for a decade, and had begun to fight back against the Gap Gang. In his memoir, Parker wrote about his area of southern Pennsylvania, "Kidnapping was so common . . . that we were kept in constant fear. We would hear of slaveholders or kidnappers every two or three weeks; sometimes a party of white men would break into a house and take a man away, no one knew where; again a whole family might be carried off. There was no power to protect them, nor prevent it."

Parker judged most whites in the area to be "negro-haters" who didn't much care whom the Gap Gang seized.

At least one of the federal posse in Christiana was a member of the gang. The leader of the posse, abolitionists later said, was "the notorious, lying, slave-catching Deputy Marshal Kline," from Philadelphia.

Ultimately almost 40 rebels were tried for treason in Philadelphia, and acquitted. The number of defendants made it the largest treason trial in U.S. history. The occurrence of armed black resistance shook the divided nation like no other event until John Brown's raid at Harpers Ferry in 1859.

IN FICTION, AND IN HISTORICAL MEMORY, THE MOST VIVID FUGITIVE SLAVE tableau is the scene in *Uncle Tom's Cabin* where the young Eliza, bearing her child in her arms, crosses the ice-choked Ohio River with slave catchers in hot pursuit. But that scene is mere melodrama compared to real-life incidents.

In Cincinnati in late January 1856, a Kentucky slave owner and federal agents cornered a group of fugitives, including a mother named Margaret Garner who had vowed never to let her children return to slavery. As the agents broke into their hiding place, Garner cut her young daughter's throat and was trying to kill two of her boys.

Despite protests, a federal magistrate ruled that Garner and her surviving children should be returned to their owner. The owner decided to sell them to the Deep South. On the journey, literally down the river into slavery, Garner's youngest child died along with two dozen other people in a boat accident. Garner eventually was sold in New Orleans.

Garner's gruesome story counterpoints the more common and more calculated manhunts conducted by kidnappers, who lured their victims into capture and often operated under the guise of law. Kidnappers might accuse their victims of petty crimes or enlist accomplices to testify, falsely, that they were escaped slaves.

The legal tricks employed by kidnappers had their roots in the original fugitive slave law of 1793, signed by George Washington. Intended

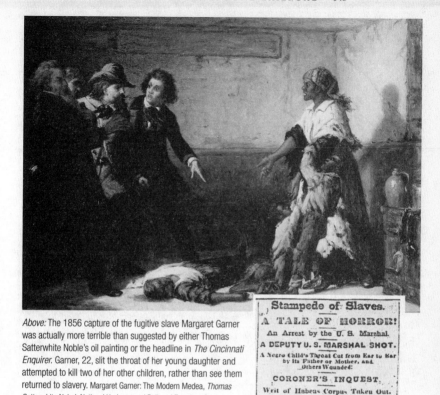

Above: The 1856 capture of the fugitive slave Margaret Garner was actually more terrible than suggested by either Thomas Satterwhite Noble's oil painting or the headline in *The Cincinnati Enquirer.* Garner, 22, slit the throat of her young daughter and attempted to kill two of her other children, rather than see them returned to slavery. Margaret Garner: The Modern Medea, *Thomas Satterwhite Nobel, National Underground Railroad Freedom Center*

Right: The Cincinnati Enquirer. *Used with permission*

Stampede of Slaves.

A TALE OF HORROR!

An Arrest by the U. S. Marshal.

A DEPUTY U. S. MARSHAL SHOT.

A Negro Child's Throat Cut from Ear to Ear by Its Father or Mother, and Others Wounded:

CORONER'S INQUEST,

Writ of Habeas Corpus Taken Out.

GREAT EXCITEMENT!

The city was thrown into much excitement yesterday morning by the information that a party of slaves, sixteen in all, had made a stampede from Kentucky to this side of the river.

to fill a void in the Constitution concerning the extradition of criminals, the law gave citizens the right to pursue fugitives, including escaped slaves, across state lines. Blacks accused of being runaways had almost no legal recourse.

By 1799, blacks in Philadelphia felt sufficiently threatened by kidnappings that they submitted a petition to Congress equating them with the African slave trade. Callous men, it said, "are employed in kidnapping those of our Brethren that are free" and "these poor, helpless victims like droves of cattle are seized, fettered and hurried into places provided for this horrid traffic, such as dark cellars and garrets, as is notorious at Northurst, Chester-town, Eastown and divers other places."

Philadelphia had a large free black community and one of the earliest abolition societies, of which Benjamin Franklin had once been president. Nevertheless, even the most prominent black people became targets of kidnappers. Richard Allen, who was born a slave in Philadelphia and returned a free man to establish the American Methodist Episcopal Church, was once accosted by a slave catcher who claimed him as a runaway. Allen was so well known that he was able to have the slave catcher arrested.

Few blacks were that fortunate. False seizure and outright abduction occurred with such frequency that some states, including Ohio, Pennsylvania, and New York, began to pass laws specifically aimed at preventing kidnapping. The federal fugitive slave law, however, remained intact.

Born a slave in Philadelphia, Richard Allen had bought his freedom and risen to prominence as a founder of the first independent black church in the United States when he successfully resisted a kidnapping that would have returned him to slavery. *Moorland-Spingarn Research Center, Howard University*

The conflict between the state and federal laws led to the most significant slavery case to be heard by the U.S. Supreme Court before the *Dred Scott* case.

In 1842, Justice Joseph Story of Massachusetts wrote that a Maryland slave catcher named Prigg had the right to retrieve a black woman and her two young children from Pennsylvania. The woman, Margaret Morgan, was only technically a slave. Her original owner had treated her as a free person, allowing her to marry a free black man and move to Pennsylvania, where at least one of their children was born. She was seized in 1837, when she had been living in York County, Pennsylvania, for five years.

Story, who was a professor of law at Harvard at the same time he served as a Supreme Court justice, had written another famous decision the year before, freeing the captives from the slave ship *Amistad*. Story wrote several decisions against the slave trade, but his belief in federal power led him to make a proslavery ruling in *Prigg v. Pennsylvania*. It undercut Northern states' ability to protect free blacks and laid the foundation for the Fugitive Slave Act of 1850.

William Lloyd Garrison called the decision "the additional ounce that breaks the camel's back," since it allowed the slaveholding South "to roam without molestation through the Northern states, 'seeking whom it may devour,' and dragging into its den the victims of its lust."

BECAUSE THE FUGITIVE SLAVE LAWS WERE SO SUSCEPTIBLE TO FRAUD, the legal distinction between free blacks and escaped slaves was often blurred. But the most notorious kidnappers, like the Cannon gang, didn't even bother with legal masks and still managed to carry on their marauding for years.

The Cannon gang may have begun its outright man-stealing soon after the United States shut down the foreign slave trade in 1808. The gang is first mentioned in a court record in 1811, when Cannon's first son-in-law was imprisoned for kidnapping. He escaped, only to be re-captured and hanged as a murderer.

United States Supreme Court Justice Joseph Story of Massachusetts earned a reputation as the nation's leading legal scholar and wrote two famous slavery decisions. One freed the *Amistad* captives, but the other, *Prigg v. Pennsylvania*, reinforced Southerners' rights to hunt down fugitive slaves. *Engraving from original full-length oil painting by Alonzo Chappel, 1862*

Patty Cannon was born about 1774, the daughter of an English immigrant. Her husband, Jesse Cannon, came from a prominent Sussex County, Delaware, family. Patty herself became locally famous as "the fascinating hostess" at the tavern owned by her daughter's second husband, Joe Johnson. "Tradition tells that Patty Cannon was fond of music, dancing and sensual pleasures," a Cannon family biographer later wrote. "As strong as a man, she was witty, black-eyed and the reputed brains and accomplice of a notorious kidnapping ring."

Given the tendency of law officers to ignore crimes against blacks, the gang must have operated brazenly to have attracted the attention it did. In 1816, as punishment for kidnapping, Jesse Cannon was rumored to have been sentenced to have his ears nailed to a pillory, and upon release to have his earlobes cut off.

If the sentence was carried out, it wasn't much of a deterrent. In late 1821, Jesse was again arrested for kidnapping, but this time, so was his entire family. The indictment named his wife (identified as "Martha," perhaps Patty's real name), their son Jesse Jr., their daughter, and her husband, Joe Johnson.

Apparently only Johnson was prosecuted. Found guilty in April 1822, he was sentenced to be whipped and, like his father-in-law, to have his ears nailed to a pillory, and then have his earlobes cut off. (The governor withdrew the latter part of the sentence.) Shortly after that, Jesse, the father, is believed to have died, leaving his wife and her son-in-law at the head of the gang.

It may have been at about that time that they decided to shift their hunt for victims north.

In the summer of 1825, according to the *African Observer* newspaper, black youths began to disappear from Philadelphia and its suburbs. At first no one saw a pattern. Ranging in age from eight to sixteen, the youths were thought to have drowned or to have run away. No runaways returned, however, and by the end of the summer, suspecting kidnappers, the black community finally persuaded the police to investigate. There were vague reports that some of the missing youths had been seen in Delaware. But, according to the *African Observer,* "the whole transaction remained a profound mystery."

Then, in January 1826, the mayor of Philadelphia, Joseph Watson, received letters from two plantation owners in Rocky Springs, Mississippi. A man named Ebenezer Johnson had shown up there weeks earlier trying to sell several youths. One of the plantation owners, John Hamilton, told the mayor he'd become suspicious of Johnson after sixteen-year-old Samuel Scomp secretly told him he'd been kidnapped from Philadelphia. As proof, Scomp removed his shirt to show Hamilton the scars from beatings he said he'd suffered on his journey south.

Hamilton summoned a magistrate, who demanded to see Johnson's ownership papers. Johnson produced a bill of sale, but at the same time implicated his brother Joe. It was Joe, Ebenezer said, who had bought the slaves for him on commission.

Now more suspicious than ever, the Mississippians let Ebenezer leave, supposedly to get better proof of ownership. But Hamilton kept the young slaves and, while Johnson was gone, he and a neighbor questioned them more closely. They took a sworn statement from Scomp and included it in their letter to Mayor Watson, urging him to publish the details and start an investigation. Watson did both, and later took his own deposition from Scomp.

Scomp said he'd never been a slave, but rather an apprentice who'd run away from his New Jersey master to find work in Philadelphia. One morning on the Market Street wharf, "in watermelon and peach time," a mulatto man offered him a quarter to help unload watermelons. The man, who said his name was Smith, led him to a small sloop.

On board, a white man greeted them, and then invited them into a cabin below for a drink. The white man followed them down, and immediately tied Scomp and Smith by the hands, telling Smith that Scomp was an escaped slave from Maryland and threatening to cut Scomp's throat if he protested.

The white man let Smith go with a warning that he never wanted to see him again. The white man's name, Scomp remembered, was Joseph Johnson, and he soon learned that Smith was his accomplice. Locked in the hold of the sloop, Scomp met two other boys who said Smith had taken them the night before. Later that same day, Smith brought in two more boys, one of them a chimney sweep. The sloop, with five boys to sell, set sail that night.

A week later by Scomp's reckoning they arrived at Johnson's house somewhere in Maryland or Delaware. Always bound by ropes or irons, they were transferred to what Scomp understood to be Jesse Cannon Jr.'s house and then to Patty Cannon's. Along the way they were joined by Ebenezer Johnson and another kidnap victim, a woman.

All six captives were soon back on a boat, headed south. Apparently they landed somewhere in Alabama, where Johnson owned property and where Scomp said they began a 600-mile trek that would end in Mississippi.

Johnson rode in a light carriage with his wife, while the smaller boys drove a supply wagon. The bigger boys walked most of the way, barefoot. One boy, thought to be about ten, was sold in Tuscaloosa for $400.

When the boys complained of sore feet and frostbite, they were beaten. Once Scomp, realizing they were passing through Choctaw Indian territory, tried to escape. But an Indian he met returned him to Johnson, who flogged him with a saw blade and hickory sticks. The beating left the scars Scomp showed Hamilton.

The young chimney sweep, who had the same name as his captor, Joe Johnson, suffered the most. Lame and frostbitten, he began to fall frequently, prompting more beatings. Scomp said he heard Ebenezer's wife say it did her good to see him beat the boys. Little Joe Johnson died just before the party reached Rocky Springs, and rescue.

Although Hamilton might easily have kept them all, the plantation owner promised to send the survivors home. Unlike the gang's usual backwoods customers, Hamilton was a wealthy planter who disapproved of illegal slave dealing, perhaps because it threatened the institution of slavery itself.

In Philadelphia, Mayor Watson obtained indictments against the Johnson brothers and two accomplices. But in Mississippi, Ebenezer Johnson sued Hamilton for the return of his property, challenging him to prove the captives were stolen. That burden rebounded to Philadelphia, where witnesses were hard to find. As Watson later wrote, "the great difficulty is to procure even the written testimony of white people, to establish the identity of black children, more particularly, if they have been out of sight a year or two." If the kidnap victims were street waifs, no white might recognize them. If the victims were very young, their chances of being identified diminished even further because they might grow so much during captivity.

Ultimately, at least Samuel Scomp and another of the originally kidnapped boys, who was said to be ten, got back to Philadelphia. The publicity their case generated brought reports about the gang's past activity.

But Watson's investigation lagged. "I regret to say that these attempts at kidnapping, notwithstanding the vigilance of the police, are frequently made, and all too often with success," Watson admitted in corresponding with Hamilton.

Then, in December 1826, Watson received another letter from Mississippi, this one from Natchez, sent by former governor David Holmes and a friend. It said new slaves in the neighborhood were claiming to have been kidnapped from Philadelphia by Joseph and Ebenezer Johnson. Enclosed was a statement from one of the victims, a boy named Peter Hook.

Hook's account mirrored Scomp's, although it described kidnapping on a larger scale.

Hook said he was born in Philadelphia and in June 1825 had been lured aboard Joe Johnson's boat by a black man. He'd soon found himself chained in the hold with four other boys. Their next stop was Johnson's tavern, where they were chained to the floor of an attic. Two girls were prisoners elsewhere in the attic. The number of victims increased as six more boys and a young man were added. Hook said the young man, named Henry, told him he had been kidnapped on the way to visit his mother.

All 14 were imprisoned in the attic for what Hook judged to be six months. Joe Johnson then took them south, in what appears to have been a true coffle. Johnson marched the bigger boys chained in pairs, and usually he stuck to secondary roads and camped at night. He whipped any who dared to say they were free. After traveling a month, he sold the lot to a pair of slave traders in North Carolina.

The new owners later acquired 4 stolen slaves and 2 more kidnapped Philadelphians from other sellers. At one point a planter bought 10 of the boys, then demanded his money back when they convinced him that they were from the North. Eventually most were dispensed in the Natchez area. Hook said that he was sold with 3 other boys for $450 apiece.

The report from Natchez roused Mayor Watson again. He got more arrest warrants and, in February 1827, published a proclamation offering a $500 reward for "the apprehension and prosecution to conviction of any person concerned in the forcible abduction of free colored persons from the city of Philadelphia." He also sent the city's top constable to the South to gather evidence and to retrieve whatever kidnap victims he could. Neither effort yielded much success. By the summer of 1828, only 10 of the three dozen kidnap victims eventually identified had been returned.

Only two gang members were arrested, both accomplices who acted as beards for the business. One, the owner of an oyster cellar who said Joe Johnson paid him $25 per boy, died awaiting trial. The other was the man who had lured both Scomp and Hook aboard Johnson's boat. His real name was John Purnell. Convicted on just two counts of kidnapping, Purnell was fined $4,000 and sentenced to 42 years in jail.

Both of the men arrested were black; no white was charged.

It appeared that the Cannon gang had finally been broken up, although rumor and legend began to supplant already-elusive fact.

Both Johnson brothers were thought to have fled south to start their own plantations with their kidnapping loot. Both Cannon children were thought to have left the area even before the Philadelphia kidnappings came to light. Since Jesse Cannon Sr. was already dead, that left the matriarch.

Presumed to be about sixty, Patty Cannon apparently had felt secure enough to stay in the area, reportedly entertaining friends with stories and earning money as a fortune-teller. In April 1829, she was living just over the state line in Maryland when the skeletons were discovered on her former farm.

Within days, a Sussex County grand jury indicted her for four mur-

2d lieutenant L. F. Carter, of the 7th infantry, to be assistant commissary of subsistence, 12th February, 1829

TRANSFERS.

Willoughby Morgan, lieut. col. of the 5th infantry, transferred to the 3d infantry.

Enos Cutler, lieut. col. of the 3d infantry, transferred to the 5th infantry.

Waddy V. Cobbs, captain of the 1st infantry, transferred to the 2d infantry.

Thomas J. Beall, captain of the 2d infantry, transferred to the 1st infantry.

Joseph P. Taylor, captain of the 3d artillery, transferred to the 2d artillery.

Elijah Lyon, captain of the 2d artillery, transferred to the 3d artillery.

☞ Since the date of his brevet nomination in May, lieut. col. Lawrence has received the promotion of full colonel of the 5th regiment of infantry; and first lieut. Allen, of the 4th infantry, has been promoted to the rank of captain in his regiment, since the date of his nomination for brevet promotion.

ORDER—NO. 10.

ADJUTANT GENERAL'S OFFICE,
Washington, 21st March, 1829.

The officers whose promotions, appointments, and transfers, are promulgated in the above order of the secretary of war, and herewith announced to the army, will report for duty, accordingly. Regimental officers will report to their respective colonels.

By order of major general Macomb.
R. JONES, adjutant general.

A HORRIBLE DEVELOPEMENT.

From the Delaware Gazette of April 17.

The murders in Sussex—We stated briefly in our paper of Friday last, some circumstances respecting a most diabolical course of conduct which, for some years past, has been carried on in Sussex county, in this state, the evidences of which have just been brought to light; and promised, in our next number, to give further particulars.

From our correspondent's account we gather the following particulars: About ten days previous to his writing, a tenant, who lives on the farm where Patty Cannon and her son-in-law, the celebrated Joseph Johnson, negro trader, lived for many years, in Northwest Fork Hundred, near the Maryland line, was ploughing in the field, in a place generally covered with water, and where a heap of brush has been laying for years, when his horse sunk in a grave and on digging, he found a blue painted chest, about three feet long, and in it were found the bones of a man. The news flew like wild fire, and people from many miles around visited the place; among whom it was universally agreed that a negro trader from Georgia, named Bell or Miller, or perhaps both, had been murdered, by Johnson and his gang, about 10 or 12 years ago, and that the bones now discovered were those of one of them: as the man or men had been missed about that time, and the horse on which one of them rode was found at Patty Cannon's, who laid claim to the animal, until a person from Maryland, who had lent the horse, came forward and claimed his property; and she alleged, at the time, that Bell or Miller had sailed a short time previous, with a cargo of negroes for the south. Since that time he has not been heard of, and it is said that a few days before he was missed, he was heard to say that he had with him fifteen thousand dollars, with which he purposed to purchase negroes The supposition now is that the knowledge of his having this money in his possession, formed the inducement to take his life, and that to conceal the body it had been deposited in the place where the bones have been found.

The excitement produced by this discovery, as may naturally be supposed, was very great in the neighborhood, and on the second instant, one of Johnson's gang, named Cyrus James, who has resided in Maryland, was caught in this state, and brought before a justice of the peace at Seaford, and on examination stated that Joseph Johnson, Ebenezer F. Johnson, and old Patty Cannon,

had shot the man while at supper in her house, and that he saw them all engaged in carrying him in the chest and burying him; and stated, moreover, that many others also had been killed, and that he could show where they had been buried. The officers and citizens accordingly accompanied him to the places which he pointed out, and made the necessary search. In one place, a garden, they dug and found the bones of a young child, the mother of which, he stated, was a negro woman belonging to Patty Cannon, which, being a mullatto, she had killed for the reason that she supposed its father to be one of her own family. Another place a few feet distant, was then pointed out, when upon digging a few feet, two oak boxes were found, each of which contained human bones. Those in one of them had been those of a person about seven years of age, which James said he saw Patty Cannon knock in the head with a billet of wood, and the other contained those of one whom he said they considered bad property; by which, it is supposed was meant, that he was free. As there was at the time much stir about the children, and there was no convenient opportunity to send them away, they were murdered to prevent discovery. On examining the scull bone of the largest child, it was discovered to have been broken as described by James.

This fellow, James, having been bound to her at the age of seven years, and is said to have done much mischief in his time for her and Johnson.

Another witness by the name of Butler, has already been secured; and it is thought that some others will be brought forward who are acquainted with the bloody deeds of Patty and Joe. This woman is now between 60 and 70 years of age, and looks more like a man than a woman; but old as she is, she is believed to be as heedless and heartless as the most abandoned wretch that breathes.

As stated by us on Friday last, Patty Cannon had been lodged in the jail at Georgetown; James and Butler were also placed there at the same time; and it is highly probable that ere this the trial has taken place, and the result of it will soon be known.

James stated that he had not shown all the places where murdered bodies had been buried, and at the time of writing, our correspondent informs us the people were still digging.

Joe Johnson, who is said to be residing, at this time, in Alabama, is stated to have been seen in this state in December or January last; and the probability is that his business here was to do something at his old business of kidnapping. He was convicted of this crime some years since at Georgetown, and suffered the punishment of the lash and the pillory, on account of it. He is a man of some celebrity, having, for many years, carried on the traffic of stealing and selling negroes, in which he was aided and instructed by the old had, Patty Cannon, whose daughter he married, after she had lost a former husband on the gallows.

He continued to reside near his tutoress until within a few years, when a reward of $500 was offered by Mr. Watson, mayor of Philadelphia, when having obtained information of the fact before any others in his neighborhood, he suddenly decamped, and has since been very cautious in suffering himself to be seen in that part of the country.

The former husband of Joe's wife was hung for the murder of a negro trader, the plan for which is said to have been arranged at her mother's house.

From the circumstances which have already taken place, it would appear probable that such developements may be expected to take place as will present the wretched actors in the scenes of blood, which have taken place on the border of our state in Sussex county, as successful rivals in depravity of the infamous Burke, whose bloody deeds and recent execution in Scotland, have occupied so large a portion of the public prints.

[The neighborhood in which these terrible events occurred, the borders of Delaware and Maryland, has long been famous for negro stealing and negro trading—and "Patty Cannon" and "Joe Johnson" are familiar names, to us. The people thereabouts were exceedingly ignorant and desperately wicked—but we hope that some improvement has latterly taken place.]

ders. Her son-in-law Joe and his brother Ebenezer were indicted, too, and a trial was scheduled for October, assuming they could be caught. Only Patty Cannon was. According to one account, Delaware authorities nabbed her after she was tricked into crossing the state line.

A full trial would have helped prove Cannon's true role in the gang. But she died in jail in early May, amid rumors that she'd poisoned herself. An early popular account of her life said that as she lay dying, she admitted to killing 11 people with her own hands, and to poisoning her husband.

Published in 1841, *The Narrative and Confessions of Lucretia P. Cannon* was clearly dramatized, even giving her a new, more menacing, name. The account was factual enough, though, to list the murders mentioned in the Sussex County indictment. The first murder was of an infant girl killed in April 1822. In its formal language, the indictment noted, "Patty Cannon with both her hands about the neck of the said infant . . . did choke and strangle, of which said choking and strangling the said female child . . . then and there instantly died." Cannon, the Johnson brothers, and another gang member were also accused of killing a boy the same day.

The indictment was based partially on the testimony of Cyrus James, a onetime gang member. According to a Baltimore newspaper, James said one of the skeletons found on Cannon's farm was that of a mulatto child fathered by a family member. If so, the victim could have been Cannon's grandchild. The other two murders in the indictment were of a man killed in October 1820 and a black boy killed in June 1824. Patty and Joe were accused of clubbing each to death.

Even if none of the victims had been kidnapped, their remains were evidence of the gang's ruthlessness. Cannon was buried in a pauper's grave. Her body was later exhumed, and her skull studied by phrenologists. Later the skull was passed on to the public library in Dover, Delaware.

Cannon became the central figure in *The Entailed Hat*, a famous historical novel written by celebrity journalist George Alfred Townsend. The original manuscript contained so much thinly veiled fact that Townsend edited it before publication to avoid offending prominent families still living in the area.

THE DEMISE OF THE CANNON GANG DID NOT END KIDNAPPING IN Philadelphia. George V. Alberti operated in the city even longer than the Cannon gang and was even more cunning. Alberti, a slave catcher and city constable, routinely took his victims to court and exploited weak-nesses in the fugitive slave law.

As early as 1815, the Pennsylvania Abolition Society accused Alberti and an accomplice of seizing a free black, and by the 1830s, the society was referring to him as a repeat offender. The abolitionist newspaper the *Liberator*, out of Boston, reported that Alberti was wanted in Balti-more for trying to sell a pair of free black Philadelphians.

In 1850, Alberti became the central figure in one of the first cases to arise from the new fugitive slave law. He and two accomplices had seized a black man named Adam Gibson, accusing him of stealing chick-ens. They'd led Gibson at gunpoint to the office of the city's newly ap-pointed fugitive slave commissioner and said he was an escaped slave from Maryland named Emory Rice.

Under the new law, federal commissioners received a $10 fee for each fugitive they returned, compared to $5 for each person they freed. The Philadelphia commissioner decided to detain Gibson and hold a hearing. Gibson got a lawyer and found two black friends to testify to his identity. They were countered by a witness Alberti produced, a man himself under indictment for kidnapping.

The commissioner sided with Alberti and authorized him to take Gibson to Maryland. The case would have ended there, except that in Maryland Alberti tried to deliver Gibson to an apparently honest slave owner. Whoever Gibson might be, the slave owner told Alberti, he was not Emory Rice.

The fraud resulted in Alberti's arrest for kidnapping, but this crime did not end his career. That career came to a close in March 1851, when he was convicted in a case involving an escaped Maryland slave and her freeborn child. At his trial, Alberti claimed he took the child only be-cause the mother refused to leave him behind. The sentencing judge condemned Alberti and an accomplice in extreme language that seemed to be directed at a nation divided over slavery.

"Think for a moment how great the magnitude of stealing an infant, born in a free state, and binding it in the galling chains of slavery for a little money . . . ," the judge declared. "This case is without parallel in atrocity, and is the most aggravated, legally, of any of its kind that has been presented to an American court of justice."

The rhetoric hardly matched Alberti's punishment. He was fined $1,000 and ordered to do ten years hard labor. If the judge thought the aged Alberti would die before he served his time, he was wrong. Al-berti's case became an issue in that year's gubernatorial election. The winner, Democrat William Bigler, pardoned him.

Alberti never thought he'd done anything wrong. In an 1859 interview with the abolitionist *National Anti-Slavery Standard*, in which he said that he'd captured more than 100 blacks, Alberti insisted that the Bible justified slavery. "The slaveholder has as good a right to his niggers as he has to his horses; and if they run away, as a good citizen I have a right to catch them," Alberti said.

The interview must have taken place on a Saturday, because when Alberti bragged, "I would catch a nigger on Monday, if I had the chance," the reporter asked, "Why not tomorrow?"

"Because tomorrow is Sunday," Alberti responded. "I believe it would be a sin for me to do it on Sunday."

"Amalgamationists, dupes, fanatics, foreign agents, and incendiaries"—that's how the North viewed its radical abolitionists.

Eight

HATED HEROES

T HE START OF THE CIVIL WAR AS A POLITICAL WAR OVER SLAVERY can be linked to two events in 1831.

In Boston on January 1, William Lloyd Garrison began publishing the *Liberator*, the newspaper that would become the leading organ of the radical abolitionist movement.

And in Southampton County, Virginia, in August, rebel slaves led by Nat Turner killed nearly 60 whites.

Garrison's newspaper and Turner's rebellion posed double threats to the entire nation: freedom for slaves, particularly if it came suddenly, would mean social and economic chaos.

In 1831, the only kind of abolitionism that had popular support was that promoted by the American Colonization Society, which had chapters in the North and the South. The society's goal was to send freed blacks to Africa. Few white people in America, no matter how strongly they felt about slavery, thought that blacks and whites could or should ever coexist in the same society.

Radical abolitionism created a backlash, and the backlash created martyrs. The events described here show how violent that backlash was in the North, and how abolitionism itself turned violent. In 1831, Prudence Crandall, Elijah Lovejoy, and John Brown were about to be swept up in abolitionist fervor.

That year, Crandall, aged twenty-eight, opened a school in Canterbury, Connecticut, to which she would soon welcome black girls and, by doing so, invite its destruction.

Lovejoy, twenty-nine, was a schoolteacher from Maine, soon to be-come a minister and the editor of an abolitionist newspaper. He would die at the hands of an antiabolition mob in Alton, in the free state of Illinois.

Brown, thirty-one, from Connecticut, was running a tannery in New Richmond, Pennsylvania. The sensational news of Lovejoy's murder would affect him profoundly, and Brown would anoint himself slavery's avenger. By attacking a federal arsenal, he was to make himself a white Nat Turner, and meet the same fate.

Connecticut's Canterbury Tale

PRUDENCE CRANDALL'S SCHOOL IN EASTERN CONNECTICUT HAD OPER-ated less than a year when Sarah Harris, a young black woman, asked the young schoolteacher for permission to attend classes. The request sent Crandall, a Quaker turned Baptist, to her Bible, which fell open to a pas-sage from Ecclesiastes.

"So I returned and considered all the oppressions that are done

Prudence Crandall wanted to educate young black women at her school in rural Connecticut, and though she ex-pected resistance, the violence she encountered was life-threatening, both to Crandall and to her students, like Sarah Harris, *right*, shown here in later life. *Prudence Crandall portrait, Carl Henry, 1981 painting from original commis-sioned by Crandall supporters in 1834. Both courtesy of The Prudence Crandall Museum*

under the sun: and behold the tears of such as were oppressed, and they had no comforter; and on the side of their oppressors there was power; but they had no comforter," she read.

When Crandall agreed to admit Harris, community reaction was quick. The school will go under, a minister's wife warned the young schoolteacher. "It might sink then," Crandall replied, "for I should not turn her out."

As white parents began to withdraw their daughters, Crandall sought advice from William Lloyd Garrison about "changing white scholars for colored ones," and she traveled to Boston, New York, and Providence, seeking students and supporters. The battle lines were already forming when she returned in early 1833, dismissed her remaining white students, and, on March 2, ran an ad in the *Liberator* announcing that her school would reopen "for the reception of young ladies and little misses of color."

The ad listed 15 sponsors, eight white and seven black, all prominent or destined to become prominent in the new abolitionist movement.

The white men included Garrison; Unitarian minister Samuel May; Simeon Jocelyn, also a minister; and Arthur Tappan, a textile merchant. Tappan and his brother Lewis were two of the few rich New Yorkers who poured their wealth into abolitionist causes.

In Canterbury, nearly everyone opposed Crandall and her belief that education would prove blacks the equal of whites.

Andrew Harris, a doctor who lived nearby, refused to treat her black students. A week after the *Liberator* ad appeared, gubernatorial hopeful Andrew Judson, also a close neighbor and, like Harris, a former trustee of Crandall's school, spoke at a hastily called town meeting. No school for "nigger girls" would ever stand across the street from his house, he reportedly vowed, promising that if black students did show up he would use a colonial law to have them arrested as paupers.

When Samuel May, the Unitarian minister, and another abolitionist asked to speak, Judson shouted them down. The two abolitionists were confronted with "fists doubled in their faces" and driven from the church where the meeting was held.

Before the meeting Crandall had offered to move her school to the outskirts of Canterbury. After the meeting, she determined to keep it where it was.

As attempts to crush the school moved through the next year and a half from town meetings to court trials to the appeals court, Crandall and her students increasingly became targets of community anger. Local merchants would not do business with the school, and the stage driver refused to transport its students. Boys threw manure into the school's well; neighbors refused requests for pails of fresh water. Rotten eggs and rocks were thrown at the school building—Crandall kept one of the rocks on her mantel—and its students were followed through the streets, hooted at and harassed.

In a memoir written years later, Samuel May described Crandall and her students as holding out against the town "like the besieged in the immortal Fort Sumter," and Crandall herself as "animated by the spirit of a martyr." In mid-April of 1833, after the first

PRUDENCE CRANDALL,
PRINCIPAL OF THE CANTERBURY, (CONN.) FEMALE
BOARDING SCHOOL.
RETURNS her most sincere thanks to those who have patronized her School, and would give information that on the first Monday of April next, her School will be opened for the reception of young Ladies and little Misses of color. The branches taught are as follows:— Reading, Writing, Arithmetic, English Grammar, Geography, History, Natural and Moral Philosophy, Chemistry, Astronomy, Drawing and Painting, Music on the Piano, together with the French language.
☞ The terms, including board, washing, and tuition, are $25 per quarter, one half paid in advance.
☞ Books and Stationary will be furnished on the most reasonable terms.
For information respecting the School, reference may be made to the following gentlemen, viz:—
ARTHUR TAPPAN, Esq.
Rev. PETER WILLIAMS,
Rev. THEODORE RAYMOND
Rev. THEODORE WRIGHT, } N. YORK CITY.
Rev. SAMUEL C. CORNISH,
Rev. GEORGE BOURNE,
Rev. Mr. HAYBORN,
Mr. JAMES FORTEN, } PHILADELPHIA.
Mr. JOSEPH CASSEY,
Rev. S. J. MAY,—BROOKLYN, CT.
Rev. Mr. BEMAN,—MIDDLETOWN, CT.
Rev. S. S. JOCELYN,—NEW-HAVEN, CT.
Wm. LLOYD GARRISON } BOSTON, MASS.
ARNOLD BUFFUM,
GEORGE BENSON,—PROVIDENCE, R. I.

Prudence Crandall's newspaper announcement that her Connecticut school would accept "young ladies and little misses of color" listed prominent black and white supporters, including the radical abolitionist William Lloyd Garrison. Vermont Chronicle, *Windsor, Vermont, March 15, 1833. Courtesy of The Prudence Crandall Museum*

of her new students had arrived, Crandall wrote to Simeon Jocelyn, "In the midst of this affliction, I am as happy as any moment in my life."

NORTHERN HOSTILITY TO BLACK EDUCATION WAS NOT LIMITED TO CONnecticut. One of Crandall's students transferred to the integrated Noyes Academy in Canaan, New Hampshire, which opened in March 1835.

That summer, the Canaanites voted to shut down the school. A demolition crew hitched a long train of oxen to the academy and dragged it off its foundation. According to one account, the students were still inside.

Earlier, in New Haven, Connecticut, in September 1831, city residents felt the tremors of Nat Turner's rebellion when they voted 700–4 against allowing a school for young black men to open near Yale. One of the rationales was that education would do blacks more harm than good. "What benefit can it be to a waiter or coachman to read Horace, or be a profound mathematician?" read a local editorial.

In May 1833, the Connecticut legislature passed the "Black Law," making it illegal for out-of-state students of color to attend a school without local permission. Lawmakers called in a Hartford phrenologist, an expert in the then-credible "science" of determining character from the shape of a person's skull. The phrenologist testified that Negroes could not be educated beyond a certain level and could never be fit citizens. Although the committee report that backed the law decried the "horrid traffic" in human slavery and admitted a need to help "the unhappy class of beings, whose race has been degraded by unjust bondage," it concluded: "We are under no obligations, moral or political, to incur the incalculable evils of bringing into our own state colored immigrants from abroad."

Canterbury's citizens rang church bells, fired guns, and lit bonfires to celebrate the new law. A month later, on June 27, 1833, authorities arrested Crandall and her younger sister Almira, who had joined her as a teacher, for breaking the law.

While Almira, who was not yet twenty-one, was released as a minor,

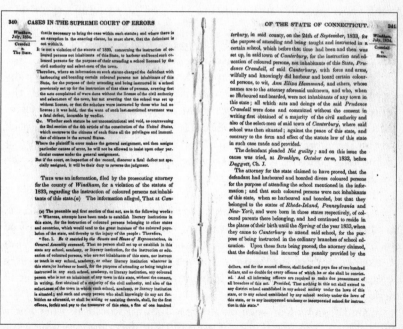

Connecticut's Black Law, directed against Prudence Crandall's school, was footnoted in the July 1834 appeal of her arrest. Two months later, a mob attacked the school, forcing it to close. Crandall v. The State of Connecticut 10 Conn. 339 (1834), Courtesy of The Prudence Crandall Museum

Crandall refused to let her supporters post bail. Samuel May wrote in his memoir that he gave her one last chance. "Oh no," she told him, "I am only afraid they will not put me in jail."

Crandall spent only one night locked up, but she had put her enemies on the defensive. Respectable white women did not go to jail. Townspeople complained bitterly that abolitionists spread the lie that Crandall had been placed in the cell that a notorious wife strangler had recently occupied. Later, Crandall explained that she'd been put in a room that the condemned man had stopped in on his way to being hanged. "I wish to say that the jailer was very polite," Crandall wrote, adding that a woman friend had been allowed to stay the night with her.

Over the next year, the hostilities continued, along with the court actions.

IN HINDSIGHT, TESTIMONY AT CRANDALL'S FIRST TRIAL IN AUGUST seems almost comical. Her students gave evasive answers, and school visitors called as witnesses said they couldn't recall whether they'd seen Crandall actually teaching. One finally testified that she'd seen Crandall giving geography and arithmetic lessons. The jury couldn't agree on a verdict.

The hung jury led to a second trial at which Crandall was found guilty, but not sentenced because her lawyers appealed.

In both trials and in the appeal, however, the testimony was less important than the lawyers' arguments and the judges' rulings. If the Canterbury school was an experiment of national significance, Crandall's arrest was a national test case. Her lawyers challenged the Black Law on the ground that it violated the clause in the Constitution that said no state could deny citizens of other states the rights it gave its own citizens.

The question was, Were black people citizens?

Arthur Tappan, the New York merchant, paid for Crandall's defense. Her lead lawyer was William W. Ellsworth, a congressman soon to be elected governor of Connecticut. Ellsworth was married to the daughter of lexicographer Noah Webster, and his father was Oliver Ellsworth, a delegate to the Constitutional Convention, and an early chief justice of the U.S. Supreme Court.

Crandall's chief prosecutor, Andrew Judson, would also become a congressman. A former legislator and a pillar of the community, he was a director of a county bank and an insurance company. The chief judge in the first trial sat on the legislative committee that had drafted the Black

Law, and he had banking ties to Judson. The chief judge in the second trial, David Daggett, as mayor of New Haven, had opposed the black school there, and was a vice president of the Hartford chapter of the American Colonization Society.

The arguments previewed those in the U.S. Supreme Court's monumental *Dred Scott* decision, still nearly a quarter century away.

Ellsworth said that blacks must be considered full citizens under the Constitution because they had fought in the Continental Army and received war pensions.

Crandall prosecutor Andrew Judson didn't want to see blacks and whites educated together, and predicted that if black people were judged to be full citizens, the country would collapse and "be given to the African race!"
Courtesy of The Prudence Crandall Museum

Judson responded with a catch-22 argument: If blacks couldn't vote—Connecticut's state constitution passed in 1818 specifically denied them the vote—then it followed that they could not be considered full citizens.

But the rhetoric reached its peak during the appeal of the case in Hartford in July 1834.

Only Southern slave states had laws as "obnoxious" as the Black Law, Ellsworth argued. "It rivets the chains of grinding bondage and makes our State an ally in the unholy cause of slavery itself." He warned that slavery threatened the nation, calling it "a volcano, the fires of which cannot be quenched, nor its ravages controlled."

Judson, too, predicted cataclysm if his opponent were to win. He said, "The consequences will inevitably destroy the government itself, and this American nation—this nation of white men—may be taken from us and given to the African race!" In closing he declared, "It rests with the Court to say whether the country shall be preserved or lost."

The appeals court ruling was anticlimactic, dismissing the case on technicalities. But because of Judge Daggett's ruling in the second trial, the case would prove an important precedent. Daggett told the jury that the case raised "the great question" of whether blacks were citizens under the U.S. Constitution, and he then answered the question for them: "To my mind, it would be a perversion of terms to say that slaves, free blacks or Indians were citizens, as the term is used in the Constitution. God forbid that I should add to the degradation of this race of men, but I am bound by my duty to say they are not citizens."

In support of his opinion, Daggett quoted from Ellsworth's father-in-law's famous dictionary, saying that Webster, "one of the most learned men of this or any country," defined "citizen"—as the term was used in the United States—as someone who could vote and own property.

In March 1857, U.S. Supreme Court Justice Roger Brooke Taney of the slave state of Maryland cited Daggett's opinion when he wrote the decisive opinion in *Dred Scott*, finding that black people could not be citizens, and that states had the right to decide whether to allow slavery. Taney pointed to Daggett's ruling in *Prudence Crandall vs. the State of Connecticut* as noteworthy because of Connecticut's reputation as a liberal state.

A colonizationist who had freed his own slaves, Taney hoped that his decision would end the conflict between North and South. Instead, it fueled the blaze. Debates over his ruling dominated the 1860 presidential campaign that ended with Abraham Lincoln's election. In that election, liberal Connecticut gave Lincoln one of his narrowest victories in New England.

1839.]   *Anti-Slavery Almanac.*   15

COLORED SCHOOLS BROKEN UP, IN THE FREE STATES.
When schools have been established for colored scholars, the law-makers and the mob have combined to destroy them;—as at Canterbury, Ct., at Canaan, N. H., ... 10, 1835, at Zanesville and Brown Co., Ohio, in 1836.

America in the 1830s was filled with proslavery mob activity, and schools that accepted black students—like Prudence Crandall's Canterbury school—were often targets of mob violence. Anti-Slavery Almanac, 1839. *Courtesy of The Prudence Crandall Museum*

DURING THE COURT CASES, CRANDALL HELD ON TO HER SCHOOL. CER-tainly, her students gave her strength. After all was lost, Crandall said of them, "It is my opinion that the colored scholars under my care made as good, if not better progress than the same number of whites taken from the same position in life."

But it didn't matter. On the night of September 9, 1834, Crandall, her husband, and some of her students were inside the Canterbury schoolhouse when they heard loud voices outside and then banging on the doors. Glass was shattered and windows were ripped from their frames. Men invaded the first floor of the school and started overturning furniture.

Accounts of what happened next vary. The attackers may have tried to set the building on fire. One student was said to be so frightened that she coughed up a pint of blood. The damage was bad enough that a friend of the schoolteacher's said it was foolish to repair the school only to have it destroyed again.

Crandall gave up. She sent her students home, put the school build-ing up for sale, and retreated to her father's farm outside the town cen-ter. Within the year, she'd left Connecticut, following in the path of her father, who, threatened for supporting her and her school, had already moved west. He was seeking, it was said, a place more peaceful than Connecticut.

She finally settled in Elk Falls, Kansas. A few years before she died in 1890, Crandall accepted a pension from the people of Connecticut. "I feel that they do owe me a just debt for all my property they destroyed, and I should like them to pay just a little of it," she said.

Minister Lovejoy

ELIJAH P. LOVEJOY'S ABOLITIONISM WAS BORN IN VIOLENCE AND ENDED in violence.

Earlier in his career, the schoolteacher and minister from Maine had been more focused on the evils of blasphemy and drinking than on American bondage. Educated at Colby College and Princeton, Lovejoy believed that slavery should and would end, someday. He was not, he told readers of the St. Louis, Missouri, newspaper he edited, an "imme-diatist," and definitely not an abolitionist.

In April 1836, however, the arrest and horrific execution of a free black man changed the course of Lovejoy's life.

Francis McIntosh, a porter on a ship docked in St. Louis, witnessed a fight between two white men on the city's waterfront. When one of the brawlers ran, police called out to McIntosh to stop him. McIntosh stepped aside, however, not wanting to get involved in a fight between whites.

He was arrested immediately. Asking about his punishment, McIntosh was told that he faced a beating and life imprisonment. According to a later account, the officers told him jokingly that he would be hanged. McIntosh had had a drink or two before leaving his ship, and he panicked. He lunged at the policemen with a pocketknife, killing one and wounding the other. Then he ran, eluding an angry crowd, but only briefly.

He was dragged at gunpoint to the city jail. Word that a "nigger" had killed a policeman spread quickly, and a white-hot crowd estimated at several thousand soon swirled outside the jail, howling, "Burn him! Burn him! Burn him!"

The sheriff fled, leaving McIntosh alone and locked in a cell. The mob broke in, carried McIntosh to a locust tree on the commons, and tied him to the tree with a chain. Rails, planking, and wood shavings were piled around his legs. Some of the wood was wet, chosen so it would not burn too quickly.

McIntosh prayed and sang hymns as he slowly burned to death. An elderly black man was given 75 cents to keep the fire burning through the night.

At noon the next day, Minister Lovejoy went to the scene.

"Awful Murder and Savage Barbarity," shouted the May 5, 1836, headline in Lovejoy's newspaper, the *Observer.* Lovejoy described McIntosh's crime and death with a ferocity and detail that shocked St. Louis. "We stood and gazed for a moment or two upon the blackened and mutilated trunk—for that was all which remained—of McIntosh before us, and as we turned away, in bitterness of heart, we prayed that we might not live."

Lovejoy did not try to exonerate McIntosh, but he decried the mob violence that had kept a free black man from being protected by the law of the land.

The judge overseeing the investigation had a different view. Francis McIntosh had been murdered by people gripped by a "mysterious metaphysical and almost electrical phrenzy," declared the judge, who had the extraordinary name of Luke Lawless. Thus the event was beyond the jurisdiction of human law. Lawless, instead, blamed the death of McIntosh on the innate violence of black men and inflammatory publications like the *Observer*. No one was charged.

But Lovejoy had been converted. In a letter to his mother, he later said the cry of the oppressed had entered his soul, "so that while I live I cannot hold my peace."

The editor began his campaign, calling for the emancipation of all enslaved people, and despite growing public outrage, he would not stop.

At the confluence of three major rivers, St. Louis was a booming frontier town. The Missouri Compromise of 1820 had provided for the admission of Missouri to the Union as a slave state. During Lovejoy's time, Missouri had a slave population of well over 25,000. Slaves were bought and sold on the streets of St. Louis.

Even before McIntosh's murder, the *Observer*'s owners had asked Lovejoy to stop his antislavery commentary. The minister refused to do so. After the murder, and after several attacks on his office and his home, Lovejoy, at the owners' urging, moved his family and the newspaper across the Mississippi River to Alton, in the free state of Illinois. The minister and his wife and baby arrived safely, but while the *Observer*'s press was stored at the dock, a small group crossed the river from St. Louis and dumped it into the river.

Alton citizens, who had welcomed the newspaper as a prestigious addition to their town, were horrified, and a former sea captain from Massachusetts spearheaded the effort to replace the press.

It seemed, briefly, that the marriage between Lovejoy and Alton, Illinois, would be a good one.

The family bought a white frame house, and Lovejoy served as minister of a small church in Upper Alton. He became close friends with Edward Beecher, an abolitionist, the president of a local college, and a brother of Harriet Beecher Stowe.

Subscriptions were increasing, to nearly 2,000 by the summer of 1837, and Lovejoy was selling papers on both sides of the Mississippi. The *Observer* was also receiving financial help from New England abolitionists. "I think I ought to get considerable aid from my native state," Lovejoy wrote to his mother back in Maine. "Mr. Adams of Brunswick, told me at the General Assembly, that he thought I was doing more to put down Slavery than any other man in the United States."

However, the moderate Elijah Lovejoy was gone. He no longer wrote about sending blacks back to Africa or about eventual emancipation.

He sent letters to leading newspapers throughout the United States, asking for their position on slavery, then published their answers with his own critical commentary. He published a passionate letter he had written in the voice of a slave. He attacked Alton's Fourth of July festivities with a bitter editorial that anticipated Frederick Douglass's famous address, 15 years later, "What to a Slave Is the Fourth of July?" He editorialized against the slave trade in Washington, D.C., saying that slavery in the nation's capital made every man a slaveholder. He became secretary of a local antislavery group, and he proposed establishing an antislavery society in Illinois. A rumor circulated that from his pulpit one Sunday he had sworn that if his wife died, he would "marry a black woman before Saturday."

Lovejoy had become a flaming abolitionist, and at the worst possible moment.

The mid-1830s were a time of violent antiabolitionist activity throughout America. In 1835, William Lloyd Garrison was dragged through Boston at the end of a rope, antiabolitionists broke up the convention of the New York State Anti-Slavery Society in Utica, and proslavery mobs and rallies occurred in all parts of the country. Leonard L. Richards, author of a study of antiabolitionist mob action in Jacksonian America, writes, "From Maine to Missouri, from the Atlantic to the Gulf, crowds gathered to hear mayors and aldermen, bankers and lawyers, ministers and priests denounce the abolitionists as amalgamationists, dupes, fanatics, foreign agents, and incendiaries."

At the beginning of his career, newspaper editor Elijah Lovejoy believed that slavery should be ended gradually, but then he saw a free black man burned alive by a mob in St. Louis, Missouri, and, as he later wrote, the cry of the oppressed entered his soul. His commitment to abolitionism led to his death less than two years later. *Courtesy of the Abraham Lincoln Presidential Library*

What's more, Alton, like much of the country, was in the grip of a financial crisis attributable to, among other factors, a drop in cotton prices, the failure of the nation's wheat crop, and a huge overextension of credit, fueled by massive land speculation.

Instead of blaming the government, as many newspapers did, Lovejoy blamed Americans' weakness for get-rich-quick schemes, and their fatal attraction to wealth. "Speculation had become a perfect mania and we had become a nation of gamblers," he charged in the *Observer.*

Alton's bankrupt citizenry didn't like that, nor did they like the fact that their town was becoming a hub of antislavery activity, which they thought was hurting property values. A citizens' group censured Lovejoy for his "incendiary doctrines," and the proslavery *Missouri Republican* editorialized that action needed to be taken against "that minister of mischief."

"Dear Mother," Lovejoy wrote on September 5, "my press has again been mobbed down."

The threats and acts of destruction continued through the fall, but the minister held his ground even as some of his supporters doubted the wisdom of continuing the battle.

A FEW HOURS BEFORE DAWN ON NOVEMBER 7, 1837, A NEW PRESS FOR the *Observer* arrived on the steamboat *Missouri Fulton*. A group guarded the press as it was hoisted to the top floor of a stone warehouse. Although they heard the long, low sound of a horn, and then an answering horn, they saw no mob gathering. Edward Beecher and Lovejoy urged the others to go home while they stayed with the press.

Beecher later recalled that Lovejoy was tranquil as they kept watch. "The sky and the river were beginning to glow with the approaching day, and the busy hum of business to be heard. I looked with exultation on the scene below. I felt that a bloodless battle had been gained for God and for the truth." At daybreak they went to Lovejoy's house, where they said prayers and had breakfast with his wife.

That night, Lovejoy and about 60 volunteers again guarded the warehouse. Lovejoy said he expected to make an absolute stand against any mob that might materialize, and that he was willing to die, but that he did not expect anyone else to make the same sacrifice. No one left, at first. But when the night remained quiet, all eventually went home, except for Lovejoy and about a dozen others.

The mob arrived at about 10 p.m. "We want that printing press!" one man shouted. During the next hour, the assailants threw rocks at the warehouse and battered at its heavy door. Many had come directly from saloons, and were drunk and firing weapons. One man among them was fatally shot as the mob was getting warmed up, but this didn't dim its fury.

When Mayor John Krum arrived, pleading with the crowd to stop firing, a barefoot farmer screamed at him, "How would you like a damned

On the night of November 7, 1837, a proslavery mob intent on destroying Elijah Lovejoy's press set fire to the roof of his editorial offices. In the ensuing melee, Lovejoy was fatally shot. The young editor's death, reformer Wendell Phillips said, "scattered a world of dreams." *Courtesy of the Abraham Lincoln Presidential Library*

nigger going home with your daughter?" Krum went inside the warehouse and begged Lovejoy and the others to surrender the press to save their lives. They refused.

Outside the warehouse, a makeshift ladder had quickly been assembled, and buckets of flaming pitch were carried over. The crowd was getting increasingly agitated. There were cries of "Burn 'em out!" and "Shoot every damned abolitionist as he leaves!" James Rock, a riverfront lowlife who hated abolitionists, volunteered to climb the ladder and set fire to the wooden roof.

It was near midnight. Two men in the mob, both doctors, positioned themselves so they could see if anyone emerged from the warehouse to shoot at Rock. As the roof caught fire, Lovejoy and Royal Weller ran from the building and aimed up at Rock, but Dr. Thomas Hope and Dr. Horace Beale, covered by darkness, had perfect sight of the open door, and they shot both.

Weller was only wounded, but Lovejoy took five bullets, including three in his chest and one in his stomach. He staggered back into the warehouse and fell dead at the feet of his defenders.

The fire was extinguished. Some of the crowd entered the building and shoved the printing press into the street below. One witness later testified that the machinery was destroyed in "a quiet sort of way. They seemed to be happy while engaged in breaking it into pieces."

Most of Lovejoy's defenders had fled, chased by rioters' buckshot, but Thaddeus Hurlbut, the assistant editor of the *Observer*, stayed by Lovejoy's body through the night.

By 2 a.m., the crowd had largely dispersed, and at daylight Lovejoy was carried home. The wagon that held his body was jeered and scoffed at by the remains of the mob lingering in the streets. One rioter mockingly pretended to play a funeral fife.

No one was found guilty of Lovejoy's murder. The defenders of the press and the warehouse were charged with inciting a riot, but they were acquitted. Illinois Attorney General Usher Linder defended Lovejoy's killers and prosecuted the case against the minister's allies.

In his argument for the prosecution, Linder said Lovejoy and his group had taken the law into their own hands. "And for what? For a press! A printing press! A press brought here to teach the slave rebellion; to excite the slaves to war, to preach murder in the name of religion; to strike dismay in the hearts of people and spread desolation over the face of this land. Society honors good order more than such a press."

Two days after he was killed, on what would have been his thirty-fifth birthday, Lovejoy was buried in Alton between two oak trees. A cold, heavy rain fell on the small group that gathered for the funeral. His brother said the expression on his face was one of great calm, and the black man who dug Lovejoy's grave refused to be paid for his work.

The Meteor

When John Brown stood up at a memorial service for Elijah Lovejoy and dedicated his life to ending slavery, it was his first public declaration of war against bondage in America. But he had been preparing for the battle most of his life.

Brown had two enemies in his sights: the South, with its plantation economy, and the North, whose apathy toward slavery he'd grown to despise.

A century and a half after his death, there is an aura of inevitability around John Brown. Every passive blow against slavery had, before him, been ineffective. Less ambitious violent acts against the institution had also failed. He was the product of these earlier failures, the omen, the streak against the night sky that revealed how dark the landscape truly was.

Many saw the rangy New Englander as crazy, others as merely passionate in his hatred for slavery—a system in which people had been taken from their homeland, denied their human rights, and forced into servitude. Regardless of the viewpoint, Brown's interpretation of American slavery as a war has a sharp ring of modernity. Brown actually drafted a constitution for the new world he envisioned. In it he asserted that slavery represented "none other than a most barbarous, unprovoked, and unjustifiable war of one portion of [America's] citizens upon another portion."

If blacks in America were war victims, Brown was the nation's terrorist against oppression.

JOHN BROWN WAS born in 1800 on his family's farm in Torrington, Connecticut. His mother died when he was eight. His father, Owen, moved the family to Hudson, Ohio, and established a tannery. John had little formal education, once remarking that he knew as much about grammar as a calf.

When the boy was twelve, he drove a herd of cattle by himself from Ohio to Mich-

The earliest known photograph of abolitionist John Brown contains a clue to his plan for the future of America. Photographed by a black daguerreotypist named Augustus Washington, Brown clutches a homemade flag for his "Subterranean Pass-Way"—a mountain passage through which he planned to lead black people to freedom. *National Portrait Gallery, Smithsonian Institution / Art Resource, New York*

igan to provision British military outposts there. A man living near the garrisons invited him to stay in his home and was exceedingly kind to him. An orphaned black boy Brown's age also lived in the house. In an account of his childhood, Brown, referring to himself in the third person, wrote: "The Negro boy was badly clothed, poorly fed; & lodged in cold weather; & beaten before his eyes with Fire Shovels or any other thing that came first to hand. This brought John to reflect on the wretched, hopeless condition of Fatherless & Motherless slave children."

"It was no abolition lecturer that converted him," Henry David Thoreau was later to remark of Brown.

BROWN SPENT MUCH OF HIS LIFE FAILING AT VARIOUS BUSINESSES. He opened tanneries, speculated in land sales, and raised sheep. But he was consumed with the cause of enslaved people.

In 1848, he traveled to Peterboro, New York, to meet philanthropist Gerrit Smith, who was giving land grants in the Adirondacks to poor blacks. Smith accepted Brown's proposal to start a farm where he could help those trying to establish communities there, and Brown moved his family to his own paradise. North Elba, on the rim of Lake Placid, was a chance for Brown and his family to live side by side with black men and women in the way he envisioned for the country. It was too cold to raise corn there and winter lasted until the middle of May, but Brown said the Adirondacks "remind one of omnipotence."

Worcester, Massachusetts, minister and abolitionist Thomas Wentworth Higginson, who supported Brown to the very end, said the remote notch where Brown built his house was "beyond the world."

Abolitionist Richard Henry Dana, author of the maritime best seller *Two Years Before the Mast*, met Brown in 1849 while hiking in the Adirondacks and got a taste of his egalitarianism. Welcomed to a meal of venison and speckled brook trout at the Brown family table, black people actually dined with them. "I observed that he called the two Negroes by their surnames, with the prefixes of Mr. and Mrs. He introduced them to us in due form,—'Mr. Dana, Mr. Jefferson,' etc."

The experience appears to have made Dana uncomfortable.

IN 1856, JOHN BROWN JOINED several of his sons at the epicenter of the country's slavery dispute. Two years earlier, Senator Stephen A. Douglas of Illinois had proposed a bill in Congress that—in its final version—would admit the territories of Kansas and Nebraska to the Union "with or without slavery," reopening the national political battle over the balance of power and reigniting the dispute over slavery.

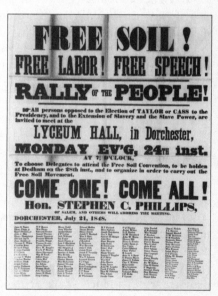

The Free-Soil settlers of Kansas didn't want to see slavery made legal in the territory, but for many settlers the issue was not the human rights of black people but a desire to protect Western lands for white labor and white families.
Courtesy, American Antiquarian Society

By then, Kansas had two illegal governments, two capitals, and an atmosphere of harassment and unrest. There were constant skirmishes between "free-soilers" and "border ruffians" from slavery-legal Missouri. In a few hours on a windy May night on Pottawatomie Creek, Brown raised the ante. A small band of his followers, including several of his sons, hacked to death five settlers who did not own slaves but were known to be proslavery.

He had wanted to create "a restraining fear" among those who favored slavery, Brown said. James Hanway, a free-state settler and rifleman with Brown who survived Kansas to become a judge, recalled the mood of foreboding before the mission. A man approached Brown, urging him to be cautious.

"Caution, caution, sir!" Brown exploded. "I am eternally tired of hearing that word caution—it is nothing but the word of cowardice."

For Brown, the South's attitude toward slavery was a given. It was the North's attitude, its apathy, that enraged him.

Even before Kansas, he was an outsider and a burr in abolitionist circles of New England. When he returned from the West, he went on a speaking tour of his home region, trying to raise money for his great plan to end slavery once and for all. He did very poorly, and left the region filled with contempt. "Farewell to the Plymouth Rocks, Bunker Hill monuments, Charter Oaks and Uncle Tom's Cabins," he said bitterly.

His attitude toward the abolitionist movement, by then more than a quarter-century old? "Talk, talk, talk."

But the feelings were mutual. He scared many abolitionists, who believed that slavery should end, but without violence. *Liberator* publisher and editor William Lloyd Garrison believed that a just society should *want* to end slavery, and many Northerners believed, even at that late date, that slavery would, eventually, wither away.

The issue dominated the national discussion. "Is there nothing in life but Negro slaves?" groaned an exasperated editor at a Connecticut newspaper in 1859.

After Kansas, after his New England tour, John Brown had even less patience with patience. If slavery would not be ended, then the Union that sheltered it would have to end. If the nation was, in Lincoln's famous phrase, a house divided against itself, Brown said: Tear the house down.

SHORTLY BEFORE IT ALL ENDED FOR HIM AT HARPERS FERRY, JOHN Brown discussed his plan to create a slavery-free world with a group of free blacks and other supporters in Ontario, Canada. James M. Jones, a gunsmith and black abolitionist from Ohio, was part of the group, and he explained later that Brown's actions would be aimed at the North as much as at the South.

"In [Brown's] conversations with me he led me to think that he intended to sacrifice himself and a few of his followers for the purpose of arousing the people of the North from the stupor they were in on the subject [of slavery]," Jones said. "He well knew that the sacrifice of any number of Negroes would have no effect."

During the decades after Elijah Lovejoy's death, as Brown fought his crusade for black emancipation—his "mistaken and deranged idea of what was right," as a New England newspaper described it—the nation fought to find a way to keep the two regions joined in a mutually profitable harness.

But as Brown saw more clearly than almost anyone else, a compromise on slavery was impossible. Despite a legal election in October 1859 that yielded a clear victory for Free-State Kansas, more people were enslaved in America than ever before in the nation's history. The U.S. Senate was dominated by Southerners who wanted to permanently table any discussion of emancipation. Some even wanted to reenter the international slave trade, closed to Americans since 1808.

THE FEDERAL ARMORY AT HARPERS FERRY ON VIRGINIA'S NORTHERN border was thought to contain more than $1 million in weapons and ammunition. Brown's plan was to take it over, use its arms to free the 10,000 slaves in Jefferson County and work his way south through the slave states. He assumed that blacks would flock to his standard as the ever-growing army moved from armory to armory. The success of his guerrilla-style fighting in Kansas had convinced him that small numbers of armed men, committed to a cause as mighty as ending slavery, could triumph against huge odds.

He also had the financial and tactical support of a half-dozen abolitionists, later known as "the Secret Six." They were philanthropist Gerrit Smith; physician Samuel Gridley Howe, husband of Julia Ward Howe; Worcester minister Thomas Wentworth Higginson; Boston minister and reformer Theodore Parker; businessman George Stearns; and teacher Franklin Sanborn of Concord.

In July 1859, under a pseudonym, Brown rented a dilapidated Mary-

When John Brown and his men captured the government arsenal at Harpers Ferry, he took a small number of white planters and their slaves as hostages, but no one, black or white, voluntarily joined his two-day insurrection.
The Western Reserve Historical Society, Cleveland, Ohio

land farm about seven miles from Harpers Ferry. At the core of his plan were 21 men—16 whites and 5 blacks. Three were his sons; two others were related to him by marriage.

From the farm, Watson Brown, twenty-four years old and father of a newborn son he had not yet seen, wrote to his wife that one of the black men in their group had a wife and seven children in slavery. During the short time the men had been encamped, five slaves who lived near the farm had been murdered or had committed suicide. "I sometimes feel as though I could not make the sacrifice," Watson wrote, "but what would I want others to do, were I in their place?"

On the evening of October 16, Brown and his men armed themselves and set out for Harpers Ferry. Reaching the covered bridge at the Potomac River, they subdued the guard, then moved quietly into the town. Before midnight, Brown had command of the armory, and by 4 a.m. he held a few neighboring planters and their slaves as captives.

But Brown had already made his fatal mistake by stopping—and then, inexplicably, letting through—a regularly scheduled train, which quickly spread news of the uprising.

Local militias from Maryland and Virginia began to pour into town, while President James Buchanan in Washington, 60 miles away, mobilized artillery units and the U.S. Marines. Hundreds of spectators gathered, while telegraph lines buzzed with accounts of the nation's mightiest black uprising since Nat Turner.

Shots were exchanged during the daylong siege, at the end of which Brown's sons Watson and Oliver lay dead beside their wounded father. Brown had received bayonet cuts to his side and a deep scalp wound. His captors, who included Robert E. Lee, the future general of the Confederacy, helped Brown to lie down on a pile of clothes.

While a crowd estimated at 2,000 howled for his blood, Brown spoke calmly, and for several hours, with Lee; Governor Henry Wise of Virginia; James Mason, the Virginia senator who later headed a congressional investigation into the raid; and a correspondent from the abolitionist-hating *New York Herald*.

Asked by the New York reporter what he would do if he "had every nigger in the United States," Brown said simply, "Set them free."

REACTION IN THE SOUTH, PREDICTABLY, WAS A KIND OF TRIUMPHANT rage—Harpers Ferry proved that Northerners meant to invade Southern states and violently separate Southerners from their way of life. It was noted approvingly that no enslaved people had willingly joined Brown's invasion.

Reaction in the North was mixed, and less predictable. Even many hard-line emancipationists who admired Brown's courage were appalled. This was not "moral suasion," this was an attempted takeover of government property involving militias, the U.S. Marines, and a threat to many lives.

William Lloyd Garrison described the attempt as "wild, misguided and apparently insane," though he said no one could deny "the right of slaves to imitate the example of our fathers."

"A Northern man made an unlawful attempt against the peace of Virginia," editorialized Rhode Island's *Providence Journal*. "In the whole North he had found only twenty men to help him. . . . Not a man in a hundred thousand in the North was ever heard to counsel such a deed."

The action at Harpers Ferry proved nothing of political or social significance, wrote editor Henry Raymond in *The New York Times*. The failed insurrection showed the failure of radical action. Harpers Ferry could prove a blessing in disguise, Raymond wrote, "if the South will frankly unite with the Conservative North in keeping the whole question of slavery out of Congress and beyond the national interference."

Meanwhile, the six men who were Brown's principal supporters panicked. Brown's most generous supporter, Gerrit Smith, panicked worst, telling a New York reporter he was terrified of being indicted for treason. Smith suffered a complete nervous collapse, was confined to the Utica Insane Asylum, and, even after his release, never fully recovered. Others, including Samuel Howe, took a train to Canada and stayed there until after Brown's execution. Franklin Sanborn, who had already fled to Canada once before, wrung his hands, asked friends to destroy his letters, and returned to Canada. (Theodore Parker was dying of tuberculosis in Italy.)

Thomas Wentworth Higginson, the forthright minister from Worcester, decided he would name none of the others in Brown's support network, but that he would offer testimony or allow himself to be extradited to Virginia, if it came to that, which it did not. During the Civil War, in what he said was expiation for having abandoned Brown, Higginson raised and served as the head of a regiment of black Union soldiers from Massachusetts.

John Brown, at his weeklong trial, angrily refused to plead insanity as a defense, saying, "I look upon it as a miserable artifice . . . and I view it with contempt more than otherwise."

It took the jury 45 minutes to find him guilty of murder, treason, and inciting slaves to riot. He was sentenced to hang on December 2. In a short address to a packed and silent courtroom, Brown said, "I believe that to have interfered as I have done, as I have always freely admitted I have done, in behalf of [God's] despised poor, I did no wrong but right."

John W. Forney, editor of the Philadelphia *Press* and later an intimate of Lincoln's, said it would be easier "to string Brown up than cut him down."

In Concord, Massachusetts, on the day of Brown's execution, Henry David Thoreau asked the town's selectmen if he could ring the bells of First Parish Church in recognition of Brown's death. They refused.

FIVE AND A HALF YEARS LATER, GENERAL ROBERT E. LEE, ONE OF THE men who had urged John Brown to surrender during the siege at Harpers Ferry, put on a clean Confederate uniform and surrendered to

General Ulysses S. Grant at Appomattox, Virginia. The civil war to end slavery in America was over.

Two days after Lee's surrender, the black soldiers of a Connecticut volunteer regiment marched into Richmond to occupy the city in advance of the approaching Union army. The local newspaper the next day noted in an offended tone that as they entered the defeated capital of the Confederacy, the black soldiers were singing, *thundering*, the popular song of the day: "John Brown's Body."

Dr. Samuel Morton's collection of 600 skulls provided what may be the North's most insidious contribution to slavery: the "proof" of black inferiority that white America wanted.

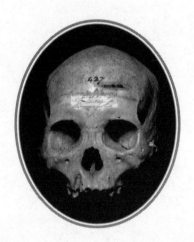

Nine

PHILADELPHIA'S RACE SCIENTIST

NEGRO, the designation of the distinctly dark-skinned, as opposed to the
fair, yellow and brown variations of mankind. . . . The negro would
appear to stand on a lower evolutionary plane than the white man, and to
be more closely related to the highest anthropoid.

Encyclopaedia Britannica, 1911

RACE, cultural construct based on the popular, but mistaken notion
that humans can be divided into biologically distinct categories by means of
particular physical features such as skin color, head shape, and other visible
traits that are transmissible by descent. . . . Genetic studies undertaken
in the last decades of the 20th century confirm that "races" do not exist
in any biological sense.

Encyclopaedia Britannica, 2002

REVOLUTIONARY IDEAS OF EQUALITY WERE IN THE AIR IN THE AU-
tumn of 1772, when John Hancock and 17 others of Boston's elite
convened to hear a case involving a teenage slave named Phillis Wheatley. The case had nothing to do with crime or Wheatley's status as property; it concerned her mental ability and, ultimately, her status as a
human being.

Wheatley was a prodigy. After arriving in Boston on a slave ship at
about age seven, she was schooled, and in early adolescence she began
to write the poetry that led to her modern celebrity as the first American

Above: Phillis Wheatley, a Boston slave, wrote "To the Rev. Mr. Pitkin on the Death of His Lady" in June 1772, when she was eighteen. Her ability to write in the style of poets like John Milton disturbed and fascinated her white readers. *The Connecticut Historical Society Museum, Hartford, Connecticut*

Right: The first lines of the poem read: "Where contemplation finds her sacred Spring/Where heav'nly music makes the centre ring/Where virtue reigns unsulled, and divine/Where wisdom thron'd and all the graces shine/There sits thy spouse amid the glitt'ring throng." *The Connecticut Historical Society Museum, Hartford, Connecticut*

slave and one of the first women to publish a book. At the time, however, Wheatley's readers regarded her as a freak, if not a fraud. The Hancock panel probed Wheatley and validated her poetry as her own. But the size and prestige of the panel—Governor Thomas Hutchinson was another member—showed how disturbing the possibility of black equality was to Bostonians, and to most other white Americans.

By 1772, color prejudice against blacks was more entrenched than slavery in the 13 original colonies. Even someone like Benjamin Franklin, a fan of Wheatley's who would preside over Philadelphia's antislavery society, placed blacks low on the chain of humanity that people then thought ascended from beast to angel.

After the Revolution—and despite its ideas—this careless, almost oblivious white prejudice against blacks began to harden into an aggressive racist ideology. Yet its first important theorist was none other than the drafter of the Declaration of Independence. In the midst of a long passage on black people in his *Notes on the State of Virginia*, Thomas Jefferson (who sniffed that Wheatley's poetry was "below the dignity of criticism") proposed that black inferiority—"in the endowment of both body and mind"—might be an unchangeable law of nature.

Jefferson's musings on blacks became a founding document in a new race science that reached its poisonous fruition in the decade before the Civil War. Famed in its heyday as the "American School of Ethnology," its reigning geniuses came from the North, or enjoyed the prestige bestowed on them by elite Northern colleges. Their rise, and temporary triumph, is essential to understanding the unique nature of American slavery.

Modern historians generally agree that the idea of fixed black inferiority evolved in tandem with the Western Hemisphere's plantation system. They also agree that slavery reached a particularly rigid form in the United States.

Previously, throughout history, slaves came in all colors and also had the hope of rising out of bondage. In America, however, being

Above left: By his death in 1851, Philadelphia physician Samuel George Morton had achieved international fame for his skull research that seemed to prove blacks were mentally inferior to whites. When *Types of Mankind,* a book based on Morton's work, was published in 1854, the respected *Putnam's Monthly Magazine* noted that his investigations "evince a scientific sagacity of the most extraordinary reach and penetration, coupled with a judicial severity of judgment." *Ewell Sale Stewart Library, The Academy of Natural Sciences of Philadelphia*

Above right: Dr. Josiah Nott was one of the South's most eminent physicians and one of the nation's leading race scientists. A coauthor of *Types of Mankind,* he denied the Bible's historical accuracy, arguing that blacks and whites were separate races who could not both be descended from Adam and Eve. *Alabama Department of Archives and History, Montgomery, Alabama*

black meant being a slave for life, with almost no chance of freedom—even for one's children. This unbroken circle turned for generations: black equaled slave equaled black.

In the nineteenth century, the race scientists made the circle even more vicious: black equaled slave equaled biologically subhuman. Their cutting-edge ideas of racial purity influenced the national debate over slavery and supported the self-image of the nation's white supremacist majority.

IF NATIONAL MEMORY COULD TOLERATE A PANTHEON OF RACE SCIENTISTS, first place might be awarded, not to Jefferson, but to Samuel George Morton, one of Philadelphia's

This photograph of Louis Agassiz is believed to have been taken shortly before his death in 1873, when he had been a Harvard professor for more than 20 years. Swiss-born, Agassiz joined with Josiah Nott to advance race-science research begun by Samuel Morton. *The Schlesinger Library, Radcliffe Institute, Harvard University*

most eminent physicians. Starting in the 1830s, Morton used measurements from his world-famous collection of skulls to show that black people had the smallest "cranial capacity" of all human types and were therefore doomed to inferiority.

Close behind Morton would come his disciples, Josiah Nott and Louis Agassiz. In the 1850s, they collaborated on a landmark 700-page treatise, *Types of Mankind*, that was dedicated to Morton and exhaustively proved that blacks were not even of the same species as whites.

All three race scientists were considered among the brightest minds of their time. After studying at the University of Pennsylvania, Nott became one of the South's leading physicians. He saw before anyone else that an insect, probably the mosquito, spread yellow fever, and he anticipated Charles Darwin's theory of evolution by challenging the biblical account of the Creation. Nott, from one of Connecticut's oldest families, glibly referred to his work on racial differences as "niggerology."

Agassiz was already a renowned Swiss zoologist and geologist when Harvard invited him to join its faculty in 1847. A towering figure for the next two decades, Agassiz came under Morton's influence when he visited him in Philadelphia in 1846 and coincidentally had his first close encounter with blacks. When they waited on him in his hotel dining room, Agassiz could barely conceal the revulsion he later described in a letter to his mother.

"Seeing their black faces with their fat lips and their grimacing teeth, the wool on the heads, their bent knees, their elongated hands, their large, curved fingernails, and above all the livid color of their palms, I could not turn my eyes from their face in order to tell them to keep their distance," Agassiz wrote.

An opponent of slavery, Dr. Benjamin Rush proposed that the apparent inferiority of black people was caused by a strain of leprosy. A signer of the Declaration of Independence, Rush is remembered as "the Father of American Psychiatry" for his enlightened treatment of the insane. *Courtesy, Pennsylvania Hospital Historic Collections, Philadelphia, Pennsylvania*

During the Civil War, when the federal government sought the Harvard scientist's advice on the best way to deal with millions of freed slaves, he said the first priority should be to avoid the potential catastrophe, to whites, of increased mixing with blacks.

"Beware of any policy which may bring our own race to their level," Agassiz warned.

NEARLY A CENTURY EARLIER, WHEN JEFFERSON DARED TO SUGGEST THAT black inferiority might be permanent, his contemporaries had tended to blame the disparity on environmental circumstance. The most illustrious may have been Dr. Benjamin Rush of Philadelphia. A signer of the Declaration of Independence and a leading early abolitionist, he earned a place in medical history by treating alcoholism as a disease.

Rush believed that Africans were afflicted with a mild strain of leprosy that turned their skin black and, if it spread to their heads, caused their lips to swell, their noses to flatten, and their hair to become woolly.

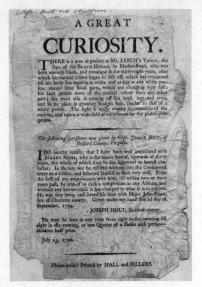

A GREAT

CURIOSITY.

THERE is a man at present at Mr. LEECH's Tavern, the sign of the BLACK HORSE, in Market-street, who was born entirely black, and remained so for thirty-eight years, after which his natural colour began to rub off, which has continued till his body has become as white and as fair as any white person, except some small parts, which are changing very fast; his face attains more of the natural colour than any other part; his wool also is coming off his head, legs and arms, and in its place is growing straight hair, similar to that of a white person. The sight is really worthy the attention of the curious, and opens a wide field of amusement for the philosophic genius.

The following certificate was given by Capt. JOSEPH HOLT, of Bedford County, Virginia.

I DO hereby certify, that I have been well acquainted with HARRY MOSS, who is the bearer hereof, upwards of thirty years, the whole of which time he has supported an honest character. In the late war he enlisted with me into the Continental army as a soldier, and behaved himself as such very well. From the first of my acquaintance with him, till within two or three years past, he was of as dark a complexion as any African, and without any known cause it has changed to what it is at present. He was free born, and served his time with Major John Brant, late of Charlotte county. Given under my hand this 2d day of September, 1794.
         JOSEPH HOLT, Bedford county.

He may be seen at any time from eight in the morning till eight in the evening, at one Quarter of a Dollar each person—children half price.

July 23, 1796.

Philadelphia: Printed by HALL and SELLERS.

Henry Moss, the "GREAT CURIOSITY" referred to in the 1796 ad shown here, caused a sensation exhibiting himself as a black man turning white. No sideshow freak, Moss attracted the interest of prominent men such as physician Benjamin Rush and abolitionist Moses Brown. *American Philosophical Society, Philadelphia, Pennsylvania*

He also thought leprosy made blacks less sensitive to pain—a purported trait slaveholders used to justify beatings.

The notion that blackness was itself a defect was embodied in Henry Moss, a slave who became a sensation in the 1790s by exhibiting himself as a black man whose skin had suddenly started to lighten, and whose hair had started to grow straight. When Rush saw Moss (who later bought his freedom with money he made exhibiting himself), he decided the black man's leprosy was curing spontaneously.

Citing Moss's whitening, Rush held out hope that a cure might one day be found for blackness. For the time being, he recommended as promising treatments the juice of unripe peaches, tight-fitting clothing, the all-purpose trio of bleeding, purging, and abstinence, and fright.

ORDINARY CHRISTIANS, HOWEVER, DIDN'T NEED MEDICAL THEORIES LIKE Rush's to explain how Africans became black, and bad. Most accepted the Bible as a basic history text and read the few lines in Genesis about the curse placed upon Noah's disobedient son Ham as the key to an operating racial myth. Its supposed truth—that Ham was black and that his progeny were doomed to slavery—became so common and so central to proslavery thought that the radical abolitionist Theodore Dwight Weld called it "a mocking lullaby, vainly wooing slumber" in a troubled nation.

Race science emerged to challenge both Ham's cursed lullaby and intellectuals like Dr. Rush, who believed that as degraded as blacks appeared to be, they at least were descended from Adam.

The science's American pioneer, Dr. Samuel Morton, has been described as tall, cadaverous, quietly urbane, and "an altogether improbable person to foment revolution in American science, to provide the boots and saddles and spurs with which to ride the mass of mankind."

Raised a Quaker, Morton graduated from the University of Pennsylvania Medical School in 1820, then got a second degree from Scotland's great Edinburgh University. He practiced medicine, but earned initial renown analyzing fossils collected by the Lewis and Clark expedition.

Working when science itself was in transition, from a discipline relying on observation—and more susceptible to being influenced by bias—to a specialized discipline defined by experimental rigor, Morton also published papers on geology and anatomy. In 1831, he was elected corresponding secretary of the Academy of Natural Sciences, a position that put him in touch with scientifically inclined men all over the world, and helped him collect human skulls.

Morton's correspondents sent him specimens from frontier outposts and lands as distant and old as India and Egypt. By 1837, he had 140 and was asking for more. Morton needed the skulls for a comparative study of American Indian populations. He published his research two years later in his book *Crania Americana*, in which he carefully explained the method he used to determine cranial capacity. He packed pepper seed into the brain cavity, then transferred the seed into a tin cylinder calibrated to measure the volume of the seeds in cubic inches.

The empirical results would have surprised no one who already assumed that whites stood at the top of the human hierarchy. Morton's sample of Caucasian skulls yielded the biggest average cranial capacity, 87 cubic inches. Mongolians, Malays, and American Indians came in at

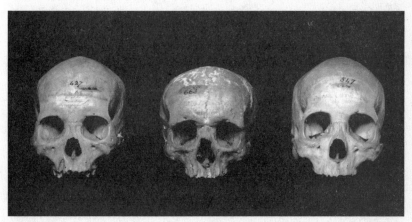

The numbered skulls shown here are samples from Samuel Morton's world famous collection known as the "American Golgotha." Morton used the skulls to measure the "cranial capacity" of various races. In the late twentieth century, scientist Stephen Jay Gould reviewed Morton's measurement methods and found them distorted by unconscious bias. *University of Pennsylvania Museum (neg. T4-2526)*

83, 81, and 80 cubic inches, respectively. Ethiopians finished at the bottom; their skulls had an average capacity of 78 cubic inches.

The data spoke for itself. But the tentative conclusion that Morton drew from the data verged on heresy. The only way he could account for the dramatic deviation in skull sizes since the Creation—then customarily dated at 4004 BC—was to presume that the Bible had been misread. Caucasians and Negroes were too different to both be descended from Adam through Noah. Morton speculated that God must have intervened at the time of the Flood to reshape mankind.

In other words, there must have been a second creation, one that made men separate and unequal.

Crania Americana appeared at a time when the idea of multiple creations was gaining credence. Morton was winning an international reputation, and his stature grew even greater after he published a sequel, *Crania Aegyptiaca*, in 1844. In it, Morton added data from the embalmed heads of ancient Egyptians that in his view confirmed the ages-old permanence of racial difference. He'd also improved his measuring method, substituting lead pellets for pepper seed.

Among the scientists who praised Morton's work was an eminent Swede who wrote that Morton had done "more for ethnography than any other living physiologist." Influential Southerners clamored for *Crania Aegyptiaca* after seeing advance copies that George Robins Gliddon, one of Morton's most important collaborators, carried on a lecture tour to South Carolina.

A professional diplomat and amateur Egyptologist, Gliddon introduced Morton's books to the Charleston Literary Club and to Governor James Henry Hammond, who vowed to use Morton's work in his proslavery writings. Gliddon's tour also took him to Washington, D.C., where he was summoned to an audience with John C. Calhoun, the powerful South Carolina senator who, between terms, was serving as secretary of state.

Calhoun hoped Morton's research might help him deal with ongoing controversies related to slavery. The strangest concerned a dispute between North and South over public health statistics reported in the 1840 federal census.

The first to survey mental illness, the census had found that Northern blacks were 10 times more prone to lunacy or idiocy than Southern blacks. Even more incredibly, the census showed that the farther north blacks lived, the more likely they were to be insane. In Maine, 1 in 14 black people was reported to be a lunatic or an idiot; in Massachusetts, it was 1 in

43; in New Jersey, 1 in 297. By contrast, the overall rate for slave states was 1 in 1,558.

Northerners demanded an investigation of the census, claiming the figures must have been falsified to support the South's contention that blacks were more suited to slavery than to freedom. Indeed, among the arguments used to defend the census figures' accuracy was that both freedom and Northern winters were bad for blacks' already weaker minds. Morton's research supported the Southern view. Reporting to Congress on the census, Calhoun wrote that its insanity data simply reflected the "deep and durable" nature of black infirmity.

Despite evidence that some of the figures were wildly out of whack, if not fabricated, the census stood unchanged, and its astonishing data on black people continued to be cited up to the Civil War.

THE CENSUS DISPUTE HAD THE INCIDENTAL EFFECT OF INTRODUCING Morton to a new collaborator, Dr. Josiah Clark Nott of Mobile, Alabama. In August 1844, Morton sent Nott a letter congratulating him on a paper he'd written in response to a medical journal article arguing that the 1840 census also showed slaves lived longer than free blacks and mulattoes.

Morton had read Nott's paper, "The Mulatto a Hybrid—Probable Extermination of the Two Races if the Whites and Blacks Are Allowed to Intermarry," in the prestigious *American Journal of the Medical Sciences*. In it, Nott elaborated on the already-current idea that the offspring of mixed-race couples tended toward sterility much as did mules, offspring of horses and donkeys.

Soon after receiving Morton's encouraging letter, Nott plunged ahead with more daring public lectures in which, invoking Galileo, he declared that science—not the Bible—must decide the true origins of mankind.

More willing than Morton to openly challenge Genesis, Nott proposed that God must have made separate races of men, just as He had made separate species of animals. Nott became so devoted to Morton that he began to visit the great man on trips to the North.

Louis Agassiz arrived in the United States already convinced that, following God's orderly plan, all living creatures occupied areas to which they were specifically suited. The only exception was man, whose unique ability to adapt had allowed him to spread over the surface of the Earth. Agassiz's opinion changed virtually overnight, however, after he

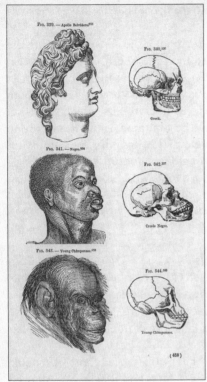 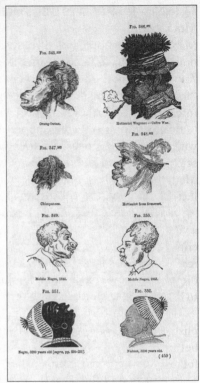

Types of Mankind contained these drawings in a chapter that discussed differences in racial anatomy. The author, Josiah Nott, wrote that, "such a head as the Greek is never seen on a Negro, nor such a head as that of the Negro on a Greek." Types of Mankind, *J. C. Nott, M.D., and Geo. R. Glidden, 1854, Special Collections of the Fisk University Franklin Library*

visited Morton, saw his skull collection, which had grown to 600, and saw blacks up close for the first time.

In January 1847, given the honor of delivering the annual Lowell Lecture in Boston, Agassiz added the weight of his reputation to the idea that blacks were a separate species.

Morton put the matter more bluntly in a letter to his chief Christian critic, a Northern-born Charleston minister named John Bachman. The Garden of Eden described in Genesis, Morton explained, was indeed the "paradise for the Adamic race." It just wasn't "the collective center for the human family."

Morton, in effect, was assuring Bachman that God did make the Garden of Eden—for whites only.

MORTON BY THEN WAS WEAKENED BY LUNG DISEASE. WHEN HE DIED IN May 1851, the *New-York Daily Tribune* noted that "one of the brightest ornaments of our age and country" had been lost. *The Charleston Medical Journal* said the South owed the Philadelphia doctor a debt of thanks "for aiding most materially in giving to the negro his true position as an inferior race."

Within months, George Gliddon had talked Nott into collaborating with him on a major new book summarizing the recent advances in race science. Morton himself had begun planning such a work. The two got Morton's widow to turn over the doctor's unpublished papers and solicited contributions from Agassiz, among others.

Nott wrote half the book, finishing in August 1853, the same month a yellow fever epidemic struck Mobile, delivering what his God-fearing critics might have seen as a divine judgment. In September, Nott, already exhausted from battling the epidemic, watched four of his children, aged two to nineteen, die in the space of a week. The loss added to his contempt for a world he considered corrupt and irrational.

Types of Mankind, the 700-page tome inspired by Morton, accomplished what Nott and Gliddon intended. The first edition sold out even before it was published in the spring of 1854. Nine more editions would follow.

Agassiz's section lent it credibility. The Harvard scientist declared each race a separate species and wrote that the differences between the races were "the same kind and even greater than those upon which the anthropoid monkeys are considered a distinct species."

In his sections, Nott concentrated on showing how wide those differences were and how urgent it was for whites to maintain their racial purity. He cited new evidence of whites' greater cranial capacity that he'd collected from hat dealers in Mobile and a hat manufacturer in New Jersey. His analysis of the figures they supplied for thousands of hats showed the average white head to be 21 inches in circumference. The data reinforced Morton's skull measurements.

While Nott found blacks were woefully lacking in brain capacity for the kind of higher-order thinking reflected in painting or sculpture, he did concede that "every Negro is gifted with an ear for music."

TYPES OF MANKIND CONFIRMED WHAT JEFFERSON HAD DARED ONLY TO speculate in his 1781 *Notes*. Its rational science supported nineteenth-

Jack, *Peabody Museum, Harvard University Photo T1873*

These daguerreotypes of slaves were taken in 1850 in the vicinity of Columbia, South Carolina, at the behest of Harvard professor Louis Agassiz, who was interested in identifying pure racial types.

Drana, Daughter of Jack, *Peabody Museum, Harvard University Photo T1871*

Renty, *Peabody Museum, Harvard University Photo T1867*

Delia, Daughter of Renty, *Peabody Museum, Harvard University Photo T1870*

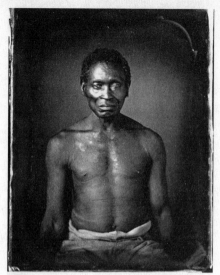

Fassena, *Peabody Museum, Harvard University Photo T1878*

century America's confident white supremacist view of itself. Even the heroes of abolition thought whites deserved the status of master race.

In 1857, the Reverend Theodore Parker of Boston, one of the few who would back John Brown's raid at Harpers Ferry, wrote in a letter, "I look with great pride on the Anglo-Saxon people. It has many faults, but I think it is the best specimen of mankind which has ever attained great power in the world."

The following year, in one of his debates with Stephen A. Douglas, Abraham Lincoln observed that whites and blacks were too different ever to live together as equals. "I as much as any other man am in favor of having the superior position assigned to the white race," Lincoln said.

The scientific theory of white supremacy was soon doomed, however. In 1859, Charles Darwin published *On the Origin of Species by Means of Natural Selection,* which would push the evolution of mankind far beyond the confines of Genesis and expose Morton's, Nott's, and Agassiz's ideas of separate creations as the fantasies they were.

Nott, who'd always scoffed at the Bible, soon bowed to Darwin. After the Civil War, he moved his medical practice to New York for a time. He wanted to live, he wrote, in a place "without morals, without political scruples and without niggers."

Agassiz was more stubborn. Ensconced at Harvard, he finally tarnished his brilliant reputation by leading the American opposition to Darwin. Wrong about evolution, wrong about blacks and whites being separate species, Agassiz and his fellow race scientists still have not been fully discredited. Their insidious legacy lives on in a world that continues to see race as biology fixed in black and white.

Two little Connecticut River towns
helped to produce music for the
middle class, at a cost of as many as
2 million African lives, sacrificed
to harvest elephant ivory.

Ten

PLUNDER FOR PIANOS

A SMALL GLASS BUILDING SHAPED LIKE A TENT STANDS IN A FIELD behind the historical society of Deep River, Connecticut. It looks like a greenhouse, but this "bleach house," as it was called, was designed not to grow plants but to expose to sunlight, for a period of 30 days, ivory piano keys cut from the tusks of African elephants.

During the latter half of the nineteenth century, in two small towns on the Connecticut River, dozens of these bleach houses, some as long as a football field, stretched over slopes that faced south. They are all gone, except for this small one, restored now to its original appearance. The enterprise these bleach houses served, transforming ivory into piano keys, billiard balls, and objects for Victorian ornament and domestic life, is also over.

Nothing about this clean, modest little structure suggests that its story is steeped in the blood of perhaps 2 million black people.

GEORGE WASHINGTON WAS ENJOYING RETIREMENT ON HIS FARM IN Virginia when Connecticut began cutting ivory. An Essex goldsmith invented a saw that could be powered by water or wind to cut the fine teeth of ivory combs. Suddenly, what had been laborious handwork was mechanized.

From Phineas Pratt's small mill on a tributary of the Connecticut River, two companies rose to become the world's leading ivory manufacturers. Connecticut's ivory businesses, located in a section of Essex later

In Connecticut's "bleach houses," the rectangles of ivory cut for piano keys were soaked in a whitening solution, then fitted into pegged wooden racks and exposed to sunlight for 30 days. *Connecticut River Museum*

named Ivoryton and in neighboring Deep River, shaped elephants' teeth into the stuff and substance of nineteenth-century life. The two companies brought constant innovation to the complex tasks of exporting ivory from Africa and cutting and refining it. At midcentury, when their market shifted from baubles and combs to home entertainment—piano keys and billiard balls—the ivory men kept pace. They mated their era's blithe derring-do and technical genius to a misplaced confidence in the renewability of natural resources.

Ivory was good for New England and for America's piano-making empire, but it was a long nightmare for African people and Africa's elephants. Even a half century after the collapse of Connecticut's ivory industry, the full human and environmental dimensions of the tragedy defy exact measurement.

When the remnants of Connecticut's ivory empire were sold at auction in the spring of 2002, there were two names on that last company: Pratt and Read. Both men were ardent abolitionists.

Abolitionist George Read was a leader in the slavery-dependent ivory business, but ivory's slaves lived in Africa, not in Connecticut. *Deep River Historical Society*

From his portrait hanging in the stone mansion that houses the Deep River Historical Society, George Read gazes mildly over his high collar. A founder of Deep River and a deacon of his church, Read was active in antislavery circles and his home was a safe place for black fugitives on their way to freedom in Canada. He provided shelter to a black man who had fled slavery in the South and settled permanently in Deep River. Read believed that a godly man should not accumulate too much personal wealth.

Like his partner, Julius Pratt was a pioneer in the antislavery movement, and an abolitionist in Connecticut at a time when slavery was still legal in the state. In the 1830s, when Read and Pratt began to militate openly against slavery in America, their position was a courageous one because abolitionists were widely despised as shrill, misguided, and liable to do more harm than good. It helped, of course, to be well-to-do, but Pratt's wealth did not protect him from the stones and jeers of a crowd when he defended a pro-emancipation speaker near Hartford.

When Pratt died in 1869, his eulogist said, "The blood of Puritans flowed generously in his veins," adding that Pratt would not "change and modify [his views] to suit a demoralized world or a time-saving church."

If Pratt was old-fashioned in his religious approach, he was completely forward-looking in his business dealings. Midway through the Civil War,

Like George Read, Julius Pratt was active in America's antislavery movement, even putting himself in harm's way to protect abolitionists. But his deep religious and social beliefs did not pose a conflict for him in his role as a captain in the ivory industry. *Deep River Historical Society*

he and George Read combined their ivory enterprises—both spin-offs of Phineas Pratt's eighteenth-century workshop—and for the next 75 years Pratt, Read & Company competed with America's other great ivory company, Comstock, Cheney & Company, just a short canter up the road.

When Samuel Merritt Comstock was born in Ivoryton in 1809 to the wife of a sea captain in the West Indies trade, the town was a crossroads with 12 houses and a different name. Comstock learned the ivory business in a family workshop, and in the early 1860s, in need of capital, he sold a quarter-interest in his company to George A. Cheney, an ivory trader who had lived for 10 years in Zanzibar, an island off the east coast of Africa that served as a world trading center for ivory.

In Connecticut, Comstock was turning tiny West Centre Brook into an ivory-town, and one of America's first planned communities. A pioneering industrialist sometimes compared to Hartford gunmaker Samuel Colt, Comstock had a vision for his town, a vision that included not only stylish homesteads on Main Street for his executives, but houses for his middle managers, modest dwellings for the immigrant families who joined his workforce, and separate dormitories for his young, unmarried, male and female workers. Comstock built churches (though no Catholic ones), places to shop, and centers for recreation—the Wheel Club was a men's cycling club.

In a town later named Ivoryton, Samuel Merritt Comstock created the nineteenth-century equivalent of a planned community around his ivory manufacturing business. History of Middlesex County, *JB Beers, 1884, Ivoryton Library Association*

Through the industry they propelled, these ivory entrepreneurs gave immigrants from Italy, Poland, and northern Europe a foothold in America, even as they depended on the labor of hundreds of thousands of enslaved people in Africa.

"IT IS SIMPLY INCREDIBLE THAT, BECAUSE IVORY IS REQUIRED, THE RICH heart of Africa should be laid waste," wrote explorer Henry M. Stanley. One of Africa's most renowned and obstreperous nineteenth-century visitors, Stanley, famous for finding the missing Dr. Livingstone, called the ivory trade "a bloody seizure."

The best ivory—the most durable and lustrous, and easiest to carve—is the soft ivory, actually the two front incisors, of *Loxodonta africana*, the African elephant. Named for the lozenge-shaped ridges on its teeth, *Loxodonta* was plentiful in eastern and central Africa—"numerous as flies," according to one Victorian-era journalist. (Bigger and crankier than the Indian elephant seen in circuses, the African species cannot be domesticated. Its ears are shaped like the continent.)

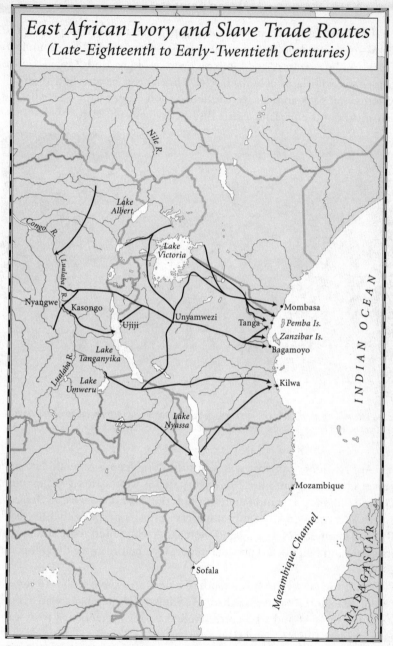

East African Ivory and Slave Trade Routes
(Late-Eighteenth to Early-Twentieth Centuries)

Nile R.

Lake Albert

Congo R.

Lualaba R.

Lake Victoria

Nyangwe

Kasongo

Ujiji

Unyamwezi

Tanga

Mombasa

Pemba Is.

Zanzibar Is.

Bagamoyo

Lualaba R.

Lake Tanganyika

Lake Umweru

Kilwa

INDIAN OCEAN

Lake Nyassa

Mozambique

Mozambique Channel

Sofala

MADAGASCAR

Ernst D. Moore documented the trade routes that were used for the transporting of ivory from the late eighteenth century until the dawn of the twentieth, when he went to Africa and became a buyer for Connecticut's ivory companies. Later, he wrote an account of the ivory trade and its immense human and environmental toll.
Map © 2005 by David Lindroth

The first big hurdle in the ivory supply system was transporting the tusks—many were as heavy as 80 pounds—from the killing grounds to coastal trading centers at Mombasa, Mozambique, and Zanzibar. The Europeans who later colonized Africa hadn't yet established their rail systems, and pack animals were killed in short order by the tsetse fly, the transmitter of the parasitic cattle disease trypanosomiasis.

For decades after the introduction of rail into Africa, the burden of moving ivory tusks to trading centers on the east coast of Africa fell squarely on ivory's human porters. *Courtesy, Ivoryton Library Association*

At first sight, Zanzibar was beautiful, "a gorgeous emerald laid on a velvet cloth of ocean blue," one ivory trader wrote. In a 1942 memoir, George Cheney's granddaughter said the island suggested fragrant spices and "perpetually sunlit minarets against a perpetually blue sky." But the energetic New England merchants who sailed there found that its blood-red flag floated above a major slave market with deep links to ivory.

"It is the custom to buy a tooth of ivory and a slave with it to carry it to the sea shore," wrote Michael W. Shepard, a merchant who visited Zanzibar in 1844 and who corresponded with Connecticut's ivory captains. "Then the ivory and slaves are carried to Zanzibar and sold."

For centuries, Arab traders had plied well-established routes through the regions later made famous by Nile River explorations. Tanganyika, Kilimanjaro, and the Zambesi River were new and magical names to the West but familiar to a trade world that was at least eight centuries old. Originally from North Africa and Egypt, the traders settled throughout eastern and central Africa and maintained trading centers on Africa's great system of rivers. Cordial, accommodating, and worldly, the traders functioned as a kind of ruling class, their influence transcending regional boundaries in a fragmented continent. They maintained cadres of armed mercenaries—Stanley called them raiders—and controlled the flow of ivory and captive Africans.

Though famously courteous to Westerners, they were unwavering in their practice of slavery. "We must differ on these subjects but we must not quarrel," said the nineteenth century's most famous trader, Hamid ibn Mohammed, to David Livingstone.

The ultimate middle men, traders such as ibn Mohammed, who was better known as Tippoo Tib—the percussive sound of his nickname was meant to suggest gunfire—dominated Africa until the early 1890s, when the scramble for Africa began in earnest and European colonizers moved in to build railroads, govern trade, and, they said, end the horrors of slavery.

But in the mid-1800s the desire of an industrialized America for luxury goods dovetailed perfectly with an Africa where slavery was legal and ivory was plentiful.

It was a system that worked for everybody—except, of course, the African tribal people. For them, it was brutal and often lethal, a system designed to exploit them even as it extracted their ivory and broke up their communities. Their villages in flames behind them, these captured people, shackled together and carrying the heavy tusks, walked as far as 1,000 miles to the coast. Many died en route, and the longer the journey, the worse the casualties.

Nothing could have prepared English missionary Alfred J. Swann for the horrors of the ivory caravans he saw in Africa in the 1880s. The feet and shoulders of ivory's black porters were a mass of open sores, made more painful by the swarms of flies that followed the march and lived on the flowing blood. Swann said the porters were "a picture of utter

Humanitarian and explorer David Livingstone became the world's most famous witness to the slave trade in Africa, and constantly militated against its practice, sometimes even freeing people bound for the slave markets. *British Information Services*

misery" and were covered with scars left by the chikote, a leather whip made of twisted rhinoceros hide.

While exploring the Zambesi River in southeastern Africa in 1858, Livingstone came upon another group of these refugees: "A long line of manacled men, women, and children came wending their way round the hill and into the valley, on the side of which the village stood. The black drivers, armed with muskets, and bedecked with various articles of finery, marched jauntily in the front, middle, and rear of the line; some of them blowing exultant notes out of long tin horns."

The guards fled when they saw Livingstone and his men, and the explorer freed the Africans. "Knives were soon busy at work cutting the women and children loose. It was more difficult to cut the men adrift, as each had his neck in the fork of a stout stick, six or seven feet long, and kept in by an iron rod which was riveted at both ends across the throat."

As pressure from the American and European ivory markets intensified, so did the misery among Africans forced into porterage.

And for those left behind in what remained of their communities, there were burdens in addition to personal loss and abandonment. His-

During the second half of the nineteenth century and well into the twentieth, 75 percent of the ivory exported from Zanzibar—including this 11-ton pile of tusks—went to two piano-key manufacturing companies in Connecticut.
Deep River Historical Society

torian Abdul Sheriff, an expert on the economics of East African slavery, writes in his *Slaves, Spices, and Ivory in Zanzibar* that subtracting the strongest from these tribal groups, many of whom were subsistence farmers, often meant starvation for those not forced into the ivory caravan.

John Bertram was a staggeringly successful Massachusetts trader (and later, a philanthropist) from whom Samuel Comstock bought ivory. In 1843, a young buyer who worked for Bertram detailed a trip to a coastal city near Mozambique, where he and his partner sold New England cottons and muskets and bought goods from African traders: "We also purchased a quantity of fine Ivory, sea horse [hippopotamus] tusk & tortoise shell from them. I here assisted Capt. Bates in the 'store' and after hours we used to walk out among the cocoa nut trees. There I saw several times gangs of Slaves just as they came in from the interior of Africa, thin almost as Skeletons. They had an iron ring round the neck & a chain went through it, thus connecting 40 or 50 in a line."

One of history's great novelists also saw the effects of the ivory trade. In the 1890s, Józef Teodor Konrad Korzeniowski, better known as Joseph Conrad, worked as a steamboat captain in the Belgian Congo.

Conrad invented the plotline for *Heart of Darkness*, his classic novella of the search upriver for the doomed ivory trader Kurtz, but insisted he did not invent what he saw in King Leopold's État Indépendent du Congo. He describes the porters:

> *Black shapes crouched, lay, sat between the trees leaning against the trunks, clinging to the earth, half coming out, half effaced within the dim light, in all the attitudes of pain, abandonment and despair. . . .*
>
> *They were dying very slowly—it was very clear. They were not enemies, they were not criminals, they were nothing earthly now—nothing but black shadows of disease and starvation, lying confusedly in the greenish gloom.*

THE SUFFERING THAT ACCOMPANIED IVORY FILLS MORE THAN A HALF century of eyewitness accounts, from the 1830s to the 1890s, decades when America at home was moving decisively against slavery. The Civil War ended slave labor in the United States, but not the idea that black people were inferior and inherently suited to physical labor, that they were made for exploitation and did not mind.

In an address to the New Haven Colony Historical Society in 1875, scholar William C. Fowler discussed the status of black people in Connecticut since their introduction into the colony in the seventeenth century. Lordly and condescending in his tone, Fowler said that blacks "being an imitative race, readily adopted the customs of the whites," and that New World slavery was an improvement over the "moral degradation" of their African homeland. Fowler's views were not regarded as racism, but as common sense.

Africa was seen as an unredeemable backwater, a primitive place, its cultures stagnant.

If Julius Pratt, George Read, and Samuel Comstock thought about it at all—and there is no evidence that they did—they probably would have regarded ivory's human victims as necessary components in their complex business. The America these men knew was in the process of freeing itself from the

David Livingstone said that it was almost impossible to write about the slave trade in East Africa without being accused of exaggeration, because the truth was so horrific. *By Permission of the British Library, 10859.m.15*

system of slavery, but the reality of involuntary labor was familiar to them, particularly the involuntary labor of black people.

Hard at work was what one historian calls "the bifurcated mind" of nineteenth-century commerce. Human rights were well and good, but successful businesses always rested on somebody's back. Even abolitionists Read and Pratt understood that. An inferior people, living in untamed wilds on the other side of the globe, were part of ivory's African supply system, but that was not the problem. The problem was maintaining the flow of high-quality ivory.

For David Livingstone, who lived in the middle of that supply system, it was another matter. Livingstone said that it was almost impossible to write about the slave trade in East Africa without being accused of exaggeration, because the truth was so horrific. He had come to Africa as a medical missionary in 1840. A natural explorer and geographer, he became convinced that Africa's lakes and rivers could be used as highways for commerce and thus end the slave trade. He spent the rest of his life exploring these rivers and documenting what he saw, becoming the slave trade's most famous witness.

In June 1868 he wrote, "Six men slaves were singing as if they did not feel the weight and degradation of the slave-sticks. I asked the cause of their mirth, and was told they rejoiced at the idea of coming back after death, and haunting and killing those who had sold them."

The chorus of their song was the names of the men who had sold them.

PIANO KEYS WERE ONCE MADE OF RARE WOODS, BUT BY THE LATE 1830S, ivory was found to be the ideal substance for the keys' veneer. Cool and smooth to the touch, never sticky or slippery yet offering a slight resistance to the fingers, ivory was also beautiful. The keys within a single keyboard were always cut from the ivory of a single tusk, because the close matching of grain and color was important. A good-sized tusk in the hands of a skillful cutter yielded the wafer-thin veneer for 45 keyboards.

Billiard balls were made from the tusks of female elephants because those tusks were straighter, and a nerve that ran down the center of the tusk caused a ball, when correctly fashioned, to roll true. A female tusk of average size yielded five billiard balls. The old sales documents sometimes refer to the ivory of female elephants as, simply, "billiard." (The harvest had a hidden cost. African elephants live in matriarchal herds, and the older females—generally those carrying the most valuable tusks—are also the source of community knowledge about where to find food and water. Their slaughter had a killing effect on the survival of younger, vulnerable herd members.)

Much of the complex technology for cutting perfectly matched keyboards and applying the ivory veneer was developed in Connecticut. When a Boston-made Chickering piano took a top prize at the Crystal Palace Exhibition in London in 1851, the demand for pianos of American manufacture was immediate and dramatic. That trendsetting piano almost certainly had a keyboard made in Deep River, because Pratt, Read was the major supplier for Jonas Chickering, who combined craftsmanship and modern industrial methods to produce a piano with superior sound.

Chickering's partner John Mackay, meanwhile, revolutionized the way pianos were sold by establishing a national network for their product. A piano in the parlor became the single most potent symbol of the cultured home. Its presence suggested refinement and an appreciation for music. "The Piano-forte is a badge of gentility," wrote one Bostonian, "being the only thing that distinguishes 'Decent people' from the lower and less distinguished kind of folks."

Everything was in place. An increasingly industrialized America had the money for luxury goods like pianos, the desire to own them, and the know-how of her Yankee ivory-cutters, who by the 1840s were cutting more than a ton of ivory every week. Depending on the weight of the tusks—and at that time an 80-pound tusk was a good average—at least a dozen elephants a week were dying to supply Connecticut's factories. And the heyday of the industry—a heyday that would last 80 years—was still to come.

IN RETROSPECT, THE DISPARATE strands of history come together as if perfectly woven. On the other side of the globe, in what seems like a diabolical coincidence, the world market for cloves, a spice grown on islands off the east coast of Africa, exploded.

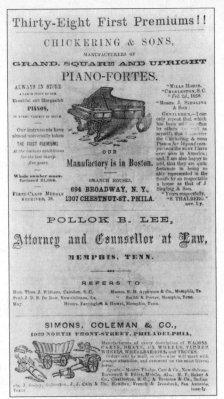

After the Civil War, a piano in the parlor became the single most potent symbol of a cultured home, and for Boston manufacturer Chickering—and its keyboard makers in Connecticut—this was good news. DeBow's Review, July 1859. Courtesy, American Antiquarian Society

Many of the enslaved Africans who managed to survive the trek with ivory to the eastern coast wound up in the slave market in Zanzibar. From there, they were sold into forced labor on clove plantations on Pemba and Zanzibar and other Indian Ocean islands, or on huge sugar plantations in Brazil, where slavery was legal until 1888. They were also sold into agricultural slavery in Arabia and North Africa.

America's first consul in Zanzibar—the United States was the first nation to have a consulate on the island—witnessed daily sales in the slave markets of as many as 100 people at a time. The consul, Richard Waters, once reported that Zanzibar's sultan purchased 700 people to work on a sugar plantation he owned. Waters also described the frenetic life onshore, with its constant deal making and politicking with the sultan, and offshore, where ships from New England and Europe were stacked up like the planes at O'Hare, waiting to ferry Africa's riches to the outer world.

He saw slave ships packed with children, most of them ten to fourteen years old. The sight "called up many unpleasant feelings," he said, although he didn't feel he could criticize the African slave trade because of America's enslaved population.

When Waters confided feelings of guilt to his journal in 1837, there were, in fact, 2 million enslaved people in America, a figure that would double before the Civil War. Waters was, like Connecticut ivory men Julius Pratt and George Read, active in the antislavery movement. But he was in Zanzibar to promote trade relations with East Africa and to help build a market that would make New Englanders rich. Waters's feelings may have been conflicted, but his mission was clear.

In another journal entry, Waters describes a Spanish slave merchant setting off with his ship full of human cargo. Though Waters tells the man that slavery is "a business which I hate from the heart," he offers to trade with him on other kinds of goods and encourages the merchant to stay in touch.

ACROSS THE STREET FROM THE TRIM REDBRICK PRATT, READ FACTORY built in 1882 is the side road where ivory tusks were brought up from the river landing in horse-drawn wagons. The factory, now an apartment complex, overshadows Deep River's main street.

Though Deep River was never a company town like Sam Comstock's Ivoryton—Deep River had shipbuilding and quarrying among other enterprises— Pratt, Read was the major employer and the center of town life. When an 1881 fire destroyed the factory, 15 tons of ivory, and everything but the company safe, about 150 men were on the payroll. At a meeting a few

Though Oscar Lynn and Louis Pratt of the Pratt, Read ivory company were jubilant when weighing the first shipment of tusks after World War II, the piano-key business was already in its twilight. *Deep River Historical Society*

days later, townspeople voted to offer the company a major tax abatement to rebuild in Deep River.

Contemporary accounts of Pratt, Read and competitor Comstock, Cheney lauded company leaders for the rigor of their work ethic and for their "native Yankee shrewdness." To a raw material imported from halfway around the world, the ivory workers applied artisan-level craftsmanship and precision machine work. This was the new American style of industry, and the result was a high-volume, high-quality product that brought the two companies contracts from throughout the country.

Correspondence from the early summer of 1876, for example, shows Comstock, Cheney supplying ivory keys to more than a dozen piano and organ manufacturers. The old letters also show a brisk business in billiard balls, combs, and many other household objects made of ivory, the plastic of its age.

For more than a century, Connecticut was a center of ivory knowledge, the center of ivory manufacturing in America, and a world leader in the business. Of the thousands of tons of ivory that passed through Zanzibar during the nineteenth and early twentieth centuries, 75 percent of the total came to Connecticut.

Smithsonian curator David Shayt, who has extensively researched Connecticut's ivory industry, has estimated that between 1884 and 1911, nearly 10 million pounds of unworked ivory were brought into the United States. The per-pound price on the New York market ranged from $1.80 to $4.00. That's a minimum figure of nearly $18 million, or about $310 million in today's currency.

That's a lot of money, and a lot of elephants, and a lot of black people carrying ivory to a port called Bagamoyo, which means, in Swahili, "lay down your heart."

A BROCHURE PRODUCED BY A GERMAN IVORY COMPANY FOR THE STORIED 1876 Centennial Exhibition in Philadelphia notes that most of the ivory harvested from Africa was just lying on the ground. In fact, early in that century great caches of available ivory had been assembled through trade with individual villages.

Africa may have been the only place ivory tusks ever served purely utilitarian purposes. Tusks were used for animal stockades and for doorposts and roof beams, and were carved into the tools of daily life, such as mortars and pestles. Henry Stanley saw tusks erected palisade-style around the graves of chieftains.

The elephant was a source of food, and for some tribal people it had a spiritual dimension and was represented in their art. In his journal in 1858 David Livingstone described the hunting and death of a female elephant in which the African hunters sang and played instruments to the elephant before killing her. "O chief! O chief! We have come to kill you," they sang.

That African people ate elephant meat and used ivory tusks to support their door frames looked like ignorance to the West. The natives clearly didn't understand the value of those tusks. But it wasn't the Africans who decimated the elephant.

By the time of the 1876 centennial, the notion of piles of ivory waiting to be scooped up was a convenient, tragic fiction.

The Smithsonian's National Museum of American History contains a chilling collection of correspondence from McLean, Morris & Company, the London broker from which Comstock, Cheney bought huge quantities of tusks during the 1870s. The handwritten letters, each still bearing its small circle of red sealing wax, detail with brutal clarity the amounts and varieties of ivory coming to market—"Zanzibar Prime" was the very best—as well as news of sales trends and anticipated shipments. The broker's cheerful communiques to Ivoryton, often several per week, and the printed circulars show annual sales of hundreds of tons of ivory. The German firm of Heinrich Adolf Meyer, a competitor of the Connecticut ivory companies, estimated that 2 million pounds of ivory were "consumed" each year worldwide.

At midcentury, English explorers had seen great herds of elephants. Livingstone once counted a group of 800. But by the 1870s, the devastating effect of all those pianos was apparent.

As elephant populations in East Africa dwindled and ivory had to be harvested from elephants in Central and West Central Africa, the journey to the coast got longer and harder for ivory's human porters. Some of the trade routes went all the way to the Belgian Congo halfway across the continent. Explorers like Stanley saw a devastated landscape of burned and empty villages. An entire frontier of ivory taking and human enslavement was moving west.

Under the weight of the tusks they were forced to carry, men and women taken from their villages by force walked hundreds of miles to the coast from inland trading centers on the Congo River and Lake Tanganyika, among other places. Ujiji, the ivory and slave-trading center on the eastern shore of Lake Tanganyika, where Stanley encountered Dr. Livingstone, was 700 miles from the coast, but the trek was often even longer.

The horrors of the ivory trade were not the temporary ravages of war or civil strife but were part of an ongoing system, one that lasted for at least 80 years and used black human beings as commercial currency.

Some of the most sustained and harrowing descriptions of the business come from a Connecticut man who was an ivory trader himself, and a very successful one.

Ernst D. Moore was twenty-three when his uncle brought him into the family ivory business. From 1907 to 1911, Moore was based primarily in Zanzibar, buying elephant tusks in the market and traveling to the interior of Africa, where he bought directly from great hunters of the day for Arnold Cheney & Company, which supplied both Pratt, Read and Comstock, Cheney.

Ernst Moore (top center) was a successful ivory trader in East Africa early in the twentieth century. After returning to Connecticut, he wrote *Ivory, Scourge of Africa,* a harrowing account of the trade. *Deep River Historical Society*

He lived in a house with carved teakwood gates, entertained Teddy Roosevelt at the Mombasa Club, bought hundreds of tons of ivory, and then came home to marry a woman in Connecticut and work for Pratt, Read as an executive in the company's player piano division. An able pianist, he loved to play Liszt.

Before his early death, Moore wrote the book *Ivory, Scourge of Africa.* Published in 1931, it is a history of the ivory trade and a cult classic. The original cover shows a slave coffle bearing tusks.

Fluent in Swahili and the language that grew out of African and Arab trade, Moore interviewed former slaves to build his story about the ivory trade, which he called "a terrible vocation."

Moore said that during the second half of the nineteenth century, the height of the ivory trade, the dhows that lay at anchor off the town were packed with slaves awaiting transport to Arabia and the Persian Gulf. Dead slaves lay rotting on Zanzibar's sloping beach until the tide carried their bodies out to sea.

Fifty years earlier, Massachusetts ivory trader Michael Shepard had seen slave-laden ships coming over to Zanzibar from the mainland, and the captives herded toward the slave market like sheep. The dead were simply thrown overboard, he wrote, and if they floated onto the shore, "the natives come with poles and push them from the beach."

Slavery was outlawed in East Africa in the decade before Moore began his career, and the railroads built by England and Germany had started carrying ivory directly from the interior to the coast. Yet human porterage and oppression continued.

A world campaign against slavery in Africa had been mounted during the decades after the American Civil War, but traders did not want to let go of a lucrative system that had worked for so long, and the priority of the West was to maintain the flow of ivory. Tens of thousands of Americans were buying pianos every year, and pianos required ivory.

The ivory and slave trades were deeply intertwined. The connection between the number of tusks gathered and human lives destroyed was understood, even in the early years of the ivory trade. The equation first formulated by Livingstone is one modern historians use as well: Five black people were killed or forced into slavery for each elephant tusk that reached the coast. Henry Stanley's number is higher. He says that for every pound of ivory, someone died.

Working from company records, scholar Donald Malcarne has estimated that between 1870 and 1900, at least 200,000 tusks were used by Comstock, Cheney. If every tusk represents the death or enslavement of five people, then the Ivoryton company affected 1 million Africans. Bring Pratt, Read into the equation—during the last decade of the nineteenth century the Deep River company actually handled more ivory than Comstock, Cheney—and the estimate becomes 2 million lives affected.

That number fails to reflect the earlier decades of Connecticut's ivory processing—by 1839 keyboards were being veneered with ivory—nor does it take into consideration the early years of the twentieth century, when Ernst Moore wrote his blood-drenched story of the ivory trade.

Two million lives is an inconceivable number, and yet the real figure is probably higher.

DURING THE LAST TWO DECADES OF THE NINETEENTH CENTURY, George Cheney was at the helm of America's ivory industry, but in 1850, when he was twenty-two, he sailed to Africa for the first time aboard the brig *Sacramento*. He was "full of high hopes," according to a family memoir, and in love with a spirited nineteen-year-old from Rhode Island.

On his rough first voyage to Zanzibar, he got on the captain's nerves with his informality and fraternizing with sailors. But once he arrived he learned Swahili, which he thought musical, as well as Portuguese, and became a formidable trader. In the employ of his future father-in-law, ivory trader Rufus Greene of Providence, Cheney established his reputation with a major early score of 60,000 pounds of ivory from a single caravan.

He read Shakespeare on Sundays, explored the island on horseback, and learned to love curry. The sultan's daughter sent him plates of fruit and flowers, and in the evenings he played cards and drank port with a trader named Jelly. A churchman of the time called Zanzibar "a cesspool of wickedness," but it sounds like Cheney had fun. A sea captain who knew him then remarked that his boyishness was disappearing.

In the diary where Cheney recorded observations to share with Sarah, his bride-to-be, he wrote that he had two servants, "two boys, an old one and a young one." He added, "They call all blacks here boys, even if they are 60 years old."

A week after their wedding in 1853, he took her with him to Zanzibar, where two of their children were born. In Sarah's letters home to her family, Cheney appears as a tender figure, attentive and eager to establish a real home for his family. He was slow to punish their servants, whom they regarded as lazy and dishonest. "George has never struck one himself," Sarah wrote, "but stands by to see it done and is pale and sick for hours after."

Cheney went into business with Samuel Comstock in 1862, put his ivory expertise to work, and helped make the company bigger and more

George Cheney was a leader in Connecticut's ivory industry, and he knew the darkest side of his business, having lived in East Africa for nearly a decade. *Ivoryton Library Association*

profitable. The boyish trader evolved into an industry captain. He bought an expensive house in Essex, had a long, happy marriage with Sarah, and died, in 1901, a very rich man.

During his career, Cheney had more direct knowledge of Africa and the costs of the ivory trade than any of his peers, because he lived in Zanzibar for most of the 1850s.

Nile explorer Richard Burton, who was notorious for hating Africans, nonetheless was horrified by the slave market, the same market Cheney would have seen. Burton said that lines of emaciated blacks, their ribs "protruding like the circles of a cask," stood mutely, like animals. Many of them lay sick on the ground, and all of them were subjected to an inspection he described as "degrading."

Between the 1790s of Phineas Pratt and the post–Civil War decades when Cheney was the most prominent name in the industry, America's relationship with slavery at home changed dramatically. Connecticut ivory cutters' exploitative compact with Africa, however, did not change. By then, the state was home to 90 percent of the nation's ivory manufacturing.

Abolitionists George Read and Julius Pratt did not see their beliefs and their work as contradictory because they understood ending slavery to be a national problem. The most pressing concern facing ivory's entrepreneurs was not the human rights of Africans but how to make their complex industry succeed. Besides, many indispensable products at the time were produced by slave labor—cotton and sugar, to name just two. While cotton might carry the suggestion of slave labor, a beautiful piano with keys made of ivory did not.

The aftermath of the Civil War brought with it a new and disabling reality, one with a ripple that reached Africa. The casualties of the United States' war were so high and communities so devastated that the national priority became the reconciliation of North and South. The other postwar agenda—to create a place in society for millions of freed blacks, most of whom were illiterate and impoverished—was essentially discarded. White America had to heal first.

In his time, and in the footsteps of earlier Connecticut ivory men, George Cheney translated a natural resource from Africa into a luxury for America, and the black people swept up into that terrible transformation simply did not figure.

AN 1881 PANORAMIC MAP IN THE LIBRARY OF CONGRESS DEPICTS ESSEX and its villages of Centerbrook and Ivoryton as a single, peaceful shire.

Sails dot the Connecticut River, tree-covered hills slope gently, and factories, including the "Comstock, Cheney & Co. Piano Key Manufactory," look solid and prosperous.

The immense wooden factory shown on the map exists now only in photographs, though a later brick building survives, as does the "sharp shop," where workers polished the ebony sharps and flats. The sight of this worn, ghostly complex is difficult to reconcile with the bursting folders of nineteenth-century correspondence at the Smithsonian.

Pratt, Read and Comstock, Cheney, which competed for nearly 75 years, merged during the Great Depression. Piano sales, which had plummeted during the 1930s, recovered a little during the 1940s, but ivory's reign was over. A final shipment of four tons was delivered in the early 1950s, but after 1957 American-made keyboards were no longer veneered with real ivory. Nascent environmentalism was less a cause than were the extraordinary difficulties of getting a reliable supply of ivory from Africa.

And at its core, despite the elaborate machinery and many technical innovations, ivory cutting had remained an artisan's craft. The home entertainment business it once served began to change, and the piano was replaced by radios and then televisions. It was no longer the "badge of gentility."

A worried company memorandum from the 1940s decries the lack of young men willing to learn the craft, and a series of photographs taken at Pratt, Read in the mid-1950s shows mostly elderly men at the saws and worktables.

A huge archive survives from the Ivoryton and Deep River companies, which, at their peak, employed nearly 1,000 people. In museum collections in Connecticut and in Washington, D.C., there is a trove of correspondence, photographs, company manuals, account books, and such objects as George Read's "bleach house" journal, in which, more than 150 years ago, he recorded each day's weather. Days of sunlight he praised extravagantly.

Pratt, Read's logo of a jovial African elephant—its trunk curling over a keyboard—appears everywhere on company literature. When the image was drawn, extinction didn't seem like a possibility for *Loxodonta africana*, nor for the ivory industry.

"I had seen a herd of elephants travelling through dense native forest," wrote Isak Dinesen, "pacing along as if they had an appointment at the end of the world."

Once found in every middle-class home, ivory today is again regarded as precious, and most world wildlife groups list the African ele-

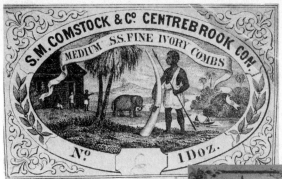

The ivory trade in Africa looked like a peaceful enterprise in nineteenth-century advertisements, and nothing about the piano in the parlor suggested its violent origins, but for countless Africans, it was a lethal endeavor. Explorer Henry Stanley called the ivory trade "a bloody seizure."

phant as endangered. Recent surveys show a population of about 600,000, and falling.

The ivory trade gave rise to beautiful Ivoryton, and to personal fortunes in Connecticut. It helped European immigrants to establish a place for themselves in the New World and to buy homes. It did not create beautiful towns or personal fortunes for Africans, because the nature of extractive cultures is to take away.

For 150 years, the ivory business subtracted elephants from an environment where they flourished. For at least a century of that time, the business also subtracted tribal people from their world.

The black man in the ivory company brochures is always barefoot. There is always a lush palm tree behind him. Sometimes there is a mountain, smoking. He always holds a spear, and balanced easily against his body is a tusk of shining white.

AFTERWORD

IN 1860, THE UNITED STATES WAS THE LARGEST SLAVEHOLDING nation in the Western Hemisphere, and one of the last.

Its nearly 4 million slaves were an asset valued at $3 billion, worth as much as all the country's factories, railroads, and livestock combined. Cotton was the single largest U.S. export, and New York City was the financial capital of the Cotton Kingdom.

The very distance that separated North from South, that separated Manhattan's Wall Street and Broadway from Southern cotton plantations, was a geographical measure of slavery's confounding paradox: It both united and divided. By splitting the nation into free and slave states, the Civil War disrupted, and masked, the economy and shared racism that bound the states together.

At this point, nearly a century and a half after Lincoln signed the Emancipation Proclamation, it is more than fair to ask, What would the United States be today if there had been no slavery?

It is obvious that, at the very least, America's extraordinary ascent into the world arena would have taken far longer than it did. At the birth of a nation, the unpaid labor of millions of human beings was a catapult, enabling America to develop, thrive, and compete with older, more established countries in a relatively short period of time.

And the complicity of the North, the deep dependence of the country's economic engine on this huge pool of unpaid labor—on slavery—allowed this to happen.

ON THE 100TH ANNIVERSARY OF THE START OF THE CIVIL WAR, THE writer Robert Penn Warren observed that twin national myths had grown from the conflict. The South's he called "the Great Alibi"; the North's "the Treasury of Virtue."

Our intention as journalists has been not so much to debunk the myth of the virtuous North as to set the record straight. Whatever readers may make of the evidence of Northern complicity, our own reactions to it varied.

One of us was most struck by the suffering of enslaved Americans. Whether they were treated better in the North than in the South is irrelevant to the institution's basic cruelty, and the irony of having legal slavery in a land defined by "liberty and justice for all."

Another was amazed by how much of its wealth America owes to slavery, and now sees the legacy of that wealth everywhere in the present.

The third was surprised over and over by how much of the history we assume we know is shaped by forgotten, or ignored, facts.

Washington Post publisher Philip L. Graham, who died in 1963, famously called journalism "a first rough draft of history." Here's the full Graham quote:

> *So let us drudge on about our inescapably impossible task of providing every week a first rough draft of a history that will never be completed about a world we can never understand.*

In *Complicity*, the three of us, all lifelong New England journalists, are doing what reporters rarely have a chance to do: present a second draft of history.

For us, this draft differs starkly from the world we thought we knew. Our hope is that it will move readers, at least a degree or two, toward a deeper understanding.

CHRONOLOGY

1631   *Massachusetts launches* Blessing of the Bay, *heralding start of New England trade to West Indies slave plantations.*

1641   *Massachusetts is first colony to recognize slavery by statute.*

1712   *The killing of 8 whites in slave rebellion in New York City leads to the death of 25 slaves.*

1741   *The Great Negro Plot in New York City results in execution of 31 blacks and 4 whites.*

1760   *Slave population of New England and the Middle Atlantic States has grown to at least 41,000.*

1772   *Newport nears peak as Triangle Trade port, as 230,000 gallons of Rhode Island rum are shipped to Africa.*

1787   *Connecticut and South Carolina delegates to Constitutional Convention in Philadelphia negotiate compromises that count a slave as three-fifths of a person and extend slave trade 20 years.*

1790   *First U.S. Census shows Connecticut and Rhode Island with a combined slave population of 3,500, Pennsylvania with 3,700 slaves, and New York with more than 20,000 black slaves. (Free and enslaved blacks make up more than 19 percent of the U.S. population.)*

1793   *Eli Whitney of Massachusetts invents his cotton gin, leading to renewed Southern demand for slave labor.*

1793 *Congress passes first fugitive slave law, setting stage for kidnapping of Northern blacks.*

1798 *The narrative of Venture Smith of Connecticut, one of the first and most important American slave narratives, is published.*

1807 *Rhode Island leads rush to import slaves before transatlantic slave trade becomes illegal on January 1, 1808. The DeWolf family ships an estimated 2,000 Africans to Charleston, South Carolina, in just seven months.*

1810 *Nearly 200 cotton mills are in operation in the North.*

1811 *New York ships 15,000 bales of cotton to Liverpool.*

1818 *The Black Ball Line begins regular packet ship runs between New York City and Liverpool, heralding New York's emergence as nation's financial and cotton trade capital.*

1819 *New England Society of Charleston, South Carolina, is founded.*

1822 *Cotton, valued at $3.9 million, is 40 percent of New York's domestic exports. Flour, the city's second-most-valuable domestic export, is valued at $794,000.*

1826 *Lowell, Massachusetts, is incorporated. Its 2,500 population includes 2,000 textile workers. By 1858, its 52 mills use 800,000 pounds of cotton every week.*

1833 *Slavery abolished in the British Empire, with compensation to slave owners.*

1834 *Antiabolitionist mob attacks Prudence Crandall's school for black girls in Canterbury, Connecticut, forcing it to close.*

1835 *Abolitionist publisher and editor William Lloyd Garrison is chased, roped, and paraded through the streets of Boston by a mob and spends the night in jail, the only place the mayor can guarantee his safety.*

1837 *Antiabolitionist mob in Alton, Illinois, kills newspaper editor Elijah Lovejoy, creating a martyr.*

1842 *U.S. Supreme Court Justice Joseph Story of Massachusetts writes* Prigg *decision, giving federal protection to slaveholders pursuing runaways in free states.*

1850   *Passage of the Fugitive Slave Act leads to mass exodus of free blacks who feel unsafe in Northern cities. Many settle in Canada.*

1854   *Publication of* Types of Mankind *marks pinnacle of work of American race scientists, who conclude blacks and whites are separate species.*

       Anthony Burns, a fugitive slave living in Boston, is returned to Virginia.

1859   *Radical abolitionist John Brown attacks arsenal at Harpers Ferry, Virginia, hoping to incite a slave rebellion and to end slavery.*

1860   *Value of cotton exported from New York is $12.4 million. Value of next largest export, flour, is $6.6 million.*

       Of 1,091 cotton mills in the country, 472 are located in New England.

1861   *Mayor Fernando Wood of New York proposes the city secede from the Union in large part so cotton trade with the South can continue.*

       The end of New York's reign as illegal slave trade hub is marked by the conviction of Nathaniel Gordon of Portland, Maine, captain of the slave ship Erie.

1862   *The Comstock, Cheney piano-key manufacturing company is formed in Ivoryton, Connecticut, joining the Pratt, Read company of Deep River as world-leading importers of African ivory, most of it harvested by slaves.*

1863   *The Emancipation Proclamation takes effect on January 1, declaring slaves held in Confederate States free.*

       Draft rioters in New York City turn against blacks, killing scores and setting fire to Colored Orphan Asylum.

NOTES

INTRODUCTION

xxvii *a "just war" against Indians:* See Donnan, *Documents Illustrative of the Slave Trade to America,* vol. 3, p. 8.

Chapter One COTTON COMES NORTH

3 *"The ships would rot . . .":* See Foner, *Business and Slavery,* p. 4. (Originally appeared in *De Bow's Review* 29:318.)

3 *"With our aggrieved brethren . . .":* Wood in "Secession Gone to Seed," *The New York Times,* January 8, 1861, p. 4. Discussion of secession speech and sentiments in Anbinder, *Fernando Wood and New York City's Secession.*

4 *cotton had already become:* Bruchey, *Cotton and the Growth,* table L, "Value of Leading Domestic Exports," p. 23.

5 *Three brothers named Lehman:* Kenneth T. Jackson, ed., *Encyclopedia of New York City,* p. 662. Also, Lehman Brothers Web site, at www.lehman.com/who/history.

5 *Junius Morgan and J. Pierpont Morgan:* Morgan, *Slavery and Servitude,* pp. 88–89.

5 *John Jacob Astor:* Kenneth Wiggins Porter, *John Jacob Astor,* pp. 672–673.

5 *Charles L. Tiffany:* Bingham, *Tiffany Fortune.* p. 122.

5 *Archibald Gracie:* McKay, *South Street,* pp. 32, 108. Also, Gracie Mansion home page, at www.historichousetrust.org/museum.

6 *New England was home to:* Hammond, *Cotton Industry,* p. 254.

6 *On the evening of October 11, 1858:* O'Connor, *Lords of the Loom,* p. 133.

7 *On the cusp of the Civil War:* Hammond, *Cotton Industry,* appendix 1 chart,

"The Cotton Production and Trade of the United States from 1784 to 1897."

7   *2,650 cotton factories:* Hammond, *Cotton Industry*, p. 252.

9   *"one negro [could] . . . clean fifty weight . . .":* Whitney's statement to Jefferson is attributed to Frederick Law Olmsted's "Memoir of Eli Whitney, Esq.," p. 17, by Bruchey in *Cotton and the Growth*, p. 61, footnote.

10   *"less than 100,000 more field hands":* Bruchey, *Cotton and the Growth*, p. 70.

10   *about 75,000 cotton plantations:* Ibid., appendix I, attributed to seventh U.S. Census.

10   Solon Robinson: Woodman, preface, *King Cotton*, pp. vii–viii.

11   *Pine Street meeting on December 15, 1860:* "The Crisis in New-York: Private Meeting to Urge the South to Postpone Disunion," *New York Times*, December 17, 1860, page 1. Also, Foner, *Business and Slavery*, pp 227–232.

12   *From 1825 on:* Albion, *Rise of New York Port*, pp. 95–121.

13   Nathaniel Prime: Chernow, *Alexander Hamilton*, p. 715.

14   discussion of the role of factors: Woodman, *King Cotton*, pt. 1, pp. 3–71, and Chandler, *The Visible Hand*, pp. 21–24.

14   Bostwick letter: Bruchey, *Cotton and the Growth*, pp. 253–254.

18   discussion of Black Ball Line and other packets: Albion, *Rise of New York Port* and *Square-Riggers on Schedule*. Also, more colorfully, McKay, *South Street*.

18   discussion of effects of cotton trade in Manhattan: Albion, *Rise of New York Port*, pp. 260–286. Especially fascinating is appendix 31, "New York Commercial Functions, 1846," p. 421, a listing of various businesses from Doggett's New York Business Directory. Also, Foner, *Business and Slavery*, pp. 1–14. *De Bow's Review*, July 1859.

24   *"the soils, seasons, climate . . . . :* Israel D. Andrews, quoted in Bruchey, *Cotton and the Growth*, pp. 71–73.

25   *"a city springing up . . . . :* John Greenleaf Whittier, quoted from his 1845 book *The Stranger in Lowell* on the Web site of the Lowell National Historical Park, at www.nps.gov.

26   *mills in Massachusetts and tiny Rhode Island:* Temin, *Engines of Enterprise*, table 3.1, p. 122.

26   *"Our local affairs are very delightful . . .":* Amos Lawrence, quoted in O'Connor, *Lords of the Loom*, p. 35.

26   *"If I have mercantile tact enough . . .":* Dalzell, *Enterprising Elite*, p. 72.

31   *"On this subject, I do not wish to think . . .":* William Lloyd Garrison, quoted in Mayer, *All on Fire*, p. 112.

31 *"There is much excitement . . .":* William Sparks, quoted in O'Connor, *Lords of the Loom*, p. 46.

32 *"I feel it to be my duty . . .":* Rufus Choate, quoted in Ibid., p. 59.

36 *"loves the black race . . .":* Amos Lawrence, quoted in Ibid., p. 97.

36 *"Where will be the patronage . . .":* Abbott Lawrence, quoted in Ibid., p. 60.

37 *"between the cotton-planters and flesh-mongers of Louisiana and Mississippi . . ."* Charles Sumner, quoted in Dalzell, *Enterprising Elite*, p. 202.

37 *"Cotton thread holds the union together . . .":* Ralph Waldo Emerson, quoted in O'Connor, *Lords of the Loom*, p. 67.

37 reactions to the Fugitive Slave Act: O'Connor, *Lords of the Loom*, pp. 93–113.

40 Peace Conference: Ibid., pp. 132–153.

43 "LEARN TO CONFORM TO CIRCUMSTANCES": Hegel, *Carriages from New Haven*, p. 27.

Chapter Two FIRST FORTUNES

45 Winthrop borrowing from the Gospel of Matthew: *John Winthrop*, Bremer, pp. 179–180.

45 Henry Winthrop lands on Barbados: Dunn, *Sugar and Slaves*, p. 50.

46 *another group of Puritans . . . slave labor:* Kupperman, *Providence Island, 1630–1641*, p. 172.

46 *"the most flourishing islands in all those American parts . . .":* See Bailyn, *New England Merchants*, p. 85.

46 English ships delivering Africans to Barbados, Jamaica, Leeward Islands: Dunn, *Sugar and Slaves*, p. 230.

46 *"a thousand Negroes . . .":* See Bailyn, *New England Merchants*, p. 85.

46 *one of earliest known New England slave voyages:* Ibid., p. 85.

48 *"New England was not a slave society . . . :* Bailyn, "Slavery and Population Growth," in Temin, *Engines of Enterprise*, pp. 254–255.

49 *plantations operated like factories:* Dunn, *Sugar and Slaves*, pp. 190–191.

49 *almost 80 percent of New England's overseas exports:* Solow, ed., *Slavery and the Rise*, p. 16; Innes, *Creating the Commonwealth*, p. 297.

51 *Towns passed ordinances:* Innes, *Creating the Commonwealth*, pp. 281–282.

51 *Transporting livestock down the Atlantic coast:* Gaddis Smith, "Agricultural Roots of Maritime History," p. 7. Also, Bowers, *Journal of Henry Bowers, Master, on Board the Brig* Gleaner.

51 Narragansett area plantation system: Fitts, *Inventing New England's Slave Paradise*, pp. 73–75.

51 New London County, Connecticut, 4,000-acre plantation: Lang, "Complicity," p. 6.

53 Slave-worked farms belonging to New Yorkers Lewis Morris and Augustus Van Cortlandt: Burrows and Wallace, *Gotham*, pp. 87, 105, 123; and Web site of New York City Department of Parks and Recreation, www.nycgovparks.org.

53 *nearly seventy distilleries:* McCusker, *Rum and the American Revolution*, pp. 438–441.

53 Molasses and rum data for 1770: Ibid., pp. 420–421.

53 Rum consumption: Ibid., p. 468.

53 Blessing of the Bay *launched:* Innes, *Creating the Commonwealth*, p. 287.

54 Boston ship ownership, 1700: Ibid., p. 297.

54 Samuel Winthrop in Antigua: Dunn, *Sugar and Slaves*, pp. 125–126.

55 Winthrop cousin in Barbados: Ibid., p. 336.

55 *"It pleased the Lord to open us a trade . . .":* Winthrop, *Journal of John Winthrop*, p. 692.

57 *"their has been a Great many Negroes . . .":* Nathaniel Russell, in Donnan, *Documents Illustrative of the Slave Trade*, vol. 4, p. 450.

Chapter Three A CONNECTICUT SLAVE

61 *"I reached out . . .":* Venture Smith, *Narrative of the Life*, p. 19. (Venture Smith's *Narrative* is available online, at www.docsouth.unc.edu/neh/venture/venture.html.)

62 *But in the 1790s . . . and New York had more than 20,000:* Evarts B. Greene and Virginia D. Harrington, *American Population before the Federal Census*, pp. 50, 64, 92.

62 *it didn't take long . . . as beneficial to the slave as to the owner:* William C. Fowler, "The Historical Status of the Negro in Connecticut" (a paper read before the New Haven Colony Historical Society, 1875), pp. 126–132.

64 *"The very first salute . . .":* V. Smith, *Narrative of the Life*, p. 10.

64 *"In the Area of this Quadrangle . . .":* Atkins, *Voyage to Guinea*, p. 269.

66 *"[James] would order me . . .":* V. Smith, *Narrative of the Life*, p. 15.

66 *"They gave her plenty to eat . . .":* Soujourner Truth, in Wideman, comp., *My Soul Has Grown Deep*, p. 366.

67 *"In the aftern I was att . . .":* Hempstead, *Diary of Joshua Hempstead*, p. 562.

68 *"We privately collected . . .":* V. Smith, *Narrative of the Life*, p. 17.

68   *"a very tall fellow . . .":* Hodges and Brown, *"Pretends to Be Free,"* pp. 49–50.

70   *"In the morning as I was putting . . .":* V. Smith, *Narrative of the Life,* p. 19.

73   *"What a compensation . . .":* Sojourner Truth, in Wideman, *Soul Grown Deep,* p. 365.

73   *"Being thirty-six years old . . .":* V. Smith, *Narrative of the Life,* p. 24.

Chapter Four REBELLION IN MANHATTAN

77   *"No one imagined":* Horsmanden, *New York Conspiracy,* p. 24.

78   *They fought back early and fiercely:* Bennett, *Before the Mayflower,* pp. 112–139.

79   *"in a riotous manner":* Governor Cornbury, as quoted in Burrows and Wallace, *Gotham,* p. 147.

81   *"whole town . . . under arms":* Scott, "Slave Insurrection in New York," quoting the *Boston Weekly News-Letter,* April 14, 1712.

81   *"I am informed that in the West Indies . . .":* Governor Robert Hunter, in O'Callaghan, *Documents Relative to the Colonial History,* vol. 5, pp. 341–342.

81   *"The Late Hellish Attempt . . .":* See Stokes, *Iconography of Manhattan Island,* vol. 10, p. 475.

83   *"Fire, Fire, Scorch, Scorch . . .":* See Thomas J. Davis, *Rumor of Revolt,* p. 17.

86   *"How this notion of its being lawful . . .":* Frederick Philipse II, quoted in Horsmanden, *New York Conspiracy,* p. 39.

86   *"a person of infamous character . . .":* Horsmanden, *Conspiracy,* p. 15.

87   *That any white people . . .":* Ibid., pp. 42–43.

88   *"died very stubbornly . . .":* Ibid., pp. 65–66.

89   *"Gentlemen, no scheme more monstrous . . .":* See Ibid., pp. 102–105.

92   *"obscure drudge":* McManus, *History of Negro Slavery in New York,* p. 131.

93   *The plot might have had:* Linebaugh and Rediker, *Many-Headed Hydra,* pp. 203–206.

Chapter Five NEWPORT RUM, AFRICAN SLAVES

95   Rhode Island slave trade volume: Coughtry, *Notorious Triangle,* pp. 25–26.

98   *"rum-men":* Ibid., p. 111.

98   200,000 gallons of rum; slave price of 150 gallons: Ibid., pp. 16, 68.

99   Slave merchants as Newport taxpayers: Crane, *Dependent People,* p. 25.

99 Slave captains in Fellowship Club, Trinity Church: Deutsch, "Elusive Guineaman," pp. 250–252.

99 orders to Rivera/Lopez slave captain, *"Lying any considerable time . . .":* Quoted by Roderick Terry in "Some Old Papers Relating to the Newport Slave Trade," *Newport Historical Society Bulletin,* July 1927, p. 15.

100 *"The inhabitants of Rhode Island, especially those of Newport . . .":* Samuel Hopkins, quoted in Crane, *Dependent People,* p. 21.

101 Brown indicted for slave trade violation: Coughtry, *Notorious Triangle,* p. 215.

102 DeWolf accused of drowning slave and violent reputation: Howe, *Mount Hope,* pp. 105–106.

102 Brown family background: Hedges, *Browns of Providence Plantations,* vol. 1.

102 *"She died about two months after you sailed . . .":* James Brown, quoted in Hedges, p. 71.

102 voyage of the *Sally:* Wax, "Browns of Providence," pp. 171–179; Hedges, *Browns of Providence Plantations,* pp. 75–80.

105 armaments on the *Sultan:* Coughtry, *Notorious Triangle,* p. 98.

105 insurance covers "risks of the Seas, Men of War": See Ibid., p. 99.

105 slave ship routines: Ibid., pp. 50–54, 106.

106 DeWolf slave pulled from mother: Howe, *New England Chronicle,* p. 119.

107 *"the White Man's Grave":* Coughtry, *Notorious Triangle,* p. 154.

107 Slave depression and suicide: Piersen, "White Cannibals, Black Martyrs," p. 150.

108 slave trade mentioned in draft of Declaration of Independence: "Declaring Independence: Drafting the Documents," Library of Congress Web site.

109 *"I have many times since thought . . .":* Moses Brown, in Donnan, *Documents Illustrative of the Slave Trade,* vol. 3, p. 334.

110 *"there was no more crime":* John Brown, in *United States Chronicle,* March 26, 1789.

110 John Brown remarks in Congress: In Donnan, *Documents Illustrative of the Slave Trade,* vol. 3, p. 383.

111 auction of the *Lucy:* Howe, *Mount Hope,* p. 108; Coughtry, *Notorious Triangle,* p. 218.

111 creation of Bristol customs district: Howe, *Mount Hope,* pp. 108–109; Coughtry, *Notorious Triangle,* pp. 225–229.

111 *"Theirs was one of the few fortunes":* Coughtry, *Notorious Triangle,* p. 49.

111   number of DeWolf voyages: Ibid., pp. 48–49.

111   the *Andromache*, pride of DeWolf fleet: Howe, *Mount Hope*, p. 129.

111   the DeWolfs' integrated business: Ibid., p. 110.

111   Slave shipments to South Carolina: McMillin, *Final Victims*, pp. 180–181, 215.

112   *"The people of Rhode Island have lately shown bitterness"*: Senator William Smith, quoted in Howe, *Mount Hope*, p. 190.

112   *prolific smugglers:* as described in Coughtry, *Notorious Triangle*, pp. 177–179.

113   *"This is my advice . . ."*: Simeon Potter, quoted in Howe, *Mount Hope*, p. 94.

113   George DeWolf bankruptcy: Howe, *Mount Hope*, pp. 230–233.

116   *During the long history of the slave trade . . . :* Appiah and Gates, *Africana*, p. 1867.

116   *More Africans . . . than through any other African fortress:* Joseph Opala, presentation at the Gilder Lehrman Center for the Study of Slavery, Resistance, and Abolition at Yale University, November 17, 2004.

117   *"This 24 hours Died . . ."*: Samuel Gould, "Log Book of Slave Traders," p. 42.

117   *The double doorways . . . guard stood:* Joseph Opala in conversation with Anne Farrow while touring Bunce Island, Sierra Leone, West Africa, November 2004.

118   *"On board the Good Hope . . ."*: Samuel Gould, "Log Book of Slave Traders," p. 38. In David Hancock, *Citizens of the World*, p. 426, John Stephens is listed as Bunce Island's agent for 1757–1758.

119   *"small winds"*: "Log Book of Slave Traders," p. 79.

Chapter Six NEW YORK'S SLAVE PIRATES

121   *Erie* capture: Rawley, "Captain Nathaniel Gordon," p. 216.

122   New York slave trade volume: Howard, *American Slavers*, pp. 58–65.

122   *Erie, Storm King,* and *Cora:* Ibid., p. 221. Also, British slave trade papers, vol. 47, Class A correspondence, document 42.

123   *"bearers to the tomb"*: Robert Edgar Conrad, *World of Sorrow*, p. 3.

123   Gordon death sentence protested: Rawley, "Captain Nathaniel Gordon," p. 223.

124   Gordon execution: *New York Herald*, February 22, 1862.

124   Judge Betts: Howard, *American Slavers*, pp. 161–162.

124 *"You don't have to worry . . ."*: See Ibid., p. 176.

124 U.S. Africa squadron and right to board: Ibid., pp. 59–61.

125 *"It is worse than idle . . ."*: Henry Wise, quoted in Howard, p. 11.

125 British practice of using "liberated" slaves: Ibid., p. 4.

125 Portuguese Company: Ibid., pp. 50–51.

125 the *Thomas Watson:* Reilly, in "Slavers in Disguise," documents 14 whaling ships outfitted for slave voyages. Samuel Skinner, part-owner of a New Bedford whaler seized in August 1861, may have been the first captain convicted of equipping a ship for a slave voyage. His prosecutor in Boston district court was Richard Henry Dana, best known as the author of *Two Years Before the Mast.*

125 Beebe, Dean & Donohue: Howard, *American Slavers*, p. 51.

125 *"the slave traders in this city . . ."*: *New-York Daily Tribune*, June 22, 1861.

126 Steamships carrying slaves: R. E. Conrad, *World of Sorrow*, p. 150; Karasch, *Brazilian Slavers*, p. 17.

126 Slave ship profits: Howard, *American Slavers*, p. 236: British slave trade papers, vol. 47, Class A correspondence, Havana document number 10.

127 the *Creole* and Madison Washington: Jones, "Peculiar Institution," pp. 28–33, passim.

128 the *Kentucky* and the *Porpoise:* Senate executive documents, 30th Congress, first session, document number 28; House executive documents, 30th Congress, second session, document number 61.

128 the *Hope* and concealed cargo: House executive documents, 29th Congress, first session, document number 43.

129 Boyle's testimony: Senate document number 28, pp. 71–77.

129 Page's testimony, *"If only one of two that were ironed together . . ."*: British slave trade papers, vol. 29, Class A correspondence, Rio de Janeiro, document number 201, p. 518.

130 *"Brazil is coffee and coffee is the Negro":* See R. E. Conrad, *World of Sorrow*, p. 62.

131 the *Mary E. Smith:* Howard, *American Slavers*, pp. 47, 124–126.

131 *Wanderer* voyage and reopening of slave trade: Wells, *Slave Ship* Wanderer, pp. 8–13; Sinha, *Counterrevolution of Slavery*, pp. 162–163.

131 *Wanderer* conspiracy, organized in New York: Wells, *Slave Ship* Wanderer, p. 38.

131 the *Nightingale:* Fairburn, *Merchant Sail*, vol. 6, pp. 3091–3092.

132 the *Ocilla* and *Huntress:* Senate executive documents, 38th Congress, first session, document number 56.

132 *"One cannot, to be sure, demand . . .":* Du Bois, *Suppression of the African Slave-Trade*, p. 198.

133 *"Do not imagine that because others . . .":* William Shipman, quoted in the *New York Herald*, February 22, 1862.

Chapter Seven THE OTHER UNDERGROUND RAILROAD

139 *Abolitionists claimed:* Weld, comp., "American Slavery as It Is," p. 142.

139 *an underground railroad:* Winch, "Philadelphia and the Other Underground Railroad," p. 3.

139 Patty Cannon: Carol Wilson, *Freedom at Risk*, pp. 20–23.

139 *"the celebrated Joseph Johnson":* Niles' *Register,* April 25, 1829.

140 David Ruggles: Ripley, ed., *Witness for Freedom*, p. 175; Dorothy Porter, "David M. Ruggles," pp. 136–137.

141 Fugitive Slave Act and black flight: Stanley W. Campbell, *Slave Catchers*, pp. 62–63.

141 Christiana Riot: Slaughter, *Bloody Dawn*, pp. 41–75.

142 *"the notorious, lying, slave-catching . . .":* See Ibid., p. 52.

142 impact of black armed resistance rivals John Brown's raid: Ibid., pp. x–xi.

142 Margaret Garner: S. W. Campbell, *Slave Catchers*, pp. 144–145.

142 *law of 1793 signed by George Washington:* Fehrenbacher, *Slaveholding Republic*, pp. 211–212.

143 *Callous men "are employed in kidnapping . . .":* Quoted from "Petition of People of Color," posted on the PBS Africans in America Web site, at www.pbs.org/wgbh/aia/home.html.

144 Richard Allen: Nash, *Forging Freedom*, p. 242.

144 Justice Joseph Story and *Prigg:* Holden-Smith, "Lords of Lash," pp. 1088–1137.

145 *"the additional ounce . . .":* William Lloyd Garrison, quoted in Morris, *Free Men All*, p. 105.

145 Cannon gang's early history: Shields, *Infamous Patty Cannon*, pp. 7–13.

145 *"Tradition tells . . .": Wilmington (DE) Morning News,* March 15, 1954.

146 Samuel Scomp's kidnapping: *African Observer,* pp. 39–49; Winch, "Philadelphia and the Other Underground Railroad," pp. 9–20; C. Wilson, "Freedom at Risk," pp. 23–29.

151 Cyrus James: "A Horrible Development," Niles' *Register,* April 25, 1829.

151 George Alfred Townsend novel's veiled facts: Roth, *Monster's Handsome Face*, p. 83.

151 George V. Alberti: C. Wilson, *Freedom At Risk*, pp. 50–53.

152 "Think for a moment . . .": American Memory, "Slaves and the Courts, 1740–1860" and "A review of the trial, conviction and sentence of George Alberti," at memory.loc.gov.ammem/sthtml/sthome.html.

153 *"The slaveholder has as good a right . . .":* George V. Alberti, in *National Anti-Slavery Standard*, February 19, 1859.

Chapter Eight HATED HEROES

156 *"So I returned and considered all the oppressions . . .":* See Welch, *Prudence Crandall*, p. 24.

157 *"It might sink then . . .":* See Larned, *History of Windham County*, p. 491.

157 *"changing white scholars for colored ones":* See Welch, *Prudence Crandall*, p. 25.

157 *Liberator* announcement: Ibid., p. 28.

157 *"nigger girls":* See Strane, *A Whole-Souled Woman*, p. 43.

157 *"fists doubled in their faces":* See Larned, *History of Windham County*, p. 493.

157 Canterbury hostile reaction: Ibid. p. 495; May, p. 50.

158 *"like the besieged in the immortal Fort Sumter":* May, *Life of Samuel Joseph May*, p. 50.

158 *"animated by the spirit of a martyr":* Ibid., p. 51.

158 *"In the midst of this affliction . . .":* Prudence Crandall, quoted in Welch, *Prudence Crandall*, p. 48.

158 Noyes Academy: Strane, *A Whole-Souled Woman*, p. 171.

158 New Haven school for black men rejected: Robert A. Warner, *New Haven Negroes*, pp. 55–56.

158 *". . . to read Horace . . .":* Litwack, *North of Slavery*, pp. 125–126.

159 Black Law testimony by phrenologist and "horrid traffic": Strane, pp. 74–75.

159 *"We are under no obligations . . .":* See Welch, p. 55.

159 Canterbury reaction to Black Law: Strane, p. 76.

160 *"I am only afraid they will not put me in jail.":* Prudence Crandall, quoted in May, p. 55.

160 Crandall in jail: Strane, pp. 81–85.

160 *The hung jury led . . . :* Pamphlet, Prudence Crandall Museum, Canterbury, Connecticut.

161 *"It rivets the chains . . .":* William W. Ellsworth, quoted in Welch, p. 227.

161 *"The consequences inevitably will destroy"*: Andrew Judson, quoted in Welch, pp. 227–228.

161 judge's ruling on the "great question": David Daggett, quoted in Welch p. 216.

162 *"To my mind, it would be a perversion . . ."*: Ibid., p. 218.

162 Daggett citing Webster as "one of the most learned men . . .": Ibid., p. 217.

162 Taney cites Crandall case: Ibid., p. 231.

163 September 9, 1834, attack on school: Larned, p. 501; Strane, p. 151; May, p. 71; White, *The Crandall School*, pp. 108–110.

163 pension awarded: Strane, p. 220.

163 *"I feel that they do owe me . . ."*: Crandall, quoted in *Kansas City Journal*, March 28, 1886.

164 *"We stood and gazed . . ."*: Elijah P. Lovejoy, quoted in Simon, *Freedom's Champion*, p. 48.

164 *"mysterious metaphysical . . . phrenzy,"* Judge Luke Lawless, quoted in Simon, p. 52.

165 *"so that while I live . . ."*: Elijah P. Lovejoy, quoted in Lovejoy and Lovejoy, *Memoir of the Rev. Elijah P. Lovejoy*, p. 186.

166 *"From Maine . . . and incendiaries:* Richards, *Gentlemen of Property and Standing*, p. 16.

167 *"Dear Mother . . . mobbed down"*: Elijah P. Lovejoy, quoted in Lovejoy and Lovejoy, *Memoir*, p. 232.

167 *"The sky and the river were beginning to glow . . ."*: Edward Beecher, quoted in Simon, *Freedom's Champion*, pp. 101–103.

167 *"How would you . . . with your daughter?"*: See Richards, *Gentlemen of Property*, p. 109.

169 *"And for what? . . ."*: Usher Linder, quoted in Simon, *Freedom's Champion*, p. 138.

169 *"none other than a most barbarous . . ."*: John Brown, in Sanborn, ed., *Life and Letters of John Brown*, 469–470.

170 *"The Negro boy . . ."*: Ibid., pp. 14–15.

170 *"It was no abolition lecturer . . ."*: Henry David Thoreau, "A Plea for Captain John Brown," available online at www.sas.upenn.edu/African Studies, p. 1.

171 *"I observed that he called . . ."*: Richard Henry Dana, "How We Met John Brown," *Atlantic Monthly*, July 1871, p. 6.

172 *"Caution, caution, sir!"*: John Brown, quoted in Villard, *John Brown*, p. 153.

172 *"Farewell to Plymouth Rocks . . .":* Ibid., p. 288.

173 *"In [Brown's] conversations with me . . .":* James M. Jones, quoted in James Cleland Hamilton, "John Brown in Canada," *Canadian Magazine,* December 1894, pp. 14–15.

174 *"I sometimes feel as though I could not . . .":* Watson Brown, quoted in Sanborn, ed., *Life and Letters,* p. 549.

175 *"A Northern man made an unlawful attempt . . .":* reprinted in the *Daily Courant* (Hartford, Connecticut), December 8, 1859. (*The Hartford Courant* microfilm archives.)

176 *"if the South will frankly unite . . .":* Henry Raymond, in Finkelman, ed., *His Soul Goes Marching On,* p. 119.

Chapter Nine PHILADELPHIA'S RACE SCIENTIST

179 description of Wheatley and her judges: Gates, *Trials of Phillis Wheatley,* pp. 1–20.

181 "American School of Ethnology": Fredrickson, *Black Image in the White Mind,* p. 74.

181 general agreement of historians on the idea of black inferiority and slavery: Works by Fredrickson, Winthrop D. Jordan, and Audrey Smedley are part of a vast literature on the relation of race and slavery.

182 Samuel George Morton: William R. Stanton and Stephen Jay Gould give capsule biographies.

182 Nott's life and "niggerology": Horsman, *Josiah Nott of Mobile;* Stanton, *Leopard's Spots,* p. 118.

183 Agassiz in Philadelphia and *"Seeing their black faces":* Stephen Jay Gould, *Mismeasure of Man,* pp. 76–77.

183 *"Beware of any policy":* Agassiz, quoted in Stanton, *Leopard's Spots,* p. 191.

183 Rush, leprosy theory, spontaneous cure, and treatment: Stanton, pp. 7, 13.

184 Curse of Ham and "a mocking lullaby": Braude, in "Ham and Noah," and Haynes, in *Noah's Curse,* trace curse's evolution; Haynes cites lullaby in note 40, p. 227.

184 Morton described as *"an altogether improbable person":* Stanton, *Leopard's Spots,* p. 27.

185 *Morton's sample of . . . skulls:* Stanton, *Leopard's Spots,* p. 32; Stephen Jay Gould, *Mismeasure of Man,* p. 88.

186 Creation 4004 BC: Dating is that of Archbishop James Ussher; see Horsman, *Josiah Nott of Mobile,* p. 89.

186 *Morton had done "more for ethnography":* See Stanton, *Leopard's Spots,* p. 51.

186 1840 federal census: Ibid., pp. 57–58.

187 Calhoun and *"deep and durable"*: Ibid., p. 64.

187 Nott, "The Mulatto a Hybrid": Ibid., p. 66.

187 Agassiz, creatures occupy specific areas and man the only exception: Stephen Jay Gould, *Mismeasure of Man*, p. 75; Stanton, *Leopard's Spots*, p. 101.

188 Garden of Eden the *"paradise for the Adamic race"*: Morton, quoted in Stanton, *Leopard's Spots*, p. 142.

189 New-York Daily Tribune *noted that Morton "one of brightest ornaments"*: See Stanton, p. 144.

189 Nott begins book: Horsman, *Josiah Nott of Mobile*, p. 173.

189 Nott loses four children: Ibid., p. 164.

189 Nott uses hat sizes: Ibid., p. 196.

191 *"I look with great pride"*: Parker, quoted in Fredrickson, *Black Image*, p. 100.

191 *"I as much as any other man"*: Lincoln, quoted in Stephen Jay Gould, *Mismeasure of Man*, p. 66.

191 *a place "without morals"*: Nott, quoted in Stanton, *Leopard's Spots*, p. 187.

Chapter Ten PLUNDER FOR PIANOS

195 *"The blood of Puritans . . ."*: Obituary of Julius Pratt, *Meriden (CT) Daily Republican*, August 31, 1869; collection of Connecticut State Library.

196 *"It is simply . . . a bloody seizure"*: Stanley, *In Darkest Africa*. See Matthiessen, *In African Silences*, p. 118.

198 *"perpetually sunlit minarets . . ."*: Downing, "Tales of Zanzibar," p. 1.

198 *"It is the custom to buy a tooth . . ."*: Michael W. Shepherd, quoted in Norman R. Bennett and George E. Brooks, *New England Merchants in Africa*, p. 263.

200 *"A long line of manacled men . . ."*: Livingstone, *Expedition to the Zambesi*, p. 377.

201 *"We also purchased a quantity . . ."*: See Bennett and Brooks, *New England Merchants in Africa*, p. 258.

201 *Black shapes crouched . . .* : Joseph Conrad, *Heart of Darkness*, p. 44.

202 *"the bifurcated mind"*: Anne Farrow, Interview with Jennifer Baszile, assistant professor of history, Yale University, June 2002.

203 *"Six men slaves were singing . . ."*: Livingstone, *Last Journals*, p. 245.

203 *"The Piano-forte is a badge of gentility . . ."*: See Kornblith, "Craftsman as Industrialist," p. 353.

206   *Smithsonian curator . . . today's currency:* Shayt, "Elephant under Glass,"
      p. 40.

209   *Working from company . . . lives affected:* Malcarne, "Ivoryton, Connecticut,"
      p. 286.

211   *"protruding like the circles . . .":* Richard Burton, quoted in Moorehead,
      White Nile, p. 8.

212   *"I had seen a herd of elephants . . .":* Dinesen, *Out of Africa,* p. 15.

BIBLIOGRAPHY

Books, Articles, and Unpublished Manuscripts

African Observer. Westport, CT: Negro Universities Press, 1970. Reprint of April 1827–May 1828 issues.

Albion, Robert Greenhalgh. *The Rise of New York Port, 1815–1860.* New York: Charles Scribner's Sons, 1939. Page references are to the 1967 edition.

———. *Square-Riggers on Schedule: The New York Sailing Packets to England, France, and the Cotton Ports.* Princeton: Princeton University Press, 1938. Reprint, Hamden, CT: Archon Books, 1965.

Alie, Joe A. D. *A New History of Sierra Leone.* Hampshire, England: Palgrave Macmillan, 1990.

Alpers, Edward A. *Ivory and Slaves: Changing Patterns of International Trade in East Central Africa.* Berkeley: University of California Press, 1975.

Anbinder, Tyler G. "Fernando Wood and New York City's Secession from the Union: A Political Reappraisal." *New York History* (New York State Historical Association, Cooperstown, NY) 68 (January 1987).

Andrews, William L., and Henry Louis Gates, Jr., eds. *The Civitas Anthology of African American Slave Narratives.* Washington, DC: Civitas/Counterpoint, 1999.

Appiah, Kwame Anthony, and Henry Louis Gates, Jr., eds. *Africana: The Encyclopedia of the African and African American Experience.* New York: Basic Civitas Books, 1999.

Aptheker, Herbert. *Negro Slave Revolts in the United States, 1526–1860.* New York: International Publishers, 1939.

Arnold, Samuel Greene. *History of the State of Rhode Island and Providence Plantations.* New York: D. Appleton, 1859–1860.

Atkins, John. *A Voyage to Guinea, Brazil, and the West Indies in His Majesty's Ships, the "Swallow" and "Weymouth."* 1735. A facsimile of the first edition. London: Cass, 1970.

Bailyn, Bernard. *The New England Merchants in the Seventeenth Century.* Cambridge, MA: Harvard University Press, 1955.

———. "Slavery and Population Growth in Colonial New England." In *Engines of Enterprise: An Economic History of New England*, edited by Peter Temin. Cambridge, MA: Harvard University Press, 2000.

Barry, Richard. *Mr. Rutledge of South Carolina.* New York: Duell, Sloan and Pearce, 1942.

Beckert, Sven. *The Monied Metropolis: New York City and the Consolidation of the American Bourgeoisie, 1850–1896.* Cambridge, England: Cambridge University Press, 2001.

Bennett, David R. *The John Brown Birthplace.* Torrington, CT: Torrington Historical Society, 2002.

Bennett, Lerone, Jr. *Before the Mayflower: A History of Black America.* 6th rev. ed. New York: Penguin Books, 1993.

Bennett, Norman R., and George E. Brooks. *New England Merchants in Africa: A History through Documents, 1802–1865.* Brookline, MA: Boston University Press, 1965.

Berlin, Ira. *Generations of Captivity: A History of African-American Slaves.* Cambridge, MA: Belknap Press of Harvard University Press, 2003.

———. *Many Thousands Gone: The First Two Centuries of Slavery in North America.* Cambridge, MA: Belknap Press of Harvard University Press, 1998.

Bingham, Alfred M. *The Tiffany Fortune and Other Chronicles of a Connecticut Family.* Chestnut Hill, MA: Abeel & Leet, 1996.

Blight, David W. *Race and Reunion, The Civil War in American Memory.* Cambridge, MA: Belknap Press of Harvard University Press, 2001.

Bontemps, Arna, comp. *Five Black Lives: The Autobiographies of Venture Smith, James Mars, William Grimes, the Rev. G. W. Offley, [and] James L. Smith.* Middletown, CT: Wesleyan University Press, 1971.

———. *Great Slave Narratives.* Selected and Introduced by Arna Bontemps. Boston: Beacon Press, 1969.

Bowers, Henry. *Journal of Henry Bowers, Master, on Board the Brig* Gleaner. Log 827, G. W. Blunt White Library of Mystic Seaport Museum, Mystic, CT.

Boyer, Paul S., et al. *The Enduring Vision: A History of the American People.* Concise, 4th ed. Boston, MA: Houghton Mifflin, 2001.

Braude, Benjamin. "Ham and Noah: Sexuality, Servitude, and Ethnicity." Paper presented at the Fifth Annual Gilder Lehrman Center International Conference, New Haven, 2003.

Bremer, Francis J. *John Winthrop: America's Forgotten Founding Father.* New York: Oxford University Press, 2003.

Brown, Barbara, and James M. Rose. *Black Roots in Southeastern Connecticut, 1650–1900.* Detroit, MI: Gale Research Co., 1980.

Brown, William Wells. *Narrative of William Wells Brown, a Fugitive Slave, Written by Himself.* Boston: Anti-Slavery Office, 1847.

Bruchey, Stuart. *Cotton and the Growth of the American Economy, 1790–1860: Sources and Readings.* New York: Harcourt, Brace & World, 1967.

Burrows, Edwin G., and Mike Wallace. *Gotham: A History of New York City to 1898.* New York, Oxford University Press, 1999.

Campbell, R. J. *Livingstone.* London: E. Benn, 1929.

Campbell, Stanley W. *The Slave Catchers: Enforcement of the Fugitive Slave Law, 1850–1860.* Chapel Hill: University of North Carolina Press, 1968.

Cantwell, Anne-Marie, and Diana diZerega Wall. *Unearthing Gotham: The Archaeology of New York City.* New Haven: Yale University Press, 2001.

Carosso, Vincent P. *The Morgans: Private International Bankers, 1854–1913.* Cambridge, MA: Harvard University Press, 1987.

Chadwick, Douglas H. *The Fate of the Elephant.* San Francisco, Sierra Club Books, 1993.

Chandler, Alfred D., Jr. *The Visible Hand: The Managerial Revolution in American Business.* Cambridge, MA: The Belknap Press of Harvard University Press, 1977.

Chernow, Ron. *Alexander Hamilton.* New York: Penguin Press, 2004.

Chyet, Stanley F. *Lopez of Newport: Colonial American Merchant Prince.* Detroit, MI: Wayne State University Press, 1970.

Collier, Christopher. *Roger Sherman's Connecticut: Yankee Politics and the American Revolution.* Middletown, CT: Wesleyan University Press, 1971.

Collier, Christopher, and James Lincoln Collier. *Decision in Philadelphia: The Constitutional Convention of 1787.* New York: Ballantine Books, 1986.

Conrad, Joseph. *Heart of Darkness.* 1902. New York: Penguin Books, 1989.

Conrad, Robert Edgar, ed. *In the Hands of Strangers: Readings on Foreign and Domestic Slave Trading and the Crisis of the Union.* University Park: Pennsylvania State University Press, 2001.

———. *World of Sorrow: The African Slave Trade to Brazil.* Baton Rouge: Louisiana State University Press, 1986.

Corry, Joseph. *Observations Upon the Windward Coast of Africa, The Religion, Character, Customs &c. of the Natives with System Upon Which They May be Civilized and a Knowledge Attained of the Interior of this Extraordinary Quar-*

ter of the Globe and Upon the Natural and Commercial Resources of the Country Made in the Years 1805 and 1806. 1807. London: F. Cass, 1968.

Cottrol, Robert J., ed. *From African to Yankee: Narratives of Slavery and Freedom in Antebellum New England.* New York: M. E. Sharpe, 1998.

Coughtry, Jay. *The Notorious Triangle: Rhode Island and the African Slave Trade, 1700–1807.* Philadelphia: Temple University Press, 1981.

Crane, Elaine Forman. *A Dependent People: Newport, Rhode Island, in the Revolutionary Era.* New York: Fordham University Press, 1985.

Dalzell, Robert F., Jr. *Enterprising Elite: The Boston Associates and the World They Made.* Cambridge, MA: Harvard University Press, 1987; New York: W. W. Norton, 1993.

Dart, Margaret S. *Yankee Traders at Sea and Ashore.* New York, William-Frederick Press, 1964.

Davis, David Brion. *The Problem of Slavery in Western Culture.* Ithaca, NY: Cornell University Press, 1966.

Davis, John Lawrence: *The Davis Homestead.* Stonington, CT: Stonington Historical Society, 1986.

Davis, Thomas J. *A Rumor of Revolt, The 'Great Negro Plot' in Colonial New York.* New York: Free Press, 1985.

Deetz, James. *In Small Things Forgotten: The Archaeology of Early American Life.* Garden City, NY: Anchor Books, 1977.

Deutsch, Sarah. "The Elusive Guineaman: Newport Slavers, 1735–1774." *New England Quarterly*, June 1982.

Dillon, Merton L. *Elijah P. Lovejoy, Abolitionist Editor.* Urbana: University of Illinois Press, 1961.

Dinesen, Isak [pseud.]. *Out of Africa.* 1937. New York: Modern Library, 1952.

Doggett, John, Jr., *Doggett's New York City Street Directory, 1851.* New York: John Doggett Jr., 1851.

Donald, David Herbert. *Lincoln Reconsidered: Essays on the Civil War Era.* 3rd ed., rev. & updated. New York: Vintage Books, 2001.

Donnan, Elizabeth. *Documents Illustrative of the History of the Slave Trade to America.* 4 vols. Washington, DC: Carnegie Institution of Washington, 1930–1935.

Douglass, Frederick. *Autobiographies.* New York: Literary Classics of the United States, 1994.

Downing, Harriet Cheney. "Tales of Zanzibar." 1942. Unpublished manuscript. Cheney-Downing Papers, Connecticut River Museum, Essex, CT.

Du Bois, W.E.B. *John Brown*. Centennial ed. (for the Emancipation Proclamation). New York: International Publishers, 1962. First published in 1909.

———. *The Suppression of the African Slave Trade to the United States of America, 1638–1870*. 1896. New York, Russell & Russell, 1965.

Dunn, Richard S. *Sugar and Slaves: The Rise of the Planter Class in the English West Indies, 1624–1713*. Chapel Hill: University of North Carolina Press, 1972.

Dunwell, Steve. *The Run of the Mill*. Boston: David R. Godine, 1978.

Fairburn, William Armstrong. *Merchant Sail*. 6 vols. Center Lovell, ME: Fairburn Marine Educational Foundation, 1945–1955.

Falconbridge, Alexander. *An Account of the Slave Trade on the Coast of Africa*. London: J. Phillips, 1788; New York: AMS Press, 1977.

Falconbridge, Anna Maria. *Narrative of Two Voyages to the River Sierra Leone During the Years 1791, 1792, 1793*. 1794. Liverpool: Liverpool University Press, 2000.

Farnie, D.A. *The English Cotton Industry and the World Market, 1815–1896*. Oxford: Clarendon Press, 1979.

Farrow, Anne. "Beyond Complicity: The Forgotten Story of Connecticut Slaveships." *Northeast*, April 3, 2005.

———. "Complicity: How Connecticut Chained Itself to Slavery: The Last Slaves." *Northeast*, Sept. 29, 2002.

Fehrenbacher, Don E. *The Slaveholding Republic: An Account of the United States Government's Relations to Slavery*. New York: Oxford University Press, 2001.

Feldstein, Stanley. *Once a Slave: The Slave's View of Slavery*. New York: William Morrow, 1971.

Finkelman, Paul, ed. *His Soul Goes Marching On: Responses to John Brown and the Harpers Ferry Raid*. Charlottesville: University Press of Virgina, 1995.

———. *Slavery in the Courtroom: An Annotated Bibliography of American Cases*. Washington, DC: Library of Congress, 1985.

Fitts, Robert K. *Inventing New England's Slave Paradise: Master/Slave Relations in Eighteenth-Century Narragansett, Rhode Island*. New York: Garland, 1998.

Foner, Philip S. *Business and Slavery: The New York Merchants and the Irrepressible Conflict*. Chapel Hill: University of North Carolina Press, 1941.

Foner, Philip S., and Herbert Shapiro. *Northern Labor and Antislavery: A Documentary History*. Westport, CT: Greenwood Press, 1994.

Fredrickson, George. *The Black Image in the White Mind: The Debate on Afro-*

American Character and Destiny, 1817–1914. New York: Harper & Row, 1971.

Fyfe, Christopher: *A Short History of Sierra Leone.* London: Longmans, 1962.

———., comp. *Sierra Leone Inheritance.* London: Oxford University Press, 1964.

Gates, Henry Louis, Jr. *The Trials of Phillis Wheatley: America's First Black Poet and Her Encounters with the Founding Fathers.* New York, Basic Civitas Books, 2003.

Gill, John. *Tide without Turning: Elijah P. Lovejoy and the Freedom of the Press.* Boston: Starr King Press, 1958.

Givens, Dorothy. "Nathaniel Russell's Descendants Hold Reunion." *Charleston Post and Courier,* November 22, 1992.

Gould, Samuel. "Log Book of Slave Traders Between New London, Conn., and Africa, 1757–1758." Unpublished manuscript. Collection of Connecticut State Library, Hartford.

Gould, Stephen Jay. *The Mismeasure of Man.* Rev. & expanded ed. New York: W. W. Norton, 1996.

Greene, Evarts B., and Virginia D. Harrington. *American Population before the Federal Census of 1790.* New York, Columbia University Press, 1932; Baltimore, MD: Genealogical, 1993.

Greene, Lorenzo. *The Negro in Colonial New England.* New York: Atheneum, 1968.

Haley, Alex. *Roots.* New York: Doubleday, 1976.

Hammond, M. B.: *The Cotton Industry: An Essay in American Economic History. Part 1, The Cotton Culture and the Cotton Trade, December, 1897.* Published for the American Economic Association by The Macmillan Company, New York.

Hancock, David. *Citizens of the World: London Merchants and the Integration of the British Atlantic Community, 1735–1785.* New York: Cambridge University Press, 1995.

Harms, Robert W. *River of Wealth, River of Sorrow: The Central Zaire Basin in the Era of the Slave and Ivory Trade.* New Haven: Yale University Press, 1981.

Haskell, Daniel C. *American Historical Prints, Early Views of American Cities, 1497–1891.* New York: New York Public Library, 1933.

Haynes, Stephen R. *Noah's Curse: The Biblical Justification of American Slavery.* New York: Oxford University Press, 2002.

Hedges, James B. *The Browns of Providence Plantations.* 2 vols. Cambridge, MA: Harvard University Press, 1952–1968.

Hedrick, Joan. *Harriet Beecher Stowe: A Life*. New York: Oxford University Press, 1994.

Hegel, Richard. *Carriages from New Haven: New Haven's Nineteenth-Century Carriage Industry*. Hamden, CT: Archon Books, 1974.

Hempstead, Joshua: *Diary of Joshua Hempstead of New London*. New London, CT: New London County Historical Society, 1901.

Higman, B. W. *Trade Government and Society in Caribbean History, 1720–1920*. Oxford, England: Heinemann Educational Books, 1983.

Hinks, Peter P. *To Awaken My Afflicted Brethren: David Walker and the Problem of Antebellum Slave Resistance*. University Park: Pennsylvania State University Press, 1997.

Hobhouse, Henry. *Seeds of Change: Five Plants That Transformed Mankind*. London: Sidgwick & Jackson, 1985.

Hochschild, Adam. *Bury the Chains: Prophets, Slaves, and Rebels in the First Human Rights Crusade*. Boston and New York: Houghton Mifflin, 2004.

———. *King Leopold's Ghost: A Story of Greed, Terror, and Heroism in Colonial Africa*. Boston: Houghton Mifflin, 1998.

Hodges, Graham Russell. *Root and Branch: African Americans in New York and East Jersey, 1613–1863*. Chapel Hill: University of North Carolina Press, 1999.

Hodges, Graham Russell, and Alan Edward Brown. *"Pretends To Be Free": Runaway Slave Advertisements from Colonial and Revolutionary New York and New Jersey*. New York: Garland, 1994.

Hoffer, Peter Charles. *The Great New York Conspiracy of 1741: Slavery, Crime, and Colonial Law*. Lawrence: University of Kansas Press, 2003.

Hofstadter, Richard. *America at 1750: A Social Portrait*. New York: Alfred A. Knopf, 1971; Vintage Books, 1973.

Holden-Smith, Barbara. "Lords of Lash, Loom and Law: Justice Story, Slavery, and Prigg v. Pennsylvania." *Cornell Law Review*, September 1993.

Homberger, Eric. *The Historical Atlas of New York City*. New York: Henry Holt, 1994.

Horsman, Reginald. *Josiah Nott of Mobile: Southerner, Physician, and Racial Theorist*. Baton Rouge: Louisiana State University Press, 1987.

Horsmanden, Daniel. *The New York Conspiracy, or A History of the Negro Plot, with the Journal of the Proceedings against the Conspirators at New York in the Years 1741–1742*. Edited by Thomas J. Davis. Boston: Beacon Press, 1971. First published in 1744, reissued in 1810.

Horton, James Oliver, and Lois E. Horton. *In Hope of Liberty: Culture, Commu-*

nity and Protest Among Northern Blacks, 1700–1860. Oxford and New York: Oxford University Press, 1997.

———. *Slavery and the Making of America*. Oxford and New York: Oxford University Press, 2005.

Howard, Warren S. *American Slavers and the Federal Law 1837–1862*. Berkeley: University of California Press, 1963.

Howe, George. *Mount Hope: A New England Chronicle*. New York: Viking Press, 1959.

Ignatiev, Noel. *How the Irish Became White*. New York: Routledge, 1995.

Innes, Stephen. *Creating the Commonwealth: The Economic Culture of Puritan New England*. New York: W. W. Norton, 1995.

Jackson, Kenneth T., ed. *The Encyclopedia of New York City*. New Haven: Yale University Press; New York: New-York Historical Society, 1995.

Jackson, Michael. *In Sierra Leone*, Durham, NC: Duke University Press, 2004.

Johnson, Charles, and Patricia Smith. *Africans in America: America's Journey through Slavery*. New York: Harcourt Brace, 1998.

Jones, Howard. "The Peculiar Institution and National Honor: The Case of the Creole Slave Revolt." In *Civil War History*, vol. 21. Kent, OH: Kent State University Press, 1975.

Jordan, Winthrop D. *White Over Black: American Attitudes Toward the Negro, 1550–1812*. Chapel Hill: Published for the Institute of Early American History and Culture at Williamsburg, Virginia, by University of North Carolina Press, 1968.

Kalm, Peter. *Travels in North America*. 1770. New York: Wilson-Erickson 1937.

Karasch, Mary C. "The Brazilian Slavers and the Illegal Slave Trade 1836–1851." Master's thesis, University of Wisconsin, 1967.

Kiple, Kenneth F. *The Caribbean Slave, A Biological History*. Cambridge, England: Cambridge University Press, 1984.

Kolchin, Peter. *American Slavery, 1619–1877*. New York: Hill & Wang, 1993.

Kornblith, Gary J. "The Craftsman as Industrialist: Jonas Chickering and the Transformation of American Piano Making." *Business History Review*, Autumn 1985.

Kupperman, Karen O. *Providence Island, 1630–1641: The Other Puritan Colony*. New York: Cambridge University Press, 1993.

Lang, Joel. "The Plantation Next Door." *Northeast*, Sept. 29, 2002.

Larned, Ellen. *History of Windham County, Connecticut*. Bicentennial Edition, vol. 2. Chester, CT: Plimpton Press, 1976.

Lincoln, Abraham. *Speeches and Writings, 1832–1865*. New York: Library of America, 1989.

Linebaugh, Peter, and Marcus Rediker. *The Many-Headed Hydra: Sailors, Slaves, Commoners, and the Hidden History of the Revolutionary Atlantic*. Boston: Beacon Press, 2000.

Litwack, Leon F. *North of Slavery: The Negro in the Free States, 1790–1860*. Chicago: University of Chicago Press, 1961.

Livingstone, David. *The Last Journals of David Livingstone in Central Africa*. London, 1874. New York: Harper & Brothers, 1875.

———. *Livingstone's African Journal, 1853–1856*. Vols. I–II. Edited by I. Schapera. Berkeley: University of California Press, 1963.

———. *Livingstone's Missionary Correspondence, 1841–1856*. Edited by I. Schapera. Berkeley: University of California Press, 1961.

———. *Missionary Travels and Researches in South Africa*. New York: Harper & Brothers, 1858.

———. *Some Letters from Livingstone, 1840–1872*. Edited by David Chamberlin. New York: Oxford University Press, 1940; Negro Universities Press, 1969.

Livingstone, David, and Charles Livingstone. *Narrative of an Expedition to the Zambesi and Its Tributaries: And of the Discovery of the Lakes Shirwa and Nyassa, 1858–1864*. New York: Harper & Brothers, 1866.

Log Book of Slave Traders Between New London, Conn., & Africa: The Africa, *John Easton, Commander, Jan. 18–Apr. 10, 1757;* The Good Hope, *Alexander Urqhart, Commander, Apr. 11–May 29, 1757;* The Fox, *William Tailor, Commander, Mar. 28–Aug. 10, 1758*. State Archives, Connecticut State Library.

Lopate, Phillip, ed. *Writing New York: A Literary Anthology*. New York: Library of America, 1998.

Lovejoy, Joseph C., and Owen Lovejoy. *Memoir of the Rev. Elijah P. Lovejoy*. New York: J. S. Taylor, 1838.

Malcarne, Donald L. "Ivoryton, Connecticut: The Ivory Industry and Voluntary and Involuntary Migration in the Late Nineteenth Century," *North American Archaeologist* 22 (2001).

Martin, Margaret E. "Merchants and Trade of the Connecticut River Valley, 1750–1820." Master's thesis, Smith College, 1939.

Matthiessen, Peter. *In African Silences*. New York: Random House, 1991.

May, Samuel. *Life of Samuel Joseph May*. Cambridge, MA: John Wilson and Son, 1873.

Mayer, Henry. *All on Fire: William Lloyd Garrison and the Abolition of Slavery.* New York: St. Martin's Press, 1998.

McCaffrey, Lawrence J. *The Irish Catholic Diaspora in America.* Washington, DC: Catholic University Press of America, 1997.

McCullogh, David. *John Adams.* New York: Simon & Schuster, 2001.

McCusker, John J. "Rum and the American Revolution: The Rum Trade and the Balance of Payments of the Thirteen Continental Colonies." Doctoral dissertation, University of Pittsburgh, 1970.

McKay, Richard C. *South Street: A Maritime History of New York.* 1934. New York: Haskell House, 1971.

McManus, Edgar J. *Black Bondage in the North.* Syracuse, NY: Syracuse University Press, 1973.

———. *A History of Negro Slavery in New York.* Syracuse, NY: Syracuse University Press, 1966.

McMillin, James A. "The Final Victims: The Demography, Atlantic Origins, Merchants, and the Nature of the Post-Revolutionary Foreign Slave Trade to North America, 1783–1810." Doctoral dissertation, Duke University, 1999.

Meadowcroft, Doris. "King of the Yankees." *Charleston (SC) News and Courier Journal,* June 3, 1962.

Melish, Joanne Pope. *Disowning Slavery: Gradual Emancipation and "Race" in New England, 1780–1860.* Ithaca, NY: Cornell University Press, 1998.

Menand, Louis. *The Metaphysical Club: A Story of Ideas in America.* New York: Farrar, Straus & Giroux, 2001.

Merrill, G. R., A. R. Macormac, and H. R. Mauersberger. *American Cotton Handbook.* New York: American Cotton Handbook, 1941.

Mintz, Sidney W. *Sweetness and Power: The Place of Sugar in Modern History.* New York: Viking, 1985.

Moore, Ernst D. *Ivory, Scourge of Africa.* New York: Harper & Brothers, 1931.

Moorehead, Alan. *The White Nile.* New York: HarperCollins Perennial, 2000.

Morgan, Kenneth. *Slavery and Servitude in Colonial North America: A Short History.* New York: New York University Press, 2001.

Morison, Samuel Eliot, Henry Steele Commager, and William E. Leuchtenburg, *The Growth of the American Republic.* 7th ed. New York: Oxford University Press, 1980.

Morris Thomas D. *Free Men All: The Personal Liberty Laws of the North, 1780–1861.* Baltimore, MD: Johns Hopkins University Press, 1974.

Mouser, Bruce L. *A Slaving Voyage to Africa and Jamaica: The Log of the Sandown, 1793–1794.* Bloomington: Indiana University Press, 2002.

Munro, Wilfred Harold. *Tales of an Old Sea Port.* Princeton, NJ: Princeton University Press, 1917.

Mushkat, Jerome. *Fernando Wood: A Political Biography.* Kent, OH: Kent State University Press, 1990.

Nash, Gary B. *Forging Freedom: The Formation of Philadelphia's Black Community, 1720–1840.* Cambridge, MA: Harvard University Press, 1988.

Newell, Margaret. "The Birth of New England in the Atlantic Economy: From Its Beginning to 1970." In *Engines of Enterprise: An Economic History of New England,* ed. Peter Temin. Cambridge, MA: Harvard University Press, 2002.

Newman, Richard S. *The Transformation of American Abolitionism: Fighting Slavery in the Early Republic.* Chapel Hill: University of North Carolina Press, 2002.

Oates, Stephen B. *The Approaching Fury: Voices of the Storm, 1820–1861.* New York: HarperCollins, 1997.

———. *To Purge This Land with Blood: A Biography of John Brown.* Amherst: University of Massachusetts Press, 1984.

O'Callaghan, Edmund Bailey. *Documents Relative to the Colonial History of the State of New York.* Vol. 5. Albany, NY: Weed, Parsons, 1855.

O'Connor, Thomas H. *Lords of the Loom: The Cotton Whigs and the Coming of the Civil War.* New York: Charles Scribner's Sons, 1968.

Olmsted, Frederick Law. *The Cotton Kingdom: A Traveller's Observations on Cotton and Slavery in the American Slave States, 1853–1861.* New York: Knopf, 1953.

Pares, Richard. *Yankees and Creoles: The Trade between North America and the West Indies before the American Revolution,* Cambridge, Harvard University Press, 1956.

Parker, William. *"The Freedman's Story."* Atlantic Monthly, February 1866.

Patterson, Margaret Sloane. *Views of Old New York: Catalogue of the William Sloane Collection.* New York: 1968. Privately printed.

Perkins, Mary E. *Chronicles of a Connecticut Farm, 1769–1905.* Boston: privately printed, 1905.

Piersen, William D. *Black Yankees: The Development of an Afro-American Subculture in 18th Century New England.* Amherst: University of Massachusetts Press, 1988.

———. "White Cannibals, Black Martyrs: Fear, Depression, and Religious

Faith as Causes of Suicide among New Slaves." *Journal of Negro History* (now *Journal of African American History;* Association for the Study of African American Life and History, Silver Springs, MD), April 1977.

Porter, Dorothy. "David M. Ruggles: An Apostle for Human Rights." *Journal of Negro History* (now *Journal of African American History*; Association for the Study of African American Life and History, Silver Springs, MD), January 1943.

Porter, Kenneth Wiggins. *John Jacob Astor, Business Man.* 2 vols. Cambridge, MA: Harvard University Press, 1931.

Prince, Carl E. "The Great 'Riot Year': Jacksonian Democracy and Patterns of Violence in 1834." *Journal of the Early Republic,* Spring 1985.

Raesly, Ellis Lawrence. *Portrait of New Netherland.* New York: Columbia University Press, 1945.

Rawick, George P. *From Sundown to Sunup: The Making of the Black Community.* Westport, CT: Greenwood, 1972.

Rawley, James A. "Captain Nathaniel Gordon, the Only American Executed for Violating the Slave Trade Laws." In *Civil War History,* vol. 39. Kent, OH: Kent State University Press, 1993.

Redpath, James. *The Public Life of Capt. John Brown, with an Autobiography of his Childhood and Youth.* Boston: Thayer & Eldridge, 1860.

Reilly, Kevin. "Slavers in Disguise: American Whaling and the African Slave Trade, 1845–1862." *The American Neptune* (Peabody Essex Museum, Salem, MA), Summer 1993.

Reiss, Benjamin. *The Showman and the Slave: Race, Death and Memory in Barnum's America.* Cambridge, MA: Harvard University Press, 2001.

Richards, Leonard L. *Gentlemen of Property and Standing: Anti-Abolition Mobs in Jacksonian America.* New York: Oxford University Press, 1970.

Ripley, C. Peter, ed. *Witness for Freedom: African American Voices on Race, Slavery, and Emancipation.* Chapel Hill: University of North Carolina Press, 1993.

Roediger, David, and Martin H. Blatt. *The Meaning of Slavery in the North.* New York: Garland, 1998.

Rose, James M., and Barbara W. Brown. *Tapestry: A Living History of the Black Family in Southeastern Connecticut.* New London: New London Historical Society, 1979.

Roth, Hal. *The Monster's Handsome Face: Patty Cannon in Fiction and Fact.* Vienna, MD: Nanticoke Books, 1998.

Rivard, Paul E. *A New Order of Things—How the Textile Industry Transformed New England.* Hanover, NH: University Press of New England, 2002.

Sanborn, Franklin Benjamin, ed. *The Life and Letters of John Brown: Liberator of Kansas and Martyr of Virginia.* 1885. Reprint, New York: Negro Universities Press, 1969.

Savage, J. Thomas. *Nathaniel Russell House.* Charleston, SC: Historic Charleston Foundation, 1997.

Scott, Kenneth: "The Slave Insurrection in New York in 1712," *New-York Historical Society Quarterly,* (now *New-York Journal of American History;* New-York Historical Society, New York), January 1961.

Shaw, Rosalind. *Memories of the Slave Trade: Ritual and the Historical Imagination in Sierra Leone.* Chicago: University of Chicago Press, 2002.

Shayt, David H. "Elephant under Glass: The Piano Key Bleach House of Deep River, Connecticut." *Journal of the Society for Industrial Archeology* (Michigan Technological University, Houghton, MI) 19, no. 1 (1993).

Sheriff, Abdul. *Slaves, Spices and Ivory in Zanzibar: Integration of an East African Commercial Empire into the World Economy, 1770–1873.* Athens: Ohio University Press, 1987.

Shields, Jerry. *The Infamous Patty Cannon in History and Legend.* Dover, DE: Bibliotheca Literaria Press, 1990.

Shorto, Russell. *The Island at the Center of the World: The Epic Story of Dutch Manhattan and the Forgotten Colony That Shaped America.* New York: Doubleday, 2004.

Simon, Paul. *Freedom's Champion: Elijah Lovejoy.* Carbondale: Southern Illinois University Press, 1994.

Sinha, Manisha. *The Counterrevolution of Slavery: Politics and Ideology in Antebellum South Carolina.* Chapel Hill: University of North Carolina Press, 2000.

Siskind, Janet. *Rum and Axes: The Rise of a Connecticut Merchant Family, 1795–1850.* Ithaca, NY: Cornell University Press, 2001.

Slaughter, Thomas P. *Bloody Dawn: The Christiana Riot and Racial Violence in the Antebellum North.* New York: Oxford University Press, 1991.

Slotkin, Richard: *Regeneration Through Violence: The Mythology of the American Frontier, 1600–1860.* Middletown, CT: Wesleyan University Press, 1973.

Smedley, Audrey. *Race in North America: Origin and Evolution of a Worldview.* Boulder, CO: Westview Press, 1993.

Smith, Gaddis. "Agricultural Roots of Maritime History." *The American Neptune: A Quarterly Journal of Maritime History,* 44, no. 1 (Winter 1984).

Smith, Venture. *A Narrative of the Life and Adventures of Venture, a Native of Africa: But Resident above Sixty Years in the United States of America. Related by Himself.* New London, CT: printed by S. Holt, at the Bee-Office, 1798.

Solow, Barbara, ed. *Slavery and the Rise of the Atlantic System*. New York: Cambridge University Press, 1991.

Spillsbury, Francis B.: *Account of a Voyage to the Western Coast of Africa: Performed by His Majesty's Sloop Favourite, in the Year 1805 . . .* London: *Richard Phillips, 1807.*

Stachiw, Myron O. "For the Sake of Commerce: Slavery, Antislavery, and Northern Industry." In *The Meaning of Slavery in the North,* edited by David Roediger and Martin H. Blatt. New York: Garland, 1998.

Stampp, Kenneth M. *The Peculiar Institution: Slavery in the Ante-bellum South.* New York: Knopf, 1956.

Stanley, Henry M. *How I Found Livingstone*. 1872. Reprint of 1913 edition, New York: Negro Universities Press, 1969.

———. *In Darkest Africa*. New York: Random House, 1991.

Stanton, William Ragan. *The Leopard's Spots: Scientific Attitudes toward Race in America, 1815–1859.* Chicago: University of Chicago Press, 1960.

Stauffer, John. *The Black Hearts of Men: Radical Abolitionists and the Transformation of Race.* Cambridge, MA: Harvard University Press, 2002.

Stewart, Austin. *Twenty-Two Years a Slave and Forty Years a Freeman.* 1857. Syracuse, NY: Syracuse University Press, 2002.

Stokes, I. N. Phelps. *The Iconography of Manhattan Island*. 6 vols. New York: Robert H. Dodd, 1915–1928.

Storms, Robbi, and Donald L. Malcarne. *Around Essex: Elephants and River Gods.* Charleston, SC: Arcadia Publishing, 2001.

Stowe, Harriet Beecher. "The Education of Freedmen." *The North American Review,* June 1879.

———. *Uncle Tom's Cabin*. New York: Modern Library, 2001.

Strane, Susan. *A Whole-Souled Woman: Prudence Crandall and the Education of Black Women.* New York: W.W. Norton & Co., 1990.

Strouse, Jean. *Morgan: American Financier.* New York: Random House, 1999.

Sully, Susan. *Charleston Style: Past and Present.* New York: Rizzoli, 1999.

Takaki, Ronald T. *A Pro-Slavery Crusade: The Agitation to Reopen the African Slave Trade.* New York: Free Press, 1971.

Temin, Peter, ed. *Engines of Enterprise: An Economic History of New England.* Cambridge, MA: Harvard University Press, 2000.

Tindall, George Brown, and David E. Shi. *America: A Narrative History.* 4th ed. New York: W. W. Norton, 1996.

Tucker, Barbara. *Samuel Slater and the Origins of the American Textile Industry, 1790–1860.* Ithaca, NY: Cornell University Press, 1984.

Vaughan, Alden T. *Roots of American Racism: Essays on the Colonial Experience.* New York: Oxford University Press, 1995.

Villard, Oswald G. *John Brown: A Biography Fifty Years After.* Boston: Houghton Mifflin, 1910.

Von Frank, Albert J. *The Trials of Anthony Burns: Freedom and Slavery in Emerson's Boston.* Cambridge, MA: Harvard University Press, 1998.

Walker, David. *David Walker's Appeal to the Coloured Citizens of the World.* Edited by Peter P. Hinks. University Park: Pennsylvania State University Press, 2002. First published in 1829.

Warner, Elizabeth A., for Greater Middletown Preservation Trust. *A Pictorial History of Middletown.* Norfolk, VA: Donning, 1990.

Warner, Robert A. *New Haven Negroes: A Social History.* New York: Arno Press, 1969.

Warren, Robert Penn. *John Brown: The Making of a Martyr.* New York: Payson & Clarke, 1929.

————. *The Legacy of the Civil War: Meditations on the Centennial.* New York: Random House, 1961.

Wax, Darold D. "The Browns of Providence and the Slaving Voyage of the Brig *Sally,* 1764–1765." *American Neptune* (Peabody Essex Museum, Salem, MA), July 1972.

Way, William. *History of the New England Society of Charleston, South Carolina: for One Hundred Years, 1819–1919.* Charleston, SC: New England Society of Charleston, 1920.

Webb, Richard D., ed. *The Life and Letters of Captain John Brown.* London: Smith, Elder, 1861.

Welch, Marvis Olive. *Prudence Crandall: A Biography.* Hartford CT: Jason Publishers, 1983.

Weld, Theodore Dwight, comp. *American Slavery as It Is: Testimony of a Thousand Witnesses.* New York: New York, Arno Press, 1968.

Wells, Thomas Henderson. *The Slave Ship* Wanderer. Athens: University of Georgia Press, 1968.

Wheeler, Richard Anson, *History of the Town of Stonington, . . .* New London, CT: Day Publishing, 1900.

White, David O. "The Crandall School and the Degree of Influence by Garrison and the Abolitionists Upon It." *Connecticut Historical Society Bulletin,* October 1978.

Wideman, John Edgar, comp. *My Soul Has Grown Deep: Classics of Early African-American Literature.* New York: Ballantine Books, 2003.

Wilson, Carol. *Freedom at Risk: The Kidnapping of Free Blacks in America, 1780–1865*. Lexington: University Press of Kentucky, 1994.

Wilson, Harriet E. *Our Nig, or Sketches from the Life of a Free Black*. 1859. New York: Vintage Books, 2002.

Winch, Julie. "Philadelphia and the Other Underground Railroad." *Pennsylvania Magazine of History and Biography* (Historical Society of Philadelphia), January 1987.

Winthrop, John. *The Journal of John Winthrop, 1630–1649*. Edited by Richard S. Dunn, James Savage, and Laetitia Yeandle. Cambridge, MA: Harvard University Press, 1996.

Woodman, Harold D. *King Cotton & His Retainers: Financing & Marketing the Cotton Crop of the South, 1800–1925*. Lexington, KY: University of Kentucky Press, 1968.

Electronic Sources

Africans in America. www.pbs.org/wgbh/aia/home.html.

American Memory. "Slaves and the Courts, 1740–1860." memory.loc.gov/ammem/sthtml/sthome.html.

The City of New York. "A Brief History of Gracie Mansion." www.nyc.gov/html/om/html/gracie.html.

Handler, Jerome S., and Michael L. Tuite Jr. The Atlantic Slave Trade and Slave Life in the Americas: A Visual Record. hitchcock.itc.virginia.edu/slavery/.

The Historic House Trust of New York City. www.historichousetrust.org.

Historic Hudson Valley. "A Note on Large Slaveholdings in the North." www.hudsonvalley.org/web/phil-manor_slaveholdings.html.

History Central. "General Archibald Gracie, Jr. CSA." www.historycentral.com/bio/cwcgens/csagracie.html.

The Library of Congress. www.loc.gov.

New York City Department of Parks and Recreation. www.nycgovparks.org.

The Trans-Atlantic Slave Trade. CD-ROM. Compiled by David Eltis, Stephen D. Behrendt, David Richardson, and Herbert S. Klein.

ACKNOWLEDGMENTS

The concept of history as news would be a hard one for many newspaper editors to accept, let alone get excited about. This is but a hint as to the exceptional qualities of the leaders of *The Hartford Courant*'s news operation: *Courant* editor Brian Toolan, whose curiosity started everything, and managing editor Cliff Teutsch. We are deeply grateful for their willingness to support a project that seemed to go on and on—wait a minute, it did go on and on!—and for their willingness to do without two writers and an editor for well over a year.

Thanks as well to the *Courant* staff members who worked on what we call "the first 'Complicity.'" They include editors Stephanie Summers and David Funkhouser; designers Melanie Shaffer and Josue Evilla; photo editor Bruce Moyer; graphics artist Wes Rand; writers Rick Green, Matthew Kauffman, Tina Brown, Steve Grant, and Kevin Canfield; and copy editor (plus) Vada Crosby. Freelancer Liz Petry was a strong contributing writer, Phil Lohman was an incomparable graphics researcher/artist and idea person, Megan Shutte was a tireless researcher, and Trinity College intern James Cabot a valuable backstop on the project.

In addition, Summers and Funkhouser put out *Northeast* in our absence, and for this they have our deepest thanks. Steve Courtney helped with editing and ideas, as did Kyrie O'Connor.

Thanks also to Stephen Dunn, the *Courant* photographer for the first *Complicity*. A number of the paintings he copied are included in this book.

A huge thanks to the *Courant*'s chief librarian, Kathy McKula, and to Tina Bachetti, senior information assistant in the *Courant*'s Center for News Research and Archives, who joined the chase for images and permissions and whose good cheer and organizational skills kept the effort moving forward at all times. Kathy Willard scanned and processed nearly 150 images for the book. We are grateful to *Courant* copy editor Susan Schoenberger, whose final reading of the manuscript was so helpful.

And a thanks from the four of us to Melody Guy and Danielle Durkin at Ballantine; to copy editor Janet Fletcher; to our literary agent extraordinaire, Tanya McKinnon; and, most especially, to editor Elisabeth K. Dyssegaard, without whom *Complicity* would be simply inconceivable.

THE AUTHORS AND THE IMAGES EDITOR LEANED ON SOME OF THE SAME individuals and institutions during their research. We have many to acknowledge. They include: the staff of the Connecticut Historical Society; Connecticut State Library; the New-York Historical Society; the New York Public Library; the Homer Babbidge Library at the University of Connecticut; the New Haven Colony Historical Society; the South Carolina Historical Society Reading Room; the Smithsonian Institution's National Museum of American History; Olin Library at Wesleyan University in Middletown, Connecticut; Yale's Sterling Library; Irene Axelrod and the Peabody Essex Museum in Salem, Massachusetts; and Mystic Seaport.

Also, Warren Perry and Gerald F. Sawyer of Central Connecticut State University; Patricia Kruger of the South Carolina Historical Society; Robbi Storms and Elizabeth Alvord of the Ivoryton, Connecticut, Library Association; Edith DeForest of the Deep River, Connecticut, Historical Society; Donald Malcarne of Wesleyan University; Kazimiera Kozlowski of the Prudence Crandall Museum in Canterbury, Connecticut; and Warner Lord and Brenda Milkofsky of the Connecticut River Museum.

IN THE WRITING OF MY CHAPTERS, I WAS GREATLY HELPED BY SCHOLARS, researchers, and librarians, all of whom dealt patiently with my questions and my ignorance. My north star in this endeavor has been, since the day I met him in April 2002, Robert P. Forbes, associate director of the Gilder Lehrman Center for the Study of Slavery, Resistance, and Abolition at Yale University. Rob's cheerful and constant guidance has been essential. I hope he is not dismayed by what he reads herein.

I am deeply grateful also to Joseph Opala of James Madison University, who introduced me to Sierra Leone's Bunce Island, both the place and its meaning.

I have been helped in a hundred ways by Alisandra Cummins and Kevin Farmer of the Barbados Museum & Historical Society; by Peter Hinks; by Dione Longley of the Middlesex County Historical Society; by Mark McEachern and Gail Kruppa at the Torrington Historical Society; by Paul O'Pecko, Quentin Snediker, and Eliza Garfield, all of Mystic Seaport Museum; by David Richardson at the University of Hull in England; by Patricia M. Schaefer of the New London County Historical Society; by Killingly, Connecticut, town historian Margaret Weaver; by John Wood Sweet of the University of North Carolina; and by John "Whit" Davis of Stonington, Connecticut, who made me welcome in his history and in his family's seventeenth-century home, where Venture Smith once lived. The help of the Essex Historical Society was also invaluable. Steve Courtney changed my life by finding the 1928 newspaper article that sent me to West Africa.

For their abiding hospitality and help in Sierra Leone, I am grateful to U.S. Ambassador Thomas N. Hull; his wife, Jill; and Deputy Chief of Mission James Stewart. They made Africa feel like home.

The staff at the National Museum of Sierra Leone made researching this work a joy.

The ivory chapter in this book is a modest reworking of a story that appeared in *The Hartford Courant*'s *Northeast* magazine in September 2002. In the writing and researching of that earlier story, I was guided by Edward A. Alpers of UCLA, Jennifer Baszile and David Blight of Yale University, Michael Everett of Quinnipiac University, James O. Horton and John Michael Vlach, both of George Washington University, G. Ugo Nwokeji of the University of Connecticut, and Susan Pennybacker and Andrew Walsh of Trinity College in Hartford, Connecticut.

And like every writer, I have a roster of people in this world and the next to whom I am more grateful than I can express. To my late father, my mother, my friends Robert S. Capers and Debra Campagna, my brother Charles and sister Kate, I want to say: You have blessed me.

A.F.

The debt owed to slavery scholars will be obvious from the sources listed elsewhere in this book. I pay special homage to the late Elizabeth Donnan, as a stand-in for all of them. More than 70 years ago, long before the civil rights movement changed our views of slavery, Donnan, an economics professor at Wellesley College, wrote and compiled the four-volume *Documents Illustrative of the History of the Slave Trade to America*. Containing hundreds of annotated letters, ships' logs, newspaper articles, and government records, Donnan's monumental study has only gained importance over the years.

J.L.

Thanks to Janson L. Cox, director of the South Carolina Cotton Museum, who helped this Yankee understand *Gossypium hirsutum*. Tony Ferraz, president of Brownell & Company, in Moodus, Connecticut, offered fascinating information, as well as the first edition of the *American Cotton Handbook*.

In addition to many of those mentioned above, staff at the following institutions were also helpful: Trinity College's Raether Library and its special collections in the Watkinson Library; the American Textile History Museum in Lowell, Massachusetts; and Lowell National Historical Park. Thanks also to Miriam K. Tierney, archivist at Saint Andrew's Society of the State of New York.

The late writer Robert G. Albion is listed in the bibliography, but his importance cannot be overstated. I join a long list of writers indebted to his work and to that of his wife, Jennie Barnes Pope.

Thanks to Emma Early, for her carriage research, and to her mother, Francine, who listened and read and bolstered.

In dozens of ways, Cheryl Magazine's eye and insights help deepen *Complicity*. I am grateful to her for this, and so much more.

He's in my dedication, too, but thanks, above all, to my most important editor, Kenton Robinson.

J.F.

Thanks first to the authors for their generous efforts to help identify the most appropriate illustrations. Joel Lang pointed out the rich and authoritative Web site The Atlantic Slave Trade and Slave Life in the Americas: A Visual Record, hitchcock.itc.virginia.edu/Slavery/. My appreciation goes to creators Jerome S. Handler and Michael L. Tuite, Jr. for their outstanding research database. The Library of Congress Web site, www.loc.gov, proved to be another treasure trove of images and documents. And Google's image-search tool allowed me to search digitized collections around the world.

Most of the chapters came together piece by piece, except for the ivory chapter. I am grateful to Robbi Storms of the Ivoryton Library Association, who fulfilled my every request for images and permissions relating to the ivory trade in Connecticut. Thanks also to Barbara Austen at the Connecticut Historical Society and to Carol Lovell of the Stratford Historical Society for allowing us to publish many of their treasures in this book.

C.M.

INDEX

Page numbers in *italics* refer to illustrations.

abductions of free blacks, 139–40,
   140, 141, *141*, 142–53
abolitionism, 6, 12, 28, 29–32, 33, 36,
   100, 109–10, 126, 143, 155–77,
   183, 184, 191
   abduction of free blacks and, 139,
     142, 145, 152, 153
   black education and, 156–63
   Boston, 32, *32*, 38–39, 166
   of John Brown, 169–77
   ivory trade and, 194, 195, 202, 211
   of Elijah Lovejoy, 163–69
   press, 29, *30*, 31, 152, 155, 157, 164,
     165–68, *168*, 169
   Rhode Island, 109–10
   violence and, 155–77
Academy of National Sciences, 185
Adams, John, 72, 111
advertisements:
   ivory trade, *213*
   slave, 21, 33, *34*, 35, *54*, 68, *68*,
     71, *99*
Aetna, 23
Africa, 114, *114*, 115, 116
African elephant (*Loxodonta Africana*),
   196, 203, 206–7, 212
   endangered, 212–13
African ivory trade, 196–213,
   197–200, *208*, *213*
African Observer, 146

African slave trade, xxviii, 21, 46–49,
   50, 51–53, 56, 61–62, 63–66, 80,
   96, 143, 173, 204–5
   banned by Congress (1808),
     100–101, 111–12, 120, 123
   Bunce Island, *99*, 114–19, *115–19*
   "castles," 64–65, *65*, 66, 115–19
   failed voyages, 102–5
   illegal, 112–13, 121–37
   ivory and, 196–213, *197–200*,
     208, 213
   Newport rum and, 95–113
   Sally revolt, 102–5, 109
   sea voyage and conditions, 64–66,
     96, 102–9, *106–9*, 117, 121,
     126–33, *133*, 134
   sleeping platforms aboard ships,
     106
   Triangle Trade, 48–49, *50*, 65, 98
Agassiz, Louis, 182, *182*, 183, 187–91
   Types of Mankind, 181, 182, *188*,
     189–91
agriculture, 71, 72; *see also* plantation
   labor system; *specific crops*
Alabama, 5, 10, 11, 21, 147, 187, 189
Albany, New York, 4, 6
Alberti, George V., 151–53
Allen, Richard, 144, *144*
Alton, Illinois, 156, 165–69
American Anthropology, 137

American Anti-Slavery Society, 33
American Colonization Society, 155, 161
American Journal of the Medical Sciences, 187
American Methodist Episcopal Church, 144
American Revolution, xxvi, 49, 51, 62, 75, 95, 98, 100, 104, 105, 115, 180
  black soldiers in, 73
American School of Ethnology, 181
Amistad, 127, *127*, 144, 145
Andrews, Israel D., 23–25
Andromache, 111
Antigua, 46, 54, 105
Appleton, Nathan, 35
Appleton, William, 41
Arabia, 204, 209
Arkwright, Richard, 28
armed black resistance, 142, 173–77; *see also* slave revolts
Arnold, Benedict, 63, 114–15
Arnold Cheney & Company, 208, *208*
arson, 77, 79, 80–93
Aspinwall, William H., 11
Astor, John Jacob, 5, 11
Astor, William B., 11
Atkins, John, 64–65
Austria, 7

Bachman, John, 188
Bailyn, Bernard, 45
Baltimore, 152
banknote, Sanford Bank (Maine), *35*
Baqauqua, Mahommah Gardo, 106
Barbados, 45, 46–47, 54, 55, 65, 66, 104
Barnes, Ocea Lee, *136*
barrels and casks, 80
Beale, Dr. Horace, 168
Beebe, Dean & Donohue, 125
Beecher, Edward, 165, 167
Belgian Congo, 201, 207
Belgium, 7
Belmont, August, 11
Benjamin, Asa, 61, 62
Berbice, Louis, 63
Bertram, John, 201
Betts, Samuel Rossiter, 124

Bible, 181
  race science and, 182–91
Bigler, William, 152
billiard balls, ivory, 203, 206
Black Ball Line, 16, *16*, 18
"black codes," 63, 67, 82–83, 85
Black Law, 159, *159*, 160, 161
"bleach houses," 193, *194*, 212
Blessing of the Bay, 53
blockades, 27
Boston, xxvii, 6–7, 10, 12, 25, 32, 35, 38, 40, 49, 131, 179–80, 203
  abolitionism, 32, *32*, 38–39, 166
  commerce, 38–39, 46–47, 53–55
  Lowell Lecture, 188
  shipbuilding, 53–54
  slave revolts in, 79
Boston Associates, 6, 27, 29, 35–37, 41
Boston Female Anti-Slavery Society, 32
Boston Weekly News-Letter, 81
Bostwick, William, 14
Bowen, Francis, 132
Boyle, Thomas, 129
branding of slaves, *100*, 106
Brazil, 7, 106
  slave trade to, 123–31
Bristol, Rhode Island, 56, 101, 106, 110–13
Brooklyn, New York, 79
Brown, James, 102
Brown, John (abolitionist), 39, 155, 156, 169–70, *170*, 171–77, 191
  Harpers Ferry raid, 142, 173–74, *174*, 175–77
  trial and execution of, 176
Brown, John (slave owner), 101, *101*, 102–5, 109, 110, 111
Brown, Moses, 28, 102, 109, *109*, 110, 113, 184
Brown, Nicholas, 105
Brown, Obediah, 102
Brown, Oliver, 175
Brown, Watson, 174, 175
Brown University, 97, 102
Buchanan, James, 175
Buffalo, New York, 141
Bull, William, 59
Bunce Island, *99*, 114–19, *115–19*

burning at the stake, 81, 89, *90*, 91, 92, 164
Burns, Anthony, 39, *39*
Burr, Aaron, 13
Burton, Mary, 85, 86, 87, 88, 92
Burton, Richard, 211

Calhoun, John C., 27, 37, 186–87
Canada, 46, 141, 176, 195
cannibalism, 107
Cannon, Jesse, 145, 146
Cannon, Patty, 139–40, 145–51
Cannon gang, 139–40, 145–51
    newspaper article on, *150*
Canterbury school, Connecticut, 156–58, *158*, 159–63
Cape Coast Castle, 64–65, *65*, 115
Caribbean, 46, 96
    trade, 46–49, *50*, 51–55, 61, 65–66, 78–79, 95, 104, 115, 119
    see also specific countries
carriage trade, 42–43, *43*
Cartwright, Edmund, 28
"castles," slave trade, 64–65, *65*, 66, 115–19
cattle, 51
Census, U.S., 26, 80, 186–87
Charleston, South Carolina, 3, 10, 18, 41, 56–59, 98, 99, 111, 112, 131, 186
Charleston Medical Journal, The, 189
Charter Oak Life Insurance Company, *24*
Cheney, George A., 196, 198, 210, *210*, 211
Cheney, Sarah, 210, 211
Chickering, Jonas, 203
Chickering pianos, 203, *204*
China, 132
Choate, Rufus, 32
Christiana Riot (1851), 141–42
chronology of Northern complicity, 217–19
Cincinnati, 142
Cincinnati Enquirer, The, 143
civil rights movement, xxvi
Civil War, xxvi, 7, 122, 123, 176–77, 195, 201, 215
    aftermath of, 211

beginning of, 41, 131
events leading to, 155–77
Clause, 81
Clay, Henry, 27, 37
cloves, 294
coffee, 123, 130, 134
coffle, *107*, 208
Collins, Charles, 111
Colt, Samuel, 196
Columbia, South Carolina, 190
Comfort, Gerardus, 91–92
commerce, xxvii, 14, 202
    Boston, 38–39, 46–47, 53–55
    Connecticut ivory industry, 193–94, *194*, 195–213, *213*
    Newport rum, 97–113
    New York City, 15–18, *19*, 20–25, 49, 50, 53, 80, 121–33
    West Indian, 46–49, *50*, 51–55, 61, 65–66, 78–79, 95, 102, 104, 111, 115, 119
Compromise of 1850, 37, 141
Comstock, Cheney & Company, 195–96, 206, 207, 208, 209, 210–11, 212
    advertisement, *213*
Comstock, Samuel Merritt, 195–96, *196*, 201, 202, 210
Concord, Massachusetts, 176
Confederacy, 3
Congo, 121, 131, 201, 207
Congress, U.S., 10, 36, 40, 95, 101, 110, 112, 143
    slave trade ban (1808), 100–101, 111–12, 120, 123
Connecticut, xxvi, xxviii, 23, 48, 49, 170, 177
    Black Law, 159, *159*, 160, 161
    hostility to black education, 156–63
    ivory industry, 193–94, *194*, 195–213, *213*
    slavery in, *34*, 51, *54*, 61–75, 79, 114–15, 195, 201–2
    textile industry, 6, 29
Connecticut Courant, slave ads in, *34*, *54*
Connecticut River, 51, 74, 193, 212
Conrad, Joseph, *Heart of Darkness*, 201

Constitution, U.S., 29, 36, 40, 110, 143, 160, 161, 162
    Thirteenth Amendment, 29
Continental Congress, 98
Continental Army, 161
Continental Navy, 105
Cook (G. & D.) & Company, New Haven, 42–43, *43*
Cora, 122, *122*
corn, 7, 53
Coromantees, 80–81
cotton, xxvi, xxvii, 7, 13, 46, 166, 211, 215
    bales, 13
    British trade, 5, 7, 9–10, 18, 28–29
    factor, 14
    "lords," 35
    New York trade, 3–4, *8*, 10–25, 215
    Northern trade, 3–43
    production, 7, *8*, 9–10, 13
    slaves and, 10, 26, 35–37, 100, 110
    Southern, 7, 9–10, *12*, 18, 95, 100, 110, 131, 134
cotton gin, xxvi, 7–10, *22*, 23, 26, 100, 110
    patent, 7, 9, *9*
Cotton Triangle, 18
Craft, Ellen, 38, *38*
Craft, William, 38
Crandall, Almira, 159–60
Crandall, Prudence, 155, *155*, 156–63
    education battle and court cases, 156–63
Creole, 127
Crystal Palace Exhibition (1851, London), 203
Cuba, 111, 112, 113, 122, 125, 126, 127, 131, 132
Cuffee, 84, 87–91
"cure" for blackness, 184
currency, *50*

Daggett, David, 161, 162
daguerreotypes of slaves, *190–91*
Dana, Richard Henry, 171
dance, slave trade, 107, *108*
Daphne, 133
Darwin, Charles, 182
    On the Origin of the Species by Means of Natural Selection, 191

Davis, Jefferson, 6–7
De Bow, D. B., 21
De Bow's Review, 21, *21–22*, 23
Declaration of Independence, xxvii, 53, 62, 108–9, 111, 160, 183
Deep River, Connecticut, 193–95, 203, 205–6, 209, 212
Delaware, 62, 139, 146, 147, 151
Delia, Daughter of Renty (daguerreotype), *190*
DeWolf, George, 113
DeWolf, James, 101, *101*, 102, 103, 105, 106, 110–13
Dinesen, Isak, 212
disease, 65, 102, 107, 117, 131, 182, 189, 198
Dix, John A., 12
Dodge, William E., 40
Dominican Republic, 48
Douglas, Stephen A., 38, 171, 191
Douglass, Frederick, 140–41, 166
Douglass, George, 128–30
Downing, Emanuel, xxvii, 47
Drana, Daughter of Jack (daguerreotype), *190*
Dred Scott case, 144, 161, 162
Du Bois, W.E.B., xxviii
    The Suppression of the African Slave Trade to the United States of America, 1638–1870, xxviii–xxix, 132–33
dysentery, 107, 117

East African ivory trade, 196–213, *197–200*, *208*, *213*
East Haddam, Connecticut, 74, 75
economy, xxvi, xxvii, 27, 215
    cotton, 4–5, 13, 25, 37, 166
    1857 crisis, 40
    Northern vs. Southern, 36–37
    slave, 45–55, 110, 113, 133, 215
    War of 1812 and, 27
education, black, 156, 179–80
    Northern hostility to, 156–63
Egypt, 185, 186, 199
Eliot, Samuel, 36
Ellery, William, 111, 113
Ellsworth, Oliver, 160
Ellsworth, William W., 160, 161, 162
Elmina, 115

Emancipation, 30–32, 165, 173
Emancipation Proclamation, 215
Emerson, Ralph Waldo, 37
Encyclopedia Britannica, 179
Equaino, Olaudah, 107
Erie, 121, 122, 123, 124
Erie Canal, 15
Europe, xxvii, xxix, 10, 18, 49, 95,
    115, 199, 205
    ivory markets, 199, 200
    see also specific countries
evolution, theory of, 182, 191
exports, 49, *49,* 50, *50,* 51–53, 80
    ivory, 193–213
    see also specific exports

Faneuil, Peter, 54
Fassena (daguerreotype), *191*
Fillmore, Millard, 11
Fishers Island, New York, 66, 68, 70,
    72
fishing, 72, 73
Flora (slave), 61–62, *62*
flour, 18
Fonseca, Manoel Pinto da, 128, 130
foodstuffs, 49, *49,* 50, *50,* 80, 116, 204
Forney, John W., 176
Fort Coromantine, 119
Fort George, 77, 81
    Great Negro Plot (1741), 77, 83–93
Fort Sumter, shelling of, 41, 131
Fowler, William C., 201–2
Fox, 119
France, 7, 18, 27, 83, 119
    Seven Years' War, 103
Franklin, Benjamin, 143, 180
free blacks, 73–74, 93, 183, 187, 211
    "grommetos," 118
    kidnapped and sold into slavery,
        139–40, *140,* 141, *141,* 142–53
    Prigg v. Pennsylvania ruling, 144–45
    violence toward, 163–64
Free-Soil settlers, 171, *171,* 172
Fugitive Slave Act (1793), 142–43,
    144
Fugitive Slave Act (1850), 36, 37–38,
    141–42, 144, 145

Gap Gang, 141–42
Garner, Margaret, 142, *143*

Garrison, William Lloyd, 29, *30,*
    31–32, *32,* 37, 145, 155, 157, 158,
    166, 172, 175
George III, King of England, 117
Georgia, 10, 14, 38, 116, 131, 134, 137
Germany, 7
    ivory trade, 206, 207, 209
Ghana, 64, 80, 115, 119
Gibson, Adam, 152
Gliddon, George Robins, 186, 189
gold, *50*
Gold Coast, 65
Gordon, Nathaniel, 122, 123, *123,*
    124, 132, 133
Gorée Island, 115
Gould, Sam, 114–19
Gould, Stephen Jay, 185
Gracie, Archibald, 5
Gracie Mansion, New York City, 5
Graham, Philip L., 216
Grant, Ulysses S., 177
Great Britain, xxvii, 5, 15, 16, 18, 28,
    45, 83, 112, 209
    American Revolution, 62, 100
    Industrial Revolution, 28–29
    Seven Years' War, 103
    slave trade and, 117–19, 124–25,
        133
    -South relations, 9–10
    textile industry and cotton trade, 5,
        7, 9–10, 18, 28–29
    War of 1812, 27
Great Depression, 212
Great Negro Plot (1741), 77, 83–99,
    90, 91–93
Greene, Rufus, 210
Greenwood, John, *Sea Captains
    Carousing in Surinam,* 103
Grim, David, map of New York by, *78*
Grinnell, Henry, 11
Groton, Massachusetts, 35
Gulf of Mexico, 18

Hackensack, New Jersey, 79
Haidee, 127
Haiti, 48, 54, 78–79
Hamilton, Alexander, 13
Hamilton, John, 146–48
Hammond, James Henry, 186
Hancock, John, 179, 180

hanging, 81, 84, 88, 90, 91, 92, *123*
Hanway, James, 172
Hardenburgh, Charles, 66
Hardenburgh, Johannes, 66
Harpers Ferry raid (1859), 142, 173–74, *174*, 175–77
Harris, Andrew, 157
Harris, Sarah, 156, *156*, 157–58
Hart, Elisha, 74, 75
Hartford, Connecticut, 23, 63, 79, 161
Harvard University, 35, 183, 190, 191
Havana, 126, 132
Heday, James, 68, 69
Heinrich Adolf Meyer, 207
Hempstead, Joshua, 67, 71
Henderson, Tucker, *135*
Higginson, Thomas Wentworth, 171, 173, 176
Hogg, Rebecca, 85
Hogg, Robert, 85, 86, 88
Hook, Peter, 148–49
Hope, 128
Hope, Dr. Thomas, 168
Hopkins, Esek, 103, *103*, 104, *104*, 105
Hopkins, Samuel, 99–100, 109
horses, 51
Horsmanden, Daniel, 86–93
household servants, 71–72
Howe, Julia Ward, 13, 173
Howe, Samuel Gridley, 173, 176
Hughson, John, 85, *85*, 86, 87, 88, 91, 92
Hughson, Sarah, 85, 91
Hunter, Robert, 81
Huntress, 132
Hurlbut, Thaddeus, 168
Hutchinson, Thomas, 180

Ibn Mohammed, Hamid, 199
illegal slave trade, 112–13, 121–37
    New York, 121–37
    Wanderer survivors and descendants, 134, *135–36*, 137
Illinois, 156, 165–69, 171
India, 7, 185
Indians, xxvii, 185
Industrial Revolution, 6, 7, 28–29
inferiority of black people, theory of, 179–91

insurance, 23
    slave, 23, *24*, 105
Italy, 7
ivory industry, xxvi, 193–213
    abolitionists and, 194, 195, 202, 211
    advertisements, *213*
    "bleach houses," 193, *194*, 212
    Connecticut, 193–94, *194*, 195–213, *213*
    East African supply system, 196–213, *197–200*, *208*, *213*
    piano keys and, 194, 200, 203–6, 209, 211, 212
Ivoryton, Connecticut, 194, 195, 196, 205, 207, 211, 212, 213

Jack (daguerreotype), *190*
Jamaica, 46, 51, 54
James, Cyrus, 151
Jefferson, Thomas, 9, 111, 182
    on blacks and slavery, 108–9, 180–81, 183, 189
    Notes on the State of Virginia, 180–81, 189
Jews, 98
Jocelyn, Simeon, 157, 158
Johnson, Ebenezer, 146, 147, 151
Johnson, Joseph, 139, 145–49, 151
Johnson, Tom, 137
Jones, James M., 173
Journal of Commerce, 11
Judson, Andrew, 157, 160–61, *161*

Kansas, 36, 38, 163, 171–72
    "Bleeding Kansas," 39, 171–72, 173
    Free-Soil settlers, 171, *171*, 172
Kansas-Nebraska Act, 38–39
Kentucky, 128–30
Kerry, Peggy, 84–88, 91
kidnapped free blacks, 139–40, *140*, 141, *141*, 142–53
Kilimanjaro, 198
King, James, 13–14
King, Rufus, 13
Krum, John, 167–68

Lamar, Charles A. L., 131
Lathers, Richard, 10–11
Laurens, Henry, 98, *98*, 99

Lawless, Luke, 164–65
Lawrence, Abbott, 26, 27, 35–37
Lawrence, Amos, 26, *27*, 31, 35–37,
    39, 41
Lawrence, Amos Adams, 26, *27*, 36,
    39, 41
Lawrence, Massachusetts, 6, 36
Lee, Robert E., 175, 176–77
Lee, Ward, *135*, 136
Leeds, 15
Leeward Islands, 46
Lehman Brothers, 5
leprosy, 183–84
Lewis and Clark expedition, 185
Libby, Cyrus, 128
Liberator, 29, *30*, 31, 152, 155, 157,
    172
Liberia, 117, 121
Lincoln, Abraham, xxvii, 3, 38, 40, *41*,
    123, 124–25, 162, 172, 176, 191,
    215
Linder, Usher, 169
Liverpool, 7, 10, 17, 18
livestock, 50, 51, 53, 71, 115, 215
Livingstone, David, 196, 199, *199*,
    200, 202, *202*, 203, 207, 209
London, 5, 13, 81, 207
Long Island, New York, 51, 66,
    68–69, 73, 79, 136
Lopez, Aaron, 98, 99
Louisiana, 37
Lovejoy, Elijah, 155, 156, 163–66,
    166, 167–69
    abolitionism of, 163–69
    death of, 168–69, 173
Low, Abiel Abbot, 11
Lowell, Francis Cabot, 27–28, *28*, 29
Lowell, Massachusetts, 6, 25, *25*, 26,
    28–29, 31, 35
Lowell Lecture, 188
Lucy, 111
Lynn, Oscar, *205*

Machado, John Albert, 125
Mackay, John, 203
Maine, 6, 35, 128, 132, 163, 186
Madeira, 93
malaria, 107
Malbone, Evan, 99
Malbone, Francis, 97, 99

Malbone, Godfrey, Jr., *103*
Manhattan Life, 23
Marines, U.S., 175
Mary E. Smith, 131
Maryland, 139, 147, 149–51, 152
Mason, James, 175
Massachusetts, 6, 27, 51, 53, 176
    shipbuilding, 53–54
    slavery in, 25, 36, 79, 179–80, 186
    textile industry, 6–7, 25, *25*, 26–29,
        32, 35, *35*, 36–37, 41
Massachusetts Bay Colony, xxvii,
    45–46, 53
Massachusetts General Hospital, 35
Matilda, 1795 manifest from, *49*
Maxwell, Wright & Company, 128
May, Samuel, 157, 158, 160
McIntosh, Francis, 163–65
McLean, Morris & Company, 207
mental illness, 186–87
Merrimack Manufacturing Company,
    35
Middle Atlantic States, 48, 51, 62; *see
    also* Delaware; New Jersey; New
    York State; Pennsylvania
Middle Passage, 65, *96*, 102–9, *106–9*,
    117, 121, 126–33, *133*, 134
Miner, Hempstead, 70, 72
Minkins, Frederick, 38
Minturn, Robert, 11
Mississippi, 10, 37, 147, 148, 149
Mississippi River, 165
Missouri, 112, 164–69, 172
Missouri Compromise of 1820, 165
Missouri Republican, 167
Mitchell, Ethel Lee, *136*
mixed-race couples, 187
Mobile, Alabama, 10, 187, 189
molasses trade, 47, 48, *48*, 49, *50*, 51,
    52, 53–54, *54*, 56, 74, 80
    Newport rum and African slave
        trade, 95–113
Mombasa, 198
Montgomery, Charles, 137
Moore, Ernst D., 197, 208, *208*, 209
    Ivory, Scourge of Africa, 208
Morgan, J. Pierpont, 5
Morgan, Junius, 5
Morgan, Margaret, 144
Morris, Lewis, 53

Morrisania, Bronx, New York, 53
Morton, Samuel George, *181*, 182, 184–89
  Crania Aegyptiaca, 186
  Crania Americana, 185, 186
  death of, 189
  skull research, 181–85, *185*, 186–87, 188, 189
Moss, Henry, 184, *184*
Mozambique, 128, 198, 201
mulattoes, 187
mule, *29*
Mumford, George, 68
Mumford, Robertson, 65
Mystic, Connecticut, 132

Narragansett, Rhode Island, 51, 63, 66
Narragansett Bay, 101
Narrative and Confessions of Lucretia P. Cannon, The, 151
Narrative of James Williams, an American Slave (pamphlet), 33
Nashville, 41
National Anti-Slavery Standard, 153
National Museum of American History, Smithsonian, Washington, D.C., 207
Navy, U.S., 121
  Africa squadron, 121–22, *122*, 123, 124, 127, 131, 134
Nebraska, 38, 171
"negro cloth," 26
Netherlands, 7
Newburyport, Massachusetts, 27, 29
New England, xxvi, xxviii, 45
  origins of slavery in, 45–55
  rum trade, 47–54, *48–54*, 95–113
  textile industry, 6–7, 14, 25, *25*, 26–29, *29*, 35–37, 41, 110
  see also specific states and cities
New Hampshire, 6, 35, 132
  hostility to black education, 158
New Haven, Connecticut, 42–43, 79, 158
New Haven Colony Historical Society, 201
New Jersey, 6, 62
  slavery in, 51, 71, 79, 187

New London, Connecticut, 63, 67, 71, 114–15, 119, 125
New Orleans, Louisiana, 10, *12*, 21, 33, 127, 142
Newport, Rhode Island, 21, 57, 71, *97*
  commerce, 97–113
  Redwood Library, 97, *97*
  rum and African slave trade, 95–113
New York City, xxvi, xxvii–xxviii, *15*, 40, 49, 50, 53, *78*, 215
  African Burial Ground, 82
  commerce, 15–18, *19*, 20–25, 49, 50, 53, 80, 121–33
  cotton trade, 3–4, *8*, 10–25, 215
  docks, 15–18, *15–17*
  free blacks kidnapped in, 140
  Great Negro Plot (1741), 77, 83–89, *90*, 91–93
  illegal slave trade, 121–37
  slave revolts in, 77, 79–93
  slavery in, 3–4, *20*, 23, 77–93, *82–90*, 121–33
  Wall Street, 20, *20*, 82
New York Cotton Exchange, 5
New-York Daily Tribune, 125, 189
New-York Gazette, 68, 107
New York Herald, 11, 175
New York State, xxviii, 23, 50, 62, 144
  slavery in, 51, 53, 62, 63, 66, 71, 79
New York State Anti-Slavery Society, 166
New York Times, The, 175
New York Tribune, 10
Nightingale, 131–32
Niles, Elisha, 63
Niles' Register, 150
Noble, Thomas Satterwhite, 143
North, xxv–xxix, 123, 216
  chronology of Northern complicity, 217–19
  cotton trade, 3–43
  ivory industry, 193–213
  kidnapping of free blacks from, 139–53
  postwar, 211
  textile industry, 6–7, 14, 25–29, 35–37, 41, 110

see also Middle Atlantic states; New England; *specific states and cities;* Union
North Africa, 199, 204
North Carolina, 107, 149
North Elba, New York, 171
Nott, Josiah, *181*, 182–83, 187–91
  "The Mulatto a Hybrid—Probable Extermination of the Two Races if the Whites and Blacks Are Allowed to Intermarry," 187
  Types of Mankind, 181, 182, *188*, 189–91
Noyes Academy, Canaan, New Hampshire, 158

Observer, 164, 165–68, *168*, 169
Ocilla, 132
O'Conor, Charles, 12
Ohio, 142, 143, 144, 170
onions, 49, 51
Ontario, 173
Oswald, Richard, 115
Otis, Harrison Gray, 32

packets, 15, *15*, 16, 18
Page, William, 129, 130
Paris, 13
Parker, Theodore, 173, 176, 191
Parker, William, 141–42
passive resistance, 67–68, 78
Peace Conference (1861), 40, 41
Pemba, 204
Pennsylvania, 23, 50, 62, 141–53
  slavery in, 62, 79
Pennsylvania Abolition Society, 152
Perth Amboy, New Jersey, 79
Philadelphia, xxviii, 12, 49, 142, 180
  Centennial Exhibition (1876), 206
  free blacks kidnapped in, 139, 143–53
  race science in, 182–91
  slave revolts in, 79
Philadephia *Press*, 176
Philipse, Adolphus, 80, 84, 89
Philipse, Frederick II, 86
Phillips, Wendell, 37, 168
phrenology, 159

piano keys, ivory, 194, 200, 203–6, 209, 211, 212
Pierce, Franklin, 39
piracy, 123
Pittsburgh, Pennsylvania, 141
plantation labor system, *47*, 48–49, 51–55, 95, 125, 133, 181
poisonings, 71
Porpoise, 128, 130
Portuguese Company, 125
Potter, Simeon, 103, 113
power loom, 28, *35*
Pratt, Julius, 195, *195*, 202, 205, 211
Pratt, Louis, *205*
Pratt, Phineas, 193, 195, 211
Pratt, Read & Company, 194–95, 203, 205, *205*, 206, 208, 209, 212
  advertisement, *213*
press, abolitionist, 29, *30*, 31, 152, 155, 157, 164, 165–68, *168*, 169; *see also specific publications*
Prigg v. Pennsylvania, 144–45
Prime, Nathaniel, 13
Prime, Ward & King, 13
Prince, 87–88
professions, 71–72
Providence, Rhode Island, 28, 56, *97*, 101, 102, 110
Providence Island, 46
Providence Journal, 175
Prudence Crandall vs. the State of Connecticut, 160–63
Puritans, 45–48, 55
Purnell, John, 149
Putnam's Monthly Magazine, 181

Quack, 87–91, 93
Quaco, 81, 84
Quakers, 109, 185

race science, xxviii, 159, 179–91
  environmental theories, 183–84
  mental illness theories, 186–87
  of Morton, 181–85, *185*, 186–87, 188, 189
  of Nott and Agassiz, 182–83, 187–91, *188–91*
  separate creation theories, 179–91
racism, 93, 159, 179–91, 201–2, 215

railroads, 6, 26, 35, 209, 215
Raymond, Henry, 175–76
Read, George, 194, *194*, 195, 202, 205, 211, 212
Redwood, Abraham, 97
Redwood Library, Newport, Rhode Island, 97, *97*
religion, xxix, 144, 181, 184, 186
    race science theories and, 182–91
Renty (daguerreotype), *190*
revolts, *see* slave revolts
Rhode Island, xxviii, 26, 51, 63, 56, 59, 95, 115
    abolitionism, 109–10
    illegal slave trade, 112–13
    Newport rum and African slave trade, 95–113
    slavery in, 51, 56, 57, 62, 63, 65, 66, 71, 95–113
    textile industry, 28, *29*, 110
rice, 18, 116–17
Richards, Leonard L., 166
Richmond, Virginia, 127, 177
Rio de Janiero, 123, 126, 127–28, 130
Rivera, Jacob Rodriguez, 98, 99
Robin, 81
Robinson, Solon, 10
Rochester, New York, 141
Rock, James, 168
Romeo, *135*
Roosevelt, John, 89
Roosevelt, Nicholas, 81
Roosevelt, Teddy, 208
Ruggles, David, 140, *140*, 141
rum trade, 49, *50*, 53–54, *54*, 80, 95–113
    distilleries, *52*
    Newport rum and African slaves, 95–113
runaway slaves, 33–35, 37–39, 68–70, 140–43, *143*
    advertising, 33, *34*, 35, 68, *68*, 71
    free blacks accused as, 140–44
    Garner incident, 142, *143*
Rush, Dr. Benjamin, 183, *183*, 184
Russell, Nathaniel, 56–57, *57*, 58–59
    Charleston house of, 56, *58*, 59
Russia, 7

Sacramento, 210
Sainte-Domingue, 48, 54, 78–79

St. Kitts, 119
St. Louis, Missouri, 163–69
Salem, Massachusetts, 51
Sally revolt, 102–5, 109
Sanborn, Franklin, 173, 176
Sansaverino, Sharon, *136*
Saratoga, New York, 21
Savannah, Georgia, 10, 18, 38
Scomp, Samuel, 146, 147, 148, 149
Scott, Dred, 144, 161, 162
secession, xxvii, 3–6, 23, 36, 112
Senate, U.S., 112, 125
Senegal, 115, 117
separate creation theories, 179–91
Seven Years' War, 103
shackles, *109*
Shayt, David, 206
Shepard, Michael W., 198, 209
Sheriff, Abdul, *Slaves, Spices, and Ivory in Zanzibar,* 201
shipbuilding, 53–54, 72, 121, 205
Shipman, William, 133
Sierra Leone, 116, 117
Sierra Leone River, 116
Slater, Samuel, 28, 110
slave revolts, xxvii–xxviii, 31, 48, 71, 77–93
    Amistad revolt, 127, *127*
    Creole revolt, 127
    "Great Negro Plot" (1741), 77, 83–89, *90*, 91–93
    Harpers Ferry raid, 173–77
    Kentucky revolt, 128–30
    in New York City, 77, 79–93
    Sally revolt, 102–5, 109
    Turner's rebellion, 31, 79, 155, 158
    in West Indies, 78–79
slavery, xxv–xxix, 10, 215–16
    abuse, whippings, and beatings, 66–71, 82
    advertisements, 21, 33, *34*, 35, *54*, 68, *68*, 71, *99*
    "black codes," 63, 67, 82–83, 85
    branding, *100*, 106
    in Connecticut, *34*, 51, *54*, 61–75, 79, 114–15, 195, 201–2
    cotton trade and, 10, 26, 35–37, 100, 110
    economy, 45–55, 110, 113, 133, 215

free blacks kidnapped and sold into, 139–53
insurance, 23, *24*, 105
ivory industry and, 193–213, *197–200, 208, 213*
in Massachusetts, 25, 36, 79, 179–80, 186
masters vs. traders, 108
New England origins of, 45–55
in New Jersey, 51, 71, 79, 187
in New York City, 3–4, *20*, 23, 77–93, *82–90*, 121–33
in New York State, 51, 53, 62, 63, 66, 71, 79
Northern style and conditions, 62–63, 71–72, 172
notion of black inferiority and, 179–91
passive resistance, 67–68, 78
in Pennsylvania, 62, 79
plantation labor system, *47*, 48–49, 51–55, 95, 125, 133, 181
race science and, 179–91
regional differences, 23–25, 62–63, 71, 186–87
in Rhode Island, 51, 56, 57, 62, 63, 65, 66, 71, 95–113
runaways, 33, *34*, 35, 37–39, 68–70, 71, 140–43, *143*
Southern, 23–25, 26, 33–35, 63, 71, 79, 95
textile industry and, 35–37, 41, 110
violence toward owners, 71
see also African slave trade; slave revolts
slave trade, *see* African slave trade
smallpox, 65, 102, 107
Smith, Gerrit, 171, 173, 176
Smith, Meg, 61, 69, 73, 74, 75
Smith, Oliver, 72, 73
Smith, Venture, 61–75
  freedom of, 73–75
  gravestone of, *74*, 75
  physical violence toward, 69–71
  published narrative of, 63, *64*, 68, 69
  as a runaway, 68–70
Smith, William, 89, 91, 112, 113

South, xxv, xxvii, xxix, 123, 216
  antebellum, 21
  -British relations, 9–10
  cotton, 7, 9–10, *12*, 18, 95, 100, 110, 131, 134
  postwar, 211
  secession, 3–6, 36
  slavery, 23–25, 26, 33–35, 63, 71, 79, 95
  see also Confederacy; *specific states and cities*
South America, 46, 96, 103
  slave trade to, 123–31
South Carolina, 3, 10, 11, 33, 41, 56–59, 79, 98, 111, 116, 131, 135, 137, 186, 190
  census, *135*
South Carolina Gazette, 56
Spain, 7, 83, 92, 205
  blacks, 92, 93
Sparks, Colonel William, 31
speculum oris, 108, *108*
spermaceti candles, 102, 103
spices, 204
spinning machines, 28, *29*
Stanley, Henry M., 196, 199, 206, 207, 209, 213
Stanton, Elizabeth, 61, 70
Stanton, Thomas, 69–71, 72
  house of, 69, *69*
steamships, 16, 126
Stearns, George, 173
steel, 26
Steiner, Bernard, 63
Stephens, John, 118
Stewart, A. T., 11
Stonington, Connecticut, 69, 72
Storm King, 122
Story, Joseph, 144, *145*
Stowe, Harriet Beecher, xxvi, 165
  Uncle Tom's Cabin, xxvi, 142
Stratford, Connecticut, 61
Suffolk Bank, 35
sugar trade, xxviii, 46, *47*, 48–49, *50*, 51–55, 56, 61, 80, 100, 111, 119, 131, 134, 204, 211
Sumner, Charles, 37
Supreme Court, U.S., 144, 160
  Dred Scott case, 144, 161, 162
  Prigg v. Pennsylvania, 144–45

Swann, Alfred J., 199
Switzerland, 7

Taney, Roger Brooke, 162
Tanganyika, 198, 207
Tappan, Arthur, 157, 160
Tappan, Lewis, 157
taverns, *103*
    blacks in, 85, 86, 87, 91, 92, 93
Taylor, Moses, 11
textile industry, 26–32
    Industrial Revolution and, 28–29
    New England mills, 6–7, 14, 25, *25*,
        26–29, *29*, 35–37, 41, 110
    slavery and, 35–37, 41, 110
    see also cotton
Thomas Watson, 125
Thompson, George, 31, 32
Thompson, Jeremiah, 16–18
Thoreau, Henry David, 170, 176
thumbscrews, *108*
Tiffany, Charles L., 5
Tilden, Samuel J., 11
Tillman, Benjamin R., 137
tobacco, 7, 18, 46
Torrey, Jesse, Jr., *Portraiture of
    Domestic Slavery in the U.S.*, *140*
Toussaint L'Ouverture, Francois
    Dominique, 79
Townsend, George Alfred, *The
    Entailed Hat*, 151
Triangle Trade, 48–49, *50*, 65, 98
Trumbull, Jonathan, 63
Truth, Sojourner, 66–67, *67*, 73
Turner, Nat, 31, 79, 155, 156, 158, 175
Tyler, John, 40
Types of Mankind (Nott and Agassiz),
    181, 182, *188*, 189–91

Ujiji, 207
Ulrick, John, 130
Union, 6, 36, 37
Union army, black soldiers in, 176,
    177
U.S. cotton crop, 1840–1850, *8*
University of Pennsylvania, 182, 185
upland cotton (*Gossypium hirsutum*), 7,
    7, 9
Ury, John, 92

Vaarck, Caesar, 84, 85–88
Vaarck, John, 84
Valenti, Sheryl, *136*
Van Cortlandt, Augustus, 53
Vernon, Samuel, 98
Vernon, William, 98
Vicksburg, Mississippi, 33
violence, xxvii, 66–68, 71
    abolitionism and, 155–77
    against schools with black
        students, *162*, 163
    of owners toward slaves, 66–71, 82,
        102
    slave revolts, 77–93
    of slaves toward owners, 71
    whippings and beatings, 66–71, 82
    see also slave revolts; *specific methods*
Virginia, 31, 40, 46, 51, 79, 127
    Harpers Ferry raid, 142, 173–74,
        174, 175–77
    Turner's rebellion, 31, 79, 155, 158
voting rights, 161

Wadsworth, William, 34
Waltham, Massachusetts, 28–29
Wanderer, 131, 134, *134*, 135–37
    survivors and descendants of, 134,
        135–36, 137
Wanton, Jonas, *103*
Wanton, Joseph, 103
Wanton family, 98, 99
Ward, Samuel, 13
War of 1812, 15, 27
Washington, D.C., 6, 31, 166
Washington, George, 62, 72, 110, 142,
    193
Washington, Madison, 127
Washington Post, 216
Waters, Richard, 204–5
Watson, Joseph, 146, 147, 148
Webb, Joseph, 34
Webster, Daniel, 27, 37
Weld, Theodore Dwight, 184
Weller, Royal, 168
Westervelt, Minthorne, 132
West Indies, xxvi, 7, 20
    slave revolts, 78–79
    sugar plantations, 46, *47*, 48–55, 61,
        78–79, 95, 100, 111, 131

trade, 46–49, *50*, 51–55, 61,
    65–66, 78–79, 95, 102, 104, 111,
    115, 119
Wethersfield, Connecticut, 49, 51
wheat, 7, 53, 166
Wheatley, Phillis, 179–80, *180*
    poetry by, 179–80, *180*
Whig Party, 37
white supremacy, scientific theory of,
    179–91
Whitney, Eli, 7, 9, *9*, 26, 110
Whittier, John Greenleaf, 25
Williams College, 35
Winthrop, Henry, 45–46

Winthrop, John, xxvii, 45–46, *46*, 47,
    49, 53, 54–55
Winthrop, Samuel, 54
Wise, Henry, 125, 175
Wood, Fernando, 3–4, *4*, 5–6, 23
wood and woodworking, 48, 49, 50,
    53, 71, 72, 80

Yale University, 158
yellow fever, 182, 189

Zambesi River, 198, 200
Zanzibar, 196, 198, 200, *200*, 204–11
Zenger, John Peter, 83

ABOUT THE AUTHORS

ANNE FARROW has been a writer and editor at newspapers in New England since 1976, and on the staff of *The Hartford Courant* since 1988. Farrow grew up in Connecticut and has a master's degree in English literature from the University of New Hampshire. She was a lead writer on "Complicity," *Northeast*'s first issue on slavery, and was the sole writer on the second, "Beyond Complicity: The Forgotten Story of Connecticut's Slave Ships," published April 3, 2005.

JOEL LANG has been a reporter and editor at *The Hartford Courant* since 1968, and a staff writer for *Northeast*, the paper's Sunday magazine, since 1982. He is the recipient of the New England Society of Newspaper Editors Master Reporter award for career achievement. A Rhode Island native and graduate of Wesleyan University in Connecticut, Lang was a lead writer on *Northeast*'s "Complicity" issue on slavery.

JENIFER FRANK has worked at newspapers in the New York area for 25 years, most recently at *The Hartford Courant*. A New York native, she grew up in Connecticut and is a graduate of Trinity College in Hartford. She has been editor of *Northeast* magazine since 2001, and was editor of both special issues on slavery.